Soldiers in the Southwest Borderlands 1848–1886

Soldiers in the Southwest Borderlands 1848–1886

Edited by

JANNE LAHTI

UNIVERSITY OF OKLAHOMA PRESS : NORMAN

Library of Congress Cataloging-in-Publication Data

Name: Lahti, Janne, editor, author.
Title: Soldiers in the southwest borderlands, 1848–1886 / edited by Janne Lahti.
Description: Norman : University of Oklahoma Press, 2017. | Includes index.
Identifiers: LCCN 2016036745 | ISBN 978-0-8061-5702-3 (hardcover : alk. paper)
Subjects: LCSH: Southwest, New—History, Military—19th century. | Mexican-American Border Region—History, Military—19th century. | Soldiers—United States—History—19th century. | Soldiers—United States—Biography.
Classification: LCC F786 .S68 2017 | DDC 355.00979—dc23
LC record available at https://lccn.loc.gov/2016036745

The paper in this book meets the guidelines for permanence and durability of the Committee on Production Guidelines for Book Longevity of the Council on Library Resources, Inc. ∞

1 2 3 4 5 6 7 8 9 10

Contents

Illustrations

FIGURES

MAP

Acknowledgments

I want to start by praising my group of authors. Lance Blyth, Billy Kiser, Jerry Thompson, Megan Kate Nelson, Andy Masich, Robert Wooster, James Leiker, Ty Smith, and Victoria Smith proved the kind of team any editor would hope to get. They attentively followed the general guidelines I set early on, worked diligently, and kept the deadlines with admirable precision. They also accepted my suggestions, and gave, in turn, courteous and sometimes critical, but always valuable, input. It was a pleasure working with each and every one of them. Although I had been warned beforehand that editing a book can be like "herding that many wild cats," and that it would amount to such a frustrating process that one would never voluntarily try it again, I actually found putting together my first (but hopefully not last) edited volume quite exciting. Importantly, it was both a whole lot of fun and a beneficial learning experience. Early on, planning the book, scouting for a team of authors, and pitching the idea to Chuck Rankin at the University of Oklahoma Press taught me a lot. I learned more later when carefully reading and editing each essay, accepting and offering feedback, and building the book piece by piece. I want to thank Chuck for his encouragement and Adam Kane, acquisitions editor at the University of Oklahoma Press, for his invaluable help in the latter stages of the book, especially with the introduction. Also, I want to thank copyeditor Kelly Parker. Any author would be lucky to work with a professional like her. When I first got an idea for this work in late 2013, Durwood Ball, professor of history at the University of New Mexico, proved most helpful and worked with me in finalizing the idea that the book should be about common soldiers. It is the enlisted men, not the officers, who finally deserved to be placed in the spotlight. I also want to thank Michael Coleman for his comments. Also, Billy Kiser is largely responsible for putting together a panel so that some of us got to present our research on borderlands soldiers at the 2015 meeting of the Western History Association in Portland, Oregon. This book also benefited tremendously from the funding I received from the Academy of Finland, the Finnish Cultural Foundation, and the Department of Philosophy, History, Culture and Art Studies at the University of Helsinki. The latter provided a very congenial working environment that enabled me to balance teaching with writing. Finally, I wish to thank my wife, Sanna, and our two children, Sofia and Juho, because it is they who in the end matter the most.

Soldiers in the Southwest Borderlands 1848–1886

UTAH
NEVADA
Colorado River
Fort Mojave
ARIZONA
Prescott
Mogollon Rim
White Mts.
Camp Verde
La Paz
Fort Apache
San Mateo
Black River
Salt River
Gila River
Gila River
Mogollon Mts.
San Carlos
Fort Yuma
Camp Goodwin
Fort Grant
Tucson
Silver City
Fort Bowie
Burro Mts.
Knight's Ranch
Chiricahua Mts.
Santa Cruz
San Bernardino Ranch
Janos
Sierra Madre
Sierra de Enmedio
SONORA
CHIHUAHUA
Cities
Forts and Camps
Mountains

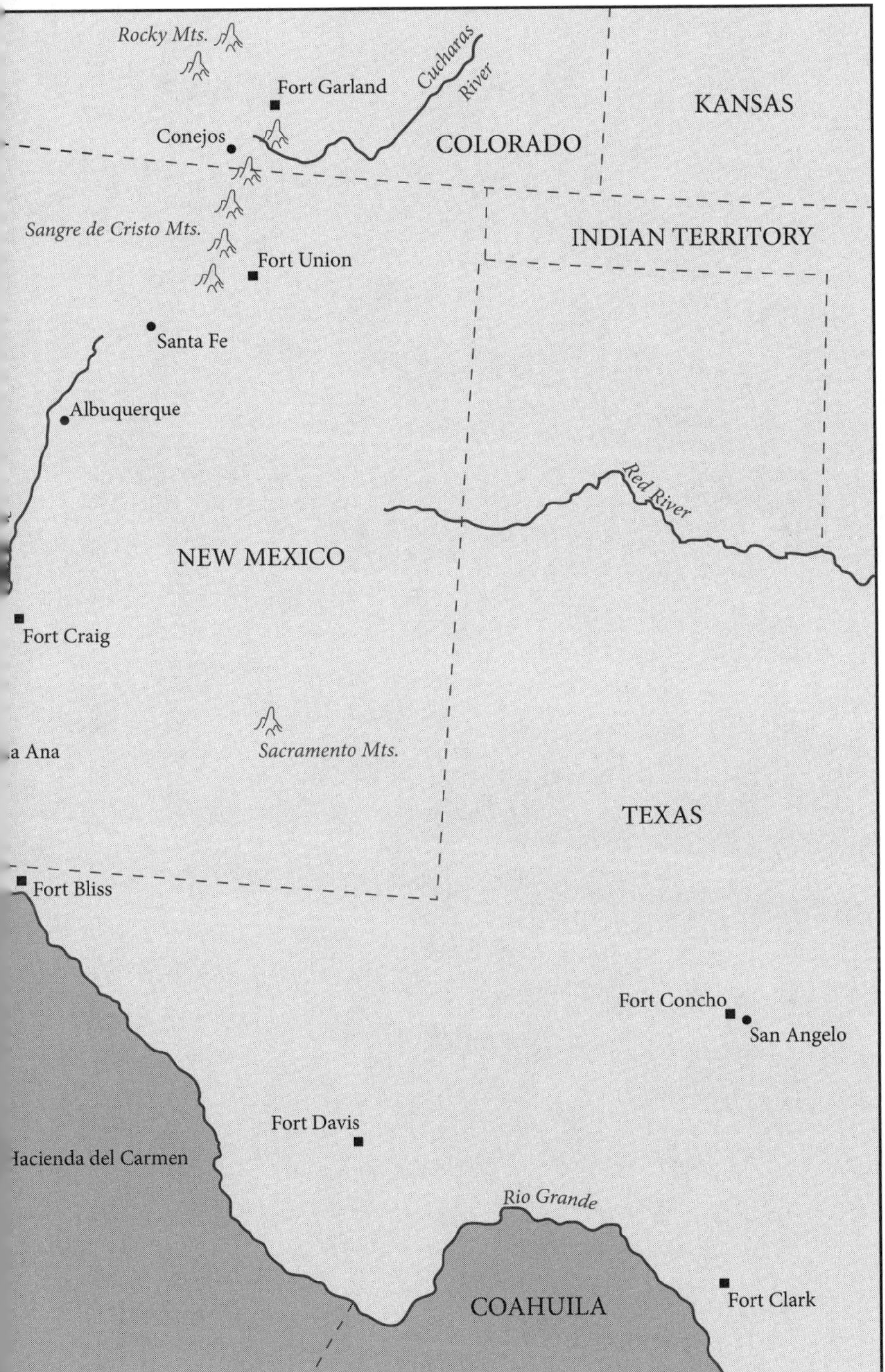

The Southwest Borderlands. Map by Chuck Grear. Copyright © 2017 by the University of Oklahoma Press.

Introduction

COMMON MEN, VIOLENCE, AND SETTLER COLONIALISM

Janne Lahti

Many U.S. Army posts in the Southwest borderlands saw summertime temperatures reach 110 degrees Fahrenheit and beyond in the shade. The thousands of men who were stationed in such places during the U.S.–indigenous wars not only struggled with the suffocating heat but battled a plethora of other concerns as well. This book concentrates on the individual in North America's Southwest borderlands.[1] It is not an anthology of leaders, but instead comprises ten biographies of common men written by proven scholars in western and military history. It is in individualizing the enlisted soldiers, telling the stories of ordinary men, and spotlighting those previously on the margins of history that this book seeks to make a meaningful contribution. It offers narratives of, and seeks to enrich our understandings of, U.S. empire building. Contributors to this volume tell stories of enlisted men and comment on and contextualize their experiences within the analytical framework of violence and settler colonialism.

Essays in this volume focus on the diversity of men who served under U.S. or Mexican flags and on the payroll of state/territorial volunteers as well as of the regular U.S. Army. The men in these biographies represented most of the major ethnicities in the West—Hispanics, African Americans, Native Americans, American-born Anglos, and recent European immigrants. They enlisted for armed service and never rose to leadership positions in the military. None of them made soldiering his sole career. In other words, the writings in this volume examine common men who took up arms at one point in their lives and who served in the Southwest borderlands after the U.S.-Mexican War and in the context of the Civil War and conflicts with indigenous peoples throughout the Southwest.

The essays address questions pertaining to military life, forms of violence, ambiguities of power, cross-cultural interactions, and dynamic, situational identities. They offer insights into common men's experiences as well as advance our understanding of the variations and contradictions in U.S. colonialism. Whether these men were cognizant of it or not, or whether they liked it or not, they operated within the global framework of settler colonialism. Used increasingly by scholars writing on American western history, settler colonialism as a research concept describes a global phenomenon usually linked to the explosive expansion of the "Anglo-World" in the 1800s in North America, Australia, and elsewhere. Paraphrasing historian Lorenzo Veracini, settler colonialism refers to types of colonial endeavors marked by the permanent movement and reproduction of communities, usually of white European extraction, and their dominance over indigenous peoples. Conquest, permanence (or at least intent of permanence), settlement, focus on the land itself, and the logic of elimination of indigenous peoples defines settler colonialism. Using different words, historian David Day applies the term "supplanting society," by which he means "a society that moves onto the land of another with the intention of making that land its own" to describe settler colonial dynamics.[2]

This book touches on the broad shifts of settler colonialism that transformed the Southwest from a syncretic, yet highly competitive, world of mixed cultures and communities of predominantly indigenous and Hispanic extraction where no single group gained dominance into a realm where Anglo settlers hardened racial boundaries, sought exclusive rights to the land, and launched extractive industries backed by outside investment. It was a period during which the U.S. government wanted the monopoly of violence to itself and the Southwest Indians lost their autonomy and were eliminated in war, segregated into reservations, and pushed to the margins of society. Violence, ranging from raids to massacres to destructive campaigns targeting whole societies, their material base, and the environment, played an integral part of the nineteenth-century Southwest.

Typically, the focus of borderlands soldiers described in this book was less on long-term political outcomes and more on issues that had direct bearing on their daily life. Their reasons were mixed: survival, social or economic mobility, adventure, patriotism, and desperation, among others.

So were their experiences. Some soldiers, like Alonzo Davis, spent much time prospecting, staking claims, and promoting the Colorado River area in local and regional papers. Others, like Alonzo Ickis, did not care much about the Southwest but instead regarded the area, in the 1860s, as foreign. Still others, like Mickey Free, a former captive and a borderlands native of Hispanic background who tried to negotiate the Apache and white worlds as something of a perpetual outsider in both, contested the impacts of settler colonialism on their lives. Through enlistment, Free and his Apache brother John Rope sought economic and physical security for themselves and their families confined in the White Mountain Reservation in Arizona.

Borderlands soldiers confronted various peoples of different ethnicities whose cultures, attitudes, and ways of life they sometimes found difficult to comprehend. Some, like Santiago Brito and Louis Geck, chased and skirmished with powerful Apache fighters, whose military skills and tactics exasperated them. Others, like Emil Bode, seemed awed by the Southern Plains warriors and Indian maidens he encountered personally. Some witnessed, underwent, and inflicted extreme violence. For George Goldsby, a former slave who ran into trouble in San Angelo, Texas, violence was interpersonal. For many, it related to excruciating military campaigns and major fights, bearing different personal outcomes. The Battle of Valverde in New Mexico in 1862 seemed only to whet Alonzo Ickis's appetite for action, while it tilted the borderlands native Homobono Carabajal toward a path that led to mental breakdown and murder. Yet some men, like Harry McConnell, who served in central Texas, witnessed very little violence at all. It was common for borderlands soldiers to encounter and negotiate class privilege, racial division, and plenty of tiresome work and ennui, but they seldom saw much professional training or possibilities for advancement.

Because these were enlisted men—of whom many were illiterate and most never penned any private accounts—extensive personal records do not often exist. This book hopes to show that, although the majority of primary sources lend themselves more easily to campaign histories and profiles of renowned officers, skillful historians can produce interesting and meaningful articles also on soldiers who left few or no personal letters or memoirs. By using various institutional, ethnographic, and other source materials, it is possible to provide a fair and substantive sense of what these soldiers' experiences and terms of service were like. Also, if we were to restrict the discussion to those soldiers who left personal texts, it would mean excluding much of the present ethnic/racial diversity in the book. The subjects of the biographies in this volume include two Hispanics, one Apache, one Pole, one German, one African American, three Anglos, and one Mickey Free (a Hispanic by birth who had a white stepfather but was raised as an Apache). This kind of a broad field has value in itself. It is a step toward richer and more inclusive understandings of common soldiers' and, more broadly, common peoples' lives in the Southwest borderlands.

• • •

Several borderlands histories have shown sensitivity to violence and ordinary peoples of various ethnicities. Juliana Barr and James Brooks, in their respective studies, make violence and gender the glue of the relational field of captivity, kinship, ethnicity, and community.[3] Gary Clayton Anderson has maintained that in the mid-1800s white Texans systematically used violence for the purposes of ethnic cleansing against the Comanches, Kiowas, Apaches, and others. Brian DeLay has, in turn, demonstrated that aggressive indigenous raiding cultures that centered on the warrior and male accomplishment degraded Mexico's ability to defend itself against U.S. aggression.[4] Ned Blackhawk argues that earliest Spanish colonization already led to waves of violence that recalibrated indigenous identities and their communal relations toward cutthroat competition, and caused Indian pain that resonated far beyond the immediate reach of the Spanish.[5] Karl Jacoby in turn has unraveled intricate webs of intimacies and violence that connected various borderlands peoples in the mid-1800s. Using the concept "communities of violence," Lance Blyth has argued that for numerous generations violence made relations—both conflictive and cooperative—within and between borderlands groups.[6]

These and other scholars have deepened and complicated our understanding of violence as a sifting relational phenomenon that underwent constant negotiation and acquired new shapes and meanings that had daily consequences on all levels of borderlands society.[7] They have also shown that in the Southwest borderlands fighting men were often celebrated at the center of rich cultures. On many occasions violence—knowledge, skills, and participation—turned boys into men. It also gave meaning to men's lives and brought wealth, status, and followers, in addition to making men desirable partners for sex and marriage. What these studies have paid scant attention to, however, are the ordinary men who operated as soldiers in the Southwest after the U.S.-Mexican War. This is hardly surprising as even most traditional military histories have been guilty of the same neglect.

While the bulk of the vast Civil War literature still tends to focus on the eastern theater,[8] traditional military histories of the Southwest often narrate the U.S.-Mexican War and the ensuing imposition of U.S. rule through the lives and careers of military officers and civil officials, not the enlisted men.[9] Although governors, generals, and Indian agents were responsible for framing civil and military policies, it was the countless ordinary men who carried out the orders from higher authorities and lived through the tumultuous times that followed.[10] Yet, while a number of studies have examined the enlisted soldiers as a group, scholars often know precious little of the individual soldier and his experiences and motivations.[11] This has not, however, prevented a practice of conflating the most violent traditions of U.S. empire building with the common soldier or writing him off as a faceless, mute, and emotionless agent of a racist colonial regime.

While seeking to change this tendency to omit and stereotype the common soldiers, this volume does not pretend to offer a comprehensive treatise or entertain illusions that it can pinpoint any kind of universal experience that would apply to all borderlands soldiers. Instead, it puts forward a cross section of ordinary men and their historical realities, allowing for a diversity of experiences and voices. It provides understandings of violence and settler colonialism in the Southwest borderlands filtered through the lives of common soldiers who represented a broad spectrum of experiences and garnered many points of view. The biographies display men who wanted to be courageous and physically capable, who grasped for military glory, engaged and encountered violence, suffered from mental exhaustion, and yearned for adventure. They show men who scoffed the borderlands peoples of different ethnicities as well as those who admired, created intimate bonds with, and partook in business ventures with them. Many of the men tried to make the most out of the opportunities represented to them. Many resented their lot, but many also found camaraderie in the military as well as a sense of purpose for their lives in service of the nation. They typically strived for emotional, economic, and physical security and well-being. While some failed miserably, others became respectable members of their communities. Unlike their officers, who usually returned to live their post-military lives in the East, several common soldiers became permanent borderlands residents.[12] Their legacies are still present in the area and their lives worth remembering.

NOTES

1. The view this study takes on the geographical parameters of the Southwest borderlands might appear a bit unusual. It can be said that it stretches the term to its limits, and some might think possibly beyond, by involving cases from the Arizona-California line to central Texas and the Indian Territory (Oklahoma). By including much of the desert Southwest and sections of the southern plains, this volume covers a greater southwestern military theater where the United States engaged in violent confrontations against communities of independent Indians after its war against Mexico.

2. Lorenzo Veracini, *Settler Colonialism: A Theoretical Overview* (New York: Palgrave Macmillan, 2010), esp. 3; David Day, *Conquest: How Societies Overwhelm Others* (New York: Oxford University Press, 2008), 5–6. Through a prolonged process, the supplanting society tries to make its claim on the land superior to the claim of the preexisting people as well as being superior to any other society that might think to challenge it. On settler colonialism, see James Belich, *Replenishing the Earth: The Settler Revolution and the Rise of the Anglo-World, 1783–1939* (Oxford: Oxford University Press, 2009); Margaret D. Jacobs, *White Mother to a Dark Race: Settler Colonialism, Maternalism, and the Removal of Indigenous Children in the American West and Australia, 1880–1940* (Lincoln: University of Nebraska Press, 2009), esp. 4–24; Patrick Wolfe, "Settler Colonialism and the Elimination of the Native," *Journal of Genocide Research* 8 (December 2006): 387–409; Walter L. Hixson, *American Settler Colonialism: A History* (New York: Palgrave Macmillan, 2013); and Daiva Stasiulis and Nira Yuval-Davis, eds., *Unsettling Settler Societies: Articulations of Gender, Race, Ethnicity and Class* (London: Sage, 1995).

3. Juliana Barr, *Peace Came in the Form of a Woman: Indians and Spaniards in the Texas Borderlands* (Chapel Hill: University of North Carolina Press, 2007); James F. Brooks, *Captives and Cousins: Slavery, Kinship, and Community in the Southwest Borderlands* (Chapel Hill: University of North Carolina Press, 2002).

4. Gary Clayton Anderson, *The Conquest of Texas: Ethnic Cleansing in the Promised Land, 1820–1875* (Norman: University of Oklahoma Press, 2005); Brian DeLay, *War of a Thousand Deserts: Indian Raids and the U.S.-Mexican War* (New Haven: Yale University Press, 2008).

5. Ned Blackhawk, *Violence over the Land: Indians and Empires in the Early American West* (Cambridge, Mass.: Harvard University Press, 2006).

6. Karl Jacoby, *Shadows at Dawn: An Apache Massacre and the Violence of History* (New York: Penguin, 2008); Lance R. Blyth, *Chiricahua and Janos: Communities of Violence in the Southwest Borderlands, 1680–1880* (Lincoln: University of Nebraska Press, 2012), esp. 5.

7. On borderlands violence, see also Nicole M. Guidotti-Hernández, *Unspeakable Violence: Remapping U.S. and Mexican National Imaginaries* (Durham, N.C.:

Duke University Press, 2011); Ana Maria Alonso, *Thread of Blood: Colonialism, Revolution, and Gender on Mexico's Northern Frontier* (Tucson: University of Arizona Press, 1995); Ian W. Record, *Big Sycamore Stands Alone: The Western Apaches, Aravaipa, and the Struggle for Place* (Norman: University of Oklahoma Press, 2008); Chip Colwell-Chanthaphonh, *Massacre at Camp Grant: Forgetting and Remembering Apache History* (Tucson: University of Arizona Press, 2007); Brendan C. Lindsey, *Murder State: California's Native American Genocide, 1846–1873* (Lincoln: University of Nebraska Press, 2012); and Benjamin Madley, "Patterns of Frontier Genocide, 1803–1910: The Aboriginal Tasmanians, the Yuki of California, and the Herero of Namibia," *Journal of Genocide Research* 6 (June 2004): 167–92. Key studies on violence and settler colonialism in general include A. Dirk Moses, ed., *Empire, Colony, Genocide: Conquest, Occupation and Subaltern Resistance in World History* (New York: Berghahn Books, 2008); and Wolfe, "Settler Colonialism."

8. Some of the more recent innovative works discuss the environmental impacts of the Civil War. See Megan Kate Nelson, *Ruin Nation: Destruction and the American Civil War* (Athens: Georgia University Press, 2012); and Lisa M. Brady, *War upon the Land: Military Strategy and the Transformation of Southern Landscapes during the American Civil War* (Athens: Georgia University Press, 2012). Fresh anthologies of the Civil War and the Southwest include Virginia Scharff, ed., *Empire and Liberty: The Civil War and the West* (Berkeley: University of California Press, 2015); and Adam Arenson and Andrew R. Graybill, eds., *Civil War Wests: Testing the Limits of the United States* (Berkeley: University of California Press, 2015). See also Jerry D. Thompson, *A Civil War History of the New Mexico Volunteers and Militia* (Albuquerque: University of New Mexico Press, 2015); Andrew E. Masich, *The Civil War in Arizona: The Story of the California Volunteers, 1861–1865* (Norman: University of Oklahoma Press, 2006); and Donald S. Frazier, *Blood and Treasure: Confederate Empire in the Southwest* (College Station: Texas A&M University Press, 1995).

9. Classic military histories of U.S.-indigenous wars in the Southwest include Robert M. Utley, *Frontiersmen in Blue: The United States Army and the Indian, 1848–1865* (New York: Macmillan, 1967); Robert M. Utley, *Frontier Regulars: The United States Army and the Indian, 1866–1891* (1973; repr., Lincoln: University of Nebraska Press, 1984); Dan L. Thrapp, *The Conquest of Apacheria* (Norman: University of Oklahoma Press, 1967); James L. Haley, *The Buffalo War: The History of the Red River Indian Uprising of 1874–1875* (Austin: State House Press, 1976); Donald E. Worcester, *The Apaches: Eagles of the Southwest* (Norman: University of Oklahoma Press, 1979); and T. R. Fehrenbach, *Comanches: The History of a People* (New York: Knopf, 1974). On newer/revisionist literature, see Janne Lahti, *Wars for Empire: Apaches, the United States, and the Southwest Borderlands* (Norman: University of Oklahoma Press, forthcoming); Edwin R. Sweeney, *From Cochise to Geronimo: The Chiricahua Apaches, 1874–1886* (Norman: University of Oklahoma Press, 2010); William S. Kiser, *Dragoons in Apacheland: Conquest and Resistance in Southern New Mexico, 1846–1861* (Norman: University of Oklahoma Press, 2012); Robert M. Utley, *Geronimo* (New Haven: Yale University Press, 2012); Durwood Ball, *Army Regulars on the Western Frontier, 1848–1861* (Norman: University of Oklahoma Press, 2001); Victoria Smith, *Captive Arizona, 1851–1900* (Lincoln: University of

Nebraska Press, 2009); Timothy Braatz, *Surviving Conquest: A History of the Yavapai Peoples* (Lincoln: University of Nebraska Press, 2003); and Jacoby, *Shadows at Dawn.*

10. Even the best studies focusing on the army's roles, policies, and wars have usually shown limited interest on the enlisted men. See Robert Wooster, *The Military and United States Indian Policy, 1865–1903* (New Haven: Yale University Press, 1988); Robert Wooster, *The American Military Frontiers: The United States Army in the West, 1783–1900* (Albuquerque: University of New Mexico Press, 2009); Utley, *Frontier Regulars*; Utley, *Frontiersmen in Blue*; and Michael L. Tate, *The Frontier Army in the Settlement of the West* (Norman: University of Oklahoma Press, 1999).

11. For studies that discuss the enlisted men as a group in the U.S. Army, see Kevin Adams, *Class and Race in the Frontier Army: Military Life in the West, 1870–1890* (Norman: University of Oklahoma Press, 2009); Janne Lahti, *Cultural Construction of Empire: The U.S. Army in Arizona and New Mexico* (Lincoln: University of Nebraska Press, 2012); Don Rickey, Jr., *Forty Miles a Day on Beans and Hay: The Enlisted Soldier Fighting the Indian Wars* (Norman: University of Oklahoma Press, 1963); Edward M. Coffman, *The Old Army: A Portrait of the American Army in Peacetime, 1784–1898* (New York: Oxford University Press, 1986); Ball, *Army Regulars*; William A. Dobak and Thomas D. Phillips, *The Black Regulars, 1866–1898* (Norman: University of Oklahoma Press, 2001); Robert Wooster, *Frontier Crossroads: Fort Davis and the West* (College Station: Texas A&M University Press, 2005); James N. Leiker, *Racial Borders: Black Soldiers along the Rio Grande* (College Station: Texas A&M University Press, 2002); and Thomas T. Smith, *The U.S. Army and the Texas Frontier Economy, 1845–1900* (College Station: Texas A&M University Press, 1999). The few published book-length studies of individual common soldiers in the Southwest discuss interpreters and scouts. Dan L. Thrapp, *Al Sieber: Chief of Scouts* (Norman: University of Oklahoma Press, 1964); Edwin R. Sweeney, *Merejildo Grijalva: Apache Captive, Army Scout* (El Paso: Texas Western Press, 1992); Allan Radbourne, *Mickey Free: Apache Captive, Interpreter, and Indian Scout* (Tucson: Arizona Historical Society, 2005).

12. On the tendency of army officers to relocate outside the Southwest after their retirement, and on the opposite trend noticeable among common soldiers, see Lahti, *Cultural Construction of Empire*, 92–97.

1
Santiago Brito

Lance R. Blyth

In November 1888, Santiago Brito entered photographer L. A. Skelly's Art Studio in Silver City, New Mexico. Dressed in his best clothes, including hat, scarf, and pocket watch with chain, he posed for a photo. He wore a pistol on his left hip, rigged for a cross-body draw but pulled forward so that it lay along his thigh, displayed clearly. Brito also held a military bugle in his right hand, its bell resting on his hip. Indeed, Brito's bearded visage, the bugle, and the pistol form a triangular centerpiece, dominating the portrait's composition. It is tempting to see the bugle and pistol as photographer's props, but in Brito's case, even if they were, they illustrate a crucial piece of his past. Before he was a miner, freighter, and pioneer of the Southwest, Brito was also a soldier of the borderlands.[1]

A BORDERLANDER AND HIS WORLD

Almost forty years earlier, on October 1, 1849, Santiago Brito had enlisted in the Colonia Militar de Janos in northwestern Chihuahua as a *clarín* (bugler). Listed as a *natural de* (native of) Janos, suggesting that he had been born there, and resident of the same at the time of his enlistment, Brito was the son of María Brito. The *contrato* (contract or enlistment paper) listed no father, something almost unheard of at Janos, but his enlistment suggests that the family had some standing in the community. Brito was fourteen years old at the time, making 1835 his birth year. He was a *labrador*, a small-scale farmer or, most likely in Brito's case, an agricultural worker. He was *soltero* (unmarried) and had a *trigueño rosado* complexion, a sort of light swarthiness, a trait listed in order to aid identification in case of desertion, and something his photo forty years later attested to. And that is all we know about Santiago Brito up to that time.[2]

Santiago Brito, 1888. Courtesy Brito Family Archive.

The paucity of information makes his ancestry quite uncertain. There was a Juana Brito married to a soldier at Janos in the mid-eighteenth century, suggesting that the family may have been in the region since that time. The Brito family remembered that Santiago had been born in 1821 in Sonora, Mexico, and was a Yaqui Indian. Santiago Brito's son, Frank, remembered him often mentioning that he was originally from Sonora and narrating how he was the descendent of Spanish Jewish emigrants to New Spain who fled the Inquisition. Short of genetic research, it is difficult to determine if Santiago Brito was a Yaqui Indian, but it is quite possible that he did have Native American ancestors.[3]

By the time of Brito's enlistment, the Chiricahua Apaches and the Presidio of Janos had experienced nearly two centuries of often conflictual, occasionally cooperative, relations that made both "communities of violence." Refugees from the Pueblo Revolt of 1680 founded Janos in 1685. Apaches, themselves possible refugees from Comanche attacks on the southern plains, followed soon afterward, some settling in the Chiricahua Mountains, for which they would be named. For both Janeros and Chiricahuas, violence was the means by which they established, maintained, or altered the relations between their two communities. Both used violence as the means to establish a path to adulthood and marriage, especially for their young men, and to provide for the families—the basic building block of a community—that resulted. And both built their communities with violence, taking captives, primarily women and children, from each other and assimilating them into their populations. So, given the length of time the Brito family had been around northwestern Chihuahua, the Britos could easily have had an Apache forebearer.[4]

The uncertainty of Brito's past was matched by the uncertainty of his community's present. The U.S.-Mexican War had ended the year previously with the Treaty of Guadalupe Hidalgo. By Article V of that treaty, a boundary line between the two nations was to run "westwardly, along the whole southern boundary of New Mexico (which runs north of the town called Paso) to its western termination." For Janos, this would divide in two what had been a whole. The jurisdiction of Janos used to reach up to Santa Rita del Cobre, near present-day Silver City, New Mexico. Now, it was to end at an undetermined line among desert sierras, only fifty miles away. The new border only complicated the increasingly hostile relations with Chiricahua Apaches. About two decades prior to Brito's enlistment, the nearly four-decade practice of Apache peace establishments, by which Apaches lived on reservations near Spanish and then Mexican military communities and received rations, came to an end. The end of the peace establishments resulted in rounds of conflict between Mexicans and Apaches, followed by regular negotiations of peace.[5]

As Brito grew up, and as he joined the company of Janos, Chiricahua Apaches and the Janos presidio waged war, made peace, then returned to war. This cycle of revenge and retaliation existed since both made ready use of violence to avenge injuries or address potential threats. Both were able to use violence, as neither side was strong enough to stop the other. Apaches were broken into factions, some desiring peace, some war, and with most somewhere in between. No one leader could make all other Apaches obey him, not even Mangas Coloradas, the premier leader of the Chiricahuas at this time, or his son-in-law Cochise. The Mexican national state during the decades after independence was unable, and often unwilling, to assist its northern citizens. It simply insisted that Apaches were Mexicans, to be kindly encouraged to settle in peace, and that violence only to be used as a last resort. Needless to say, northern Mexicans rejected this position.[6]

As Apaches were unable to deal with Mexicans—and Mexicans with Apaches—from positions of strength, their weakness made the seemingly irrational cycle of retaliation quite rational. Apaches knew that they had to raid for status and survival, forcing themselves upon Mexicans with violent assaults, even as they understood this would only bring Mexican revenge, necessitating Apache retaliation. Mexicans, left to their own defenses by the local and national state, could only dispatch pursuits after raiding parties or take revenge upon unsuspecting Apaches for previous wrongs, all the while aware that this would only bring yet more Apache assaults. Neither side felt that it had any other options.[7]

At the time of Brito's birth, these views came to a head at the mining community of Santa Rita del Cobre, some one hundred miles north of Janos, a locale that would come to play an important role in Brito's later life. Created in 1803 or 1804 by the Spanish government, El Cobre had an exposed position that was a source of great concern to the Mexicans after the outbreak of general warfare with the Apaches in 1831. Sometime in the summer of 1835, the company of Janos, minus its families, deployed to El Cobre. The soldiers of Janos were quite dissatisfied with the assignment, fearful for their families, and they immediately began to desert back to Janos, being regularly returned to El Cobre. Finally, on August 6, 1836, they refused to stand guard and sixty-two of them took up arms to protest their ten-month assignment. Other officers and sergeants soon quelled the mutineers and sent them to Galeana. There the Janos mutineers revolted a second time on September 21. A few of the soldiers who mutinied continued to serve, but most were discharged from military service in December 1836.[8] It is tempting to speculate that Brito's father was among the mutineers and that Brito obscured his connection to his dishonorably discharged sire fourteen years later by using his mother's name, but it is impossible to know.

But, now bereft of most of their military protection, the inhabitants of El Cobre grew fearfully, ultimately homicidally, wary of the Apaches. When five Apache women and three Apache men approached El Cobre in the early fall of 1836 with fifteen steers to trade, the Mexican commander at El Cobre only allowed four women to enter the town. Other Mexicans then induced the rest to enter, where they fell upon the Apaches, killing two men and one woman, in a paroxysm of violence, beating, stabbing, spearing, and shooting the victims. The Mexican commander rescued four women, and one man managed to escape. While the commander did seize two Mexicans for the murders, he had to let them go when the townspeople, accompanied by his soldiers, including some from Janos, turned on him "with their weapons in their hands." The women only escaped when the commander personally escorted them three miles beyond the town.[9]

At about the same time, in the mid-1830s, in an attempt to break the logic of revenge and retaliation via extermination, several northern Mexican states, starting with Sonora but soon joined by Chihuahua, began to offer scalp bounties, signing contracts with scalp hunters. The most infamous of these was the American James "Don Santiago" Kirker. Kirker signed a contract at the end of 1839 with the governor of Chihuahua. Kirker agreed to raise a force of two hundred men—Mexicans, Americans, Shawnee Indians—paid four pesos a day. Kirker would also receive fifty pesos for each warrior killed or captured and twenty-five for each female or child taken captive. As Kirker would have to travel to Chihuahua City to collect his payment, the governor agreed to accept scalps, referred to as *piezas*, as proof.[10]

Kirker arrived at Casas Grandes in January 1840 and learned that a large party of Apaches had encamped northeast of Janos while negotiating a peace. Shown the way by a local official, and reinforced by men from Casas Grandes, Kirker's party attacked the Apaches on January 9 along the shores of the Laguna de Ascensión. The scalp hunters killed ten men, captured twenty women and children, and drove off seventy head of livestock. Kirker continued on to Janos, where he seized the Apache leader negotiating with *Alférez* (Ensign) Baltasar Padilla, before returning to Chihuahua City. Padilla was furious with Kirker, as his attacks had disrupted ongoing negotiations, which were the only way to interrupt the cycle of violence, albeit only temporarily. Such protestations did little to deter Kirker, as he attacked several Apache camps near Janos in March and April of 1840.[11] While it is impossible to know if the four-year-old Brito was present in Janos at this time, such encounters between Mexicans and Apaches would have been among his earliest memories.

Another crucial memory for Brito likely came when he was eleven years old, at the end of 1846, when most of the Janos troop rode out of the presidio to counter the American invasion. At the Battle of Sacramento north of Chihuahua on February 28, 1847, the Mexican cavalry charged the Americans at the start of the battle but were soon repulsed by artillery fire. However capable and competent the Mexican soldiers were, they had never faced such intense artillery and rifle fire from a continuously advancing foe. Most of the troop scattered, along with the rest of the Mexican army, after the battle. Some may have gone with the Chihuahuan government as it fell back to the southern reaches of Chihuahua, only returning to Chihuahua City after the Americans left it in May. Another American incursion a year later led to another defeat of Chihuahuan forces, this time at the Battle of Santa Cruz de Rosales on March 16, 1848. It was not until the end of 1848, or the beginning of 1849, that the company of Janos began to reassemble at its garrison.[12]

With the United States now on the doorstep of northern Mexico, and Indian hostilities increasing in the aftermath of the war, President José Joaquin Herrera of Mexico ordered the establishment of military colonies along the new northern border in July 1848. The boundary was to be divided into three frontier commands—Eastern, Chihuahuan, and Western—under a colonel as inspector, with a lieutenant colonel or two as sub-inspectors. Each frontier was to have five to seven colonies, with anywhere from 100 to 150 troops. Janos was to be one of the larger colonies, with a first captain, second captain, paymaster, first lieutenant, second lieutenant, first ensign, second ensign, and a first sergeant. There were to be six second sergeants—two infantry and four cavalry—four infantry corporals, eight cavalry corporals, thirty-three infantrymen, ninety-four cavalry troopers, one drummer, and three buglers.[13]

Now the regulation for the creation and administration of these new military colonies did not reach Chihuahua until June 1849 and Janos a few days after that. In receipt of a new regulation, the company simply changed its designation from *presidio* to *colonia militar*, and just transferred all the currently serving men to the new rolls. Pay records from the time revealed the same names for the presidio of Janos as for the military colony, with four exceptions. With the new authorization for four musicians in the regulation for military colonies, the community quickly signed up four of their young men: Savas Talamantes as the *tambor* (drummer) and Teleforo Padilla (possibly related to the company's first lieutenant), Antonio Benavides, and Santiago Brito as buglers.[14]

RAIDING AND PEACE TALKS

A few weeks before Brito enlisted, thirty Chiricahua Apache warriors under the leader Irigoyen stole some cattle from Janos and then pilfered a cornfield to the north of the town. Some sixty soldiers and residents confronted Irigoyen, who, outnumbered, waved a white flag and asked to talk of peace. After several hours of talk, Irigoyen agreed to drive the stolen cattle back to Janos but ran them the other way. Pursued by only twelve Mexicans, Irigoyen turned and attacked them. In the ensuing skirmish, Apaches killed six soldiers and wounded another, but the remaining soldiers, outnumbered five to one, managed to kill four Apaches and take a saddle horse.[15]

So the company Brito joined, along with the entire community of Janos, was braced for the Apache revenge they knew must come. On a foggy morning, October 11, Brito made his way to the roof of a house on the outskirts of town, where he saw small parties of Apaches driving off the company's horse herd. One Apache waved a white flag and asked to parley. Two Apache leaders approached the northern end of town, refusing to enter. They demanded the return of Apaches held captive in Janos and in the nearby town of Corralitos. Baltasar Padilla, promoted to lieutenant, requested that the Apaches release all the horses, livestock, and captives they had recently taken first. But then, as Brito watched, a party of Americans heading for California came into view along the main road. The Apaches quickly surrounded and seized them without a fight. Padilla then told the Apaches he would surrender the captives he held for the Americans. But, before the exchange of Apaches for Americans could be made, Apaches seeking revenge for their recently dead relatives killed seven of the Americans. In the confusion, the rest of the Americans, naked and beaten, escaped into Janos.[16]

So the new sub-inspector of military colonies in Chihuahua, Col. Emilio Langberg, a Dane in the service of Mexico, led out a force and stayed in the field well into November. It is unlikely that Brito, as a green recruit and not yet an adult, took part in this campaign, which killed one Apache woman, captured six more, and recovered ten horses and four steers. Soon after, Brito would have again watched as Lieutenant Padilla led his own force out of Janos, north and east to the Sierra de Florida, capturing a Chiricahua woman, who would soon escape, rescuing a Mexican captive, and recovering 270 head of livestock. Padilla's actions were vigorous enough to give Janos and nearby towns a respite from Apache attacks from the end of November 1849 through March 1850.[17]

By the spring of 1850, the new military colony of Janos listed 64 men on its rolls, out of an authorized strength of 150. All the men, except the drummer Talamantes, were in cavalry billets—since cavalrymen and trumpeters were paid better, receiving eighteen pesos a year vice fourteen for an infantryman—and were authorized two horses per man purchased at government expense, although their upkeep was the responsibility of the soldiers. The company's weapons were simple, a lance and a short-barreled, smoothbore, flintlock, muzzle-loading firearm, typically called a *fusil*. While regulations authorized each man a pistol and a sabre, there is no evidence that either weapon was ever issued at Janos at this time. The troops' training with these weapons was equally basic, consisting primarily of firing at targets. On October 19, 1850, twenty-nine men from the company took target practice, "puntados al blanco," including Brito. Most, including Brito, only fired two cartridges. Marcos Rodriguez, for some reason, fired five shots, while Eulogio Vigil did not shoot at all, likely as his firearm malfunctioned.[18]

Mexican soldiers did not fire many shots as the short range of their fusils meant that they had to hold their fire until they were literally at point-blank range while their other principal weapon—the lance or *lanza*—had even less range. In decades past, presidial soldiers used leather armor (*cuera*) and a shield (*adarga*) to protect them from arrows, as they closed with their foes. The increase in the number of firearms used by Indians ended armor's effectiveness, however. By Brito's time, Mexican soldiers fought, on foot or mounted, in a loose skirmish line, with soldiers attempting to get close enough to their opponents to successfully discharge their firearms or wield their lances. Such skirmishes were recorded as *acciones de armas* or *funciones de guerra*. These took place, of course, only when the Apaches chose to stand and fight, which they did only irregularly, mainly when defending their encampments or ambushing Mexicans. Most of the actions carried out by Mexican soldiers by this time were pursuits of Apache raiders, called a *correduría* or *correría* (from the Spanish verb *correr*, to run), with the aim to recover the livestock they had taken. All too often, the Apaches escaped or, when caught, would simply abandon the horses and cattle and then escape.[19]

As Brito learned the craft of a bugler and soldier, the pendulum of conflict and cooperation swung back to peace. In April of 1850, an Apache woman, known to the garrison as Gertrudis, who had been captured in September 1849 but had escaped in January, came to Janos, claiming to represent ten leaders who were asking for peace. Notified of the request, the governor of Chihuahua made plans to dispatch peace commissioners at the end of May. On May 22, Brito watched seven Apache headmen, with fifty warriors, and fifty women and children, enter the community to wait for the commissioners. For two days, Apaches and Janeros eagerly gambled and traded stolen livestock for manufactured goods, cloth, and, especially, alcohol. The effects of drink only heightened the Apaches' fear of treachery. So, when the Mexican peace commissioners arrived at Janos with an escort of fifty soldiers, most of the Indians fled. Over the next few days, they returned and for three weeks negotiated with the commissioners, including Lieutenant Padilla, likely accompanied by Brito. The Mexicans agreed to release the Apache prisoners they held, and in return six Apache leaders agreed to aid any pursuits of hostile Apaches, brand their livestock, and settle near Janos, where they would receive rations. Both sides approved the peace on June 24, 1850.[20]

For the next several months, several hundred Apaches resided in camps near Janos. Brito, along with many members of the community, likely spent time among the Apaches while the Apaches spent time at Janos. By this time, both peoples were increasingly dependent upon each other for trade and exchange. Apaches wanted cloth; camp goods such as knives, kettles, and hatchets; gunpowder; and, especially, strong liquor, for which they

"Yanos" (Janos), sketch by John Russell Bartlett, August 1852. Courtesy John Carter Brown Library at Brown University.

traded the livestock they took from other Mexican towns in central Chihuahua and Sonora. Janeros were all too willing to trade for valuable horses and cattle, and they did not look too closely at the brands. Further, there is some suggestion that Apache and Mexican men gambled together; both enjoyed card games. A young man such as Brito may well have been welcomed among his erstwhile opponents.[21]

To feed this contraband trade, a number of Apaches joined a large raid into Sonora in January 1851. Several hundred warriors drove off over one thousand head of cattle and horses, killing twenty-six of their Mexican pursuers. Sonorans traced a number of these warriors, and their trade, to Janos, so, at dawn on March 5, 1851, Brito awoke in the house he shared with his mother and at least one younger brother to the sound of a Sonoran attack. Many Apaches fled into Janos, seeking safety in Mexican houses, possibly even Brito's home. Sonoran troops dragged them from these dwellings and killed some in the streets. For five days the Sonorans occupied Janos and uncovered evidence of the contraband trade between the town, including the garrison, and the Apaches. When the Sonorans finally left Chihuahua, they took six Apache men, four women, and fifty-two children as prisoners, including the mother, wife, and children of the Apache man who would be known as Geronimo, along with three hundred horses, mules, and cattle, thirty-eight of which had Sonoran brands and had been in the possession of Janeros. All the garrison could do was protest vainly.[22]

Lieutenant Padilla clearly felt that the weakness of the company had led to the Sonoran incursion and occupation. When replacement weapons and uniforms arrived at Janos at the end of March 1851, Brito was among those issued new kit on April 1. Despite being no more than sixteen years old, Brito was clearly trusted, as he received a fusil and bayonet, along with a cleaning kit and screwdriver for repairs, and a sling (*bandolera*) with a hook (*gancho*) to carry his fusil while mounted. He also received a cartridge box with forty cartridges and three flints. His uniform issue included a short jacket, a longer coat, and a cloak or *sarape*. Despite receiving the accoutrements of a soldier, Brito was still too young to partake in active service in the field. It would be two years before he saw any action.[23]

A SOLDIER AMONG VOLUNTEERS

On April 18, 1853, the now-eighteen-year-old Brito rode out on his first foray. Lieutenant Padilla led Brito and nineteen soldiers, along with forty-nine civilian volunteers from Janos and the nearby towns of Casas Grandes and Barranco, out on campaign, preceded by two friendly Apache scouts. The campaign had orders to search the sierras north of Janos up to the boundary with the United States. Any Indians located were to be attacked, and all livestock taken would be distributed among the soldiers and volunteers. The latter, as they served without pay and only received munitions and loot, were to receive "good treatment" from Padilla. Brito and the rest of the campaign rode from sunup to sundown for eight days. Finally, on April 26, one of the Apache scouts spotted the plumes of smoke that marked mescal harvesting. Padilla immediately split his force into two columns, surrounded the Apache *ranchería* (settlement), and attacked. The Mexicans managed to kill one man and capture a young woman, but most of the Apaches were dispersed, gathering mescal, and so escaped. The Mexicans thus rounded up twenty-five horses and burned all the *jacales* (huts or wickiups) before heading back to Janos.[24]

Brito did quite well in his first skirmish, well enough that it was recounted in his service record. It may have brought him a share of material benefits.

Per the Chihuahuan Ley Quinto (Fifth Law), passed on May 25, 1849, the female Apache captive was worth 150 pesos and either served as a hostage to exchange for Mexican captives, or was given to a "good family," as an observer noted, as a slave. The dead man was worth 200 pesos, if the soldiers and volunteers returned with a pieza as proof. The horses too, were valuable and necessary. While ordinances required any horses taken from enemy Indians to be turned over to civil officials so they could be reclaimed, they could be used by soldiers while awaiting their owners' arrival. As soldiers were consistently short of horses, they continually added recovered horses to their herd. But the fact that civilian volunteers outnumbered soldiers in Brito's first action revealed the central motif of his military career—the steady decline of Mexican military forces in the borderlands and their replacement by civilian volunteers.[25]

The strength of the Janos company was steadily wasting away; having been over sixty-strong in 1850, it mustered just over fifty men by 1853. This was a long-term trend, beginning decades prior, and to deal with it Mexican authorities introduced conscription, either by lottery or sentencing by civil officials. Such actions did not have the desired effect, as many men simply deserted. Forced service was seen as necessary, as many men in the Mexican north, the traditional recruiting ground for Janos, simply did not wish to serve, since they could gain the main rewards of military service—loot, supplies, status—as civilian volunteers. From the 1830s, Chihuahua state officials insisted that all men, soldier and civilian, had to carry arms in the war against the "barbarian Indians," and by 1852 the national congress recommended establishing a system of civilian guerillas. The military was to supply weapons, ammunition, and mounts to these volunteers, who would keep what they took from the Apaches as pay. In a vain attempt to deal with shrinking enlistments, in June 1853, the minister of war and the navy abandoned the military colonies and authorized reorganization of the presidial companies. The reasoning was that the troops would be "natives of those frontiers," would know the country and their foes, having spent most of their lives at war.[26]

And the war went on. In March 1854, Brito and his (now-presidial) comrades, with their civilian volunteer auxiliaries, chased a party of Indians who had robbed the nearby mining community of Barranco, taking back what they had stolen. Apaches raided Corralitos in that same month, and nine soldiers and thirty civilians pursued them into the Sierra de Enmedio, recovering seven head of livestock and capturing an Indian woman, while another chase only recovered three animals. A force of civilian volunteers came into Janos that same month, and petitioned to keep the animals they had taken from Apaches as a reward. Another party of armed civilians from Janos and Casas Grandes departed on an expedition, "mounted on good horses," in June. In August 1854 men from Janos, likely including Brito, followed an Apache party, caught them, killed three, and drove back twenty-eight cattle.[27]

We can infer that Brito took part in at least some of these pursuits, as he was promoted to the rank of *soldado* (soldier) in November 1854 and to *cabo* (corporal) on December 2, 1854, in large part due to his loyalty, steadfastness, and experience, having served five years in the company. Yet the attempt to re-create Janos as a presidio, in order to increase its numbers, had failed as the company now only had forty-eight men. Reliance upon volunteers for offensive actions meant that the presidial soldiers were scattered in small detachments across the region, guarding settlements. Corporal Brito thus found himself commanding a detachment guarding the Hacienda del Carmen, a place of no particular importance, nearly two hundred miles east and south of Janos at the end of the year. This very well may have irked Brito, as only the month prior he had requested permission to marry Georgia Abalos, a native of Janos, and had enrolled his brother Tomas in the presidial school.[28]

All these actions by Brito suggest that he was establishing his own household, perhaps because his mother had died recently. It is difficult to overstate the importance of a household for a soldier in the Mexican borderlands as there was no logistical system. By the 1850s, the supply system provided just payments of cash to be used to purchase goods, but also occasionally issues of corn. So a soldier needed a household, typically under an adult female—a wife, a mother, or even a sister—with perhaps an Apache slave girl to help, to provide the logistical functions. It was a soldier's household members who would feed him, usually drawing his rations or cash for him during his many absences on campaign, with detachments at nearby settlements carrying mail, escorting supply trains, or guarding the horse herd. Because military uniform issues were few and far between, it was the household who would clothe him. And the household nursed him when he was wounded or sick, as the presidio had no infirmary or medical personnel. For these reasons, soldiers in northern Mexico, unlike their American counterparts north of the border, were typically married, and Brito wasted no time in doing the same.[29]

In May 1855, Corporal Brito rode out of Janos in a force of soldiers and citizens, looking to intercept a party of Apaches that had crossed the border and was raiding in the vicinity of Janos. The Janeros found the trail of about twenty Indians and followed them into the mountains to the south. Several hours after sunrise the next day, the Mexicans fell upon two Indians, killing one and capturing the other. Their prisoner, Nalze, told the Mexicans that many Apache headmen wished to make peace in Chihuahua. A group of nearly three hundred had recently settled near the Hacienda del Carmen. But now Captain Padilla suspected that the Apaches wished to cross the border to harvest mescal and were talking of peace to do so unmolested. Padilla's suspicions were confirmed when the Apaches failed to come to a parley east of Janos and those at Carmen abandoned their treaty, attacking Corralitos and killing fourteen miners. Janos too came under attack in that summer of 1855, when eleven men fought off over seventy-five Apaches who were attempting to drive off the community's horse herd on June 1.[30]

But Brito, along with most of the available soldiers at Janos, only twenty in all, soon found himself assigned to a new mission, escorting the Mexican Commission of Limits from October to December as it surveyed a new boundary line south of the Gila River and even closer to Janos. It proved to be unpleasant duty. The escort ran short of supplies and lost horses and mules to Apaches, and a number of men even deserted. When Brito returned to Janos in December, it was to a new wife, Anselma Ruis of Corralitos. They had married on October 6 in the centuries-old church of San Antonio de Padua in Casas Grandes, apparently just before Brito had gone off on the escort. What happened to Georgia Abalos, the woman Brito had requested to marry in November the year before, is unknown. Perhaps she turned down his proposal or, more likely, died in childbirth or from disease.[31]

END OF THE JANOS GARRISON

For the next few months, Brito apparently remained at the presidio or led small detachments of soldiers, usually four to nine, guarding Janos, the political seat of the district at Corralitos, or Hacienda del Carmen. On May 15,

1856, however, news reached Janos of an Apache raid on Casas Grandes, killing one Mexican and driving off a herd of livestock. Brito joined a force of soldiers and mainly civilian volunteers from Janos, Barranco, and Corralitos, leaving his pregnant wife. The Mexicans trailed the Apaches, located where they forded the Río Casas Grandes, and determined that they had split into two groups, one group driving the livestock before them. Captain Padilla decided to follow the livestock, and Brito and his colleagues tracked them northward. After three days, on May 19, the Mexicans surprised four Apaches, who did not expect a pursuit that close to the border, and killed three, taking their scalps for the bounty and seizing one as a prisoner, the previously captured Nalze. They also reclaimed the livestock—Brito's service record documented that he recovered five steers—before returning to the presidio. Brito was thus able to be back at Janos when his first child, a daughter named Estanislada, was born on June 27.[32]

That August, Padilla was ultimately able to exchange Nalze for Prudencio Arelos of Janos, who had been taken by Apaches three months earlier. This allowed for yet another round of peace talks to begin at Janos; but an attack on September 2 by Mangas Coloradas, who did not approve of peace with Mexicans, abruptly brought the discussions to a halt. Padilla thus seized the Apache negotiators and their families at Janos as hostages. With few forces, now less than fifty men, and the Apaches ensconced on the American side of the border, Padilla determined upon a secret plan to gain a peace with the Apaches. He dispatched one of the Apache women he had imprisoned, known as Carlota, as an emissary to Apaches living on the Mimbres River on American soil, inviting them to cross the border to Janos and settle there in peace. Padilla provided Carlota with an escort of ten soldiers, and, while the escort's leader name was not recorded, it was very likely Brito, given his loyalty and experience. If so, Brito successfully brought Carlota across the border, to the Apaches on the Mimbres, and back to Mexico, seeing, perhaps for the first time, the "tall pines" country of southwestern New Mexico. The mission proved to be a success, and by February 1857 nearly 250 Apaches were living near Janos. While this was not the first time Janos and Brito had Apache neighbors, it would prove to be the last.[33]

But, by that time, Janos was all but done as a military force. When Corporal Brito mustered on February 1, 1857, with one horse, he was one of only thirty-seven men on the company's rolls. In an attempt to concentrate and bolster the remaining presidios, the commandant general of Chihuahua administratively consolidated the companies of Janos and San Elizario on February 5, though the companies separated a year later. All this was to no avail; Brito and his comrades were operating primarily as "auxiliaries assisting the citizenry." When 150 members of the citizenry mustered at Casas Grandes under Don Esmergildo Quintana in April, Captain Padilla feared that they would attack the Apaches living at Janos and ordered them not to advance to the presidio. When one hundred of the men did so, Padilla detained them, an action for which he was roundly chastised by the commandant general, who noted that auxiliary forces were the only ones available to "garrison that frontier."[34]

A decade of experience with the border taught Apaches that they could cross over to the other side whenever things grew too threatening on one side. So, in the summer of 1857 many Apaches, including Mangas Coloradas, relocated south to avoid an American campaign and settled at Janos. Over six hundred Indians made the transition. Yet an epidemic broke out, and, while a number of Apaches relocated to Corralitos, many returned to the United States, leaving only a few family groups in the area. When these, in the absence of rations, turned to raiding, there was little the company of Janos could do as it—along with Brito's military career—was near an end.

On April 1, 1858, Captain Padilla mustered the garrison of the Janos presidio for the last time, listing four officers, an armorer, three sergeants, a bugler, three corporals, including Brito, and nineteen soldiers by rank and name. Yet Padilla recorded the "destinos," the post or assignment, of all thirty-two men as "losses." Padilla explained in his report that the company had quit military service following the order from the commandant general of Chihuahua on March 6, 1858, in support of the Plan of Tacubaya, which would lead Mexico into the Wars of the Reform pitting liberals versus conservatives.[35]

Local, armed civilians, under their own leaders, would thus be the primary soldiers in the Chihuahuan borderlands from this time. Juan Mata Ortiz of Galeana, south of Janos, was a regular mobilizer and leader of armed civilians. In 1861 and 1863, Ortiz supported campaigns in northwest Chihuahua led by Joaquín Terrazas, the cousin of the state's governor, comprised of a few state troops and local *vecinos* (citizens). Juan José Zozaya, originally an Indian peace commissioner, and Cayetano Ortiz also led groups of state-sponsored volunteers, including many from Janos, in the late 1860s. After the end of the French Intervention, and the consolidation of political control of Chihuahua under the Terrazas clan, Joaquín Terrazas was again active. In the 1870s, he continued to rely upon armed civilians to "persecute the barbarians," with those from Janos led by Mata Ortiz as the local political chief. It was just such a force of a few national cavalrymen, state troops, and armed civilian volunteers that tracked, caught, and killed or captured most of the Apaches under Victorio at Tres Castillos in 1880.[36]

CROSSING BORDERS

Santiago Brito, however, left Mexico after the disbandment of the Janos company. He told the census taker in 1900 that he came to the United States in 1857. He headed for the copper mines at Santa Rita del Cobre in New Mexico but apparently continued regularly to cross the border into Mexico as his second daughter, Estéfana, was born there in July 1858. In 1860, gold was discovered in nearby Pinos Altos, New Mexico, causing a stampede of miners, including Santiago. By the spring of 1861, Brito was working a placer gold claim in Rich Gulch in Pinos Altos. Yet, while he was no longer a soldier, the borderlands region was still at war.

Emboldened by the removal of U.S. Army forces from the region at the start of the Civil War, and enraged by their mistreatment at the hands of the miners, Chiricahua Apaches fell upon Pinos Altos at dawn on September 27, 1861. Initially the miners were trapped in their houses and at their diggings, Brito likely among them. Slowly they fought the Apaches off, the fight then coalescing around the supply stores in the center of town. At midday, after enough men had gathered, and with the support of a small cannon loaded with nails and buckshot, the miners counterattacked and drove off the Apaches, killing at least ten and possibly as many as twenty, including several leaders. Pinos Altos lost five men killed, and many more left the settlement afterward, leaving just seventy miners. Brito again was likely one who stayed. He soon became a leading member of the community, known as "Don Santiago." His "piety and zeal" led to the erection of a cross on a mountain north and east of town, in honor of the fifth-century Byzantine empress Helene, still called Cross Mountain to this day. Brito's first son,

José Anacleto Ruis, was born on April 21, 1864. Santiago apparently did well enough from his mining efforts to establish the first stage between Silver City, ten miles to the south, and Pinos Altos and operated it throughout the 1870s.[37]

Yet borderlands war was still never far away. On several occasions, Apache raiders ran off livestock belonging to Don Santiago's neighbors and kin. His daughter Estanislada married John McDonald, who lost livestock to Apaches on three different occasions during the 1870s. In 1870, Indians took a horse and a mule near McDonald's house a mile outside of Pinos Altos. Santiago and some others followed the tracks of the Indians but did not follow them very far, a lifetime of wariness cautioning against it. Indians took another horse and mule from the nearby range in 1872 and the same in 1876. In the latter instance, Santiago and three others again followed the raiders for a short distance, but, with only four in their party, they dared not go too far. In 1880, Apaches drove off most of the cattle in the neighborhood and Santiago's neighbor, John R. Adair, lost six cows and yearlings. Santiago and Adair joined with the others who had lost stock and attempted to trail the raiders, but to no avail.[38]

Not long after the birth of his second son, Francisco, "Frank," on August 24, 1877, Santiago gave up the stage coach business and returned to his "first love—mining." For the next thirty years Santiago would mine at Pinos Altos with, as his obituary noted, "varying success." Anselma died in 1885, but Santiago married again, to Isadora, but they had no children who survived. Yet he did not forget his military past. In April 1898, he summoned his two sons, José and Frank, home from their jobs as cowboys on the Circle Bar Ranch near Silver City. He sent them to Santa Fe, to enlist in the First U.S. Volunteer Cavalry Regiment, later better known as the Rough Riders. The two brothers did not fight in Cuba, as theirs was one of four troops left behind, due to a shortage in shipping. José would later enlist in a volunteer unit for the Philippines, from which he never returned, listed as missing, and presumed as dead in 1900. Santiago continued to mine in Pinos Altos, lastly at the Arizona Mine. But in October 1908, after a month-long illness, he felt death creeping up on him. He wrote a final letter to his son Frank on the seventeenth, sending his "love and blessings." Santiago Brito died on Thursday, October 29, 1908, in Pinos Altos, New Mexico, where he was buried and his headstone remains, a true soldier of the southwestern borderlands.[39]

NOTES

1. According to Richard Rudisill, *Photographers of the New Mexico Territory, 1854–1912* (Santa Fe: Museum of New Mexico, 1973), 53, Skelly was initially active in Silver City in November 1888, before relocating the same month to Deming. My thanks to Frank J. Brito for providing this reference.

2. Contrato del Clarín, Santiago Brito, Janos, October 1, 1849, roll 32, Janos Collection (JC), Cline Library, Northern Arizona University.

3. Juana Brito, "Mission 2000 Searchable Spanish Mission Records," *Tumacácori National Historical Park*, http://home.nps.gov/applications/tuma/detail.cfm?Personal_ID=18528 (accessed September 10, 2014); Frank J. Brito, "The Brito Family—A Genealogical Works," (2013), courtesy of author; Narration by Frank C. Brito re Santiago—his father, Brito Family Archive (BFA). Stanley M. Hordes, *To the End of the Earth: A History of the Crypto-Jews of New Mexico* (New York: Columbia University Press, 2005), 118–19, finds the Brito surname among the crypto-Jews of northern New Spain.

4. For this deeper history, see Lance R. Blyth, *Chiricahua and Janos: Communities of Violence in the Southwestern Borderlands, 1680–1880* (Lincoln: University of Nebraska Press, 2012), esp. 5–121.

5. Richard Griswold del Castillo, *The Treaty of Guadalupe Hidalgo: A Legacy of Conflict* (Norman: University of Oklahoma Press, 1992), 187–88 [quotation]; Matthew Babcock, "Blurred Borders: North America's Forgotten Apache Reservations," in *Contested Spaces of Early America*, ed. Juliana Barr and Edward Countryman (Philadelphia: University of Pennsylvania Press, 2014), 163–83.

6. See Brian DeLay, *War of a Thousand Deserts: Indian Raids and the U.S.-Mexican War* (New Haven: Yale University Press, 2008), for the internal politics of Mexican Indian policy during this time.

7. Blyth, *Chiricahua and Janos*, 123–54. See also William B. Griffen, *Utmost Good Faith: Patterns of Apache-Mexican Hostilities in Northern Chihuahua Border Warfare, 1821–1848* (Albuquerque: University of New Mexico Press, 1988).

8. José J. Calvo to Comandante de Janos, August 28, 1835, Folder 37, Section 1, Janos Records, Records of the Presidio de San Felipe y Santiago de Janos, 1706–1858 (JR), Benson Latin American Collection, General Libraries, University of Texas at Austin; Para que el Teniente Rey, Cobre, n.d. (likely 1836), Folder 39, Section 1, JR; Felipe Griego to Comandante of Janos, June 4, 1836, roll 26, JC; Comandante de Janos to Comandante General, Janos, August 6, 1836, Folder 38, Section 2, JR; Mariano Varela to Mariano Ponce de Leon, September 27, 1836, roll 27, JC; Lance R. Blyth, "The Presidio of Janos: Ethnicity, Society, Masculinity, and Ecology in Far Northern Mexico, 1685–1858" (PhD diss., Northern Arizona University, 2005), 159–60.

9. William B. Griffen, *Apaches at War and Peace: The Janos Presidio, 1750–1858* (Albuquerque: University of New Mexico Press, 1988), 172. For the role that fear and a "deep, constant *apprehension*" played in such massacres, see Larry McMurtry, *Oh What a Slaughter: Massacres in the American West: 1846–1890* (New York: Simon and Schuster, 2010), 6.

10. Ralph A. Smith, *Borderlander: The Life of James Kirker, 1793–1852* (Norman: University of Oklahoma Press, 1999), 99–101; Ralph A. Smith, "The Scalp Hunter in the Borderlands 1835–1850," *Arizona and the West* 6 (Spring 1964): 5–22.

11. Smith, *Borderlander*, 102–103, 109–12.

12. Luis Jáuregui, "Chihuahua en la tormenta: su situación política durante la guerra con las Estados Unidos, Septiembre de 1846-Julio de 1848," in Josefina Zoraida Vázquez, ed., *México al tiempo de su Guerra con Estados Unidos (1846–1848)* (México, DF: El Colegio de México: Secretaría de Relaciones Exteriores: Fondo de Cultura Económica, 1997), 143–47, 153–54; Joseph C. Dawson III, *Doniphan's Epic March: The 1st Missouri Volunteers in the Mexican War* (Lawrence: University Press of Kansas, 1999), 142–62; Cadmus M. Wilcox, *History of the Mexican War* (Washington, D.C.: Church News, 1892), 541–43; Blyth, *Chiricahua and Janos*, 145

13. *Colonias Militares, Proyecto para su Establecimiento en las Fronteras de Oriente y Occidente de la Republica*, July 20, 1848 (copy, Chihuahua, June 4, 1849), roll 31, JC. Translated and edited in Odie B. Faulk, "Projected Mexican Military Colonies for the Borderlands," *Journal of Arizona History* 9 (Spring 1968): 39–45.

14. *Colonias Militares*, July 20, 1848; Pay Records, Janos, 1849–1850, both in roll 31, JC.

15. Baltasar Padilla to Inspector de las Colonias Militares, September 15, 1849, roll 32, JC; Filiaciones, Macedonio Ornelas, San Buenaventura, July 21, 1842, and José Almansa, Janos, January 16, 1849, both in Folder 48, Section 2, JR.

16. Diario de novedades, October 11–12, 1849, Folder 48, Section 2, JR.

17. Hoja de servicio, Capitán Don Baltasar Padilla, Janos, December 31, 1857, Folder 53, Section 1, JR; Bob Cunningham and Harry P. Hewitt, "A 'Lovely Land Full of Roses and Thorns': Emil Langberg and Mexico, 1835–1866," *Southwestern Historical Quarterly* 98 (January 1995): 398; Blyth, *Chiricahua and Janos*, 150.

18. Lista paso la revista, Colonia Militar de Janos, n.d. (likely May 1850); Cartucheros a puntados al blanco, Janos, October 19, 1850, both in roll 33, JC.

19. Blyth, "Presidio of Janos," 75–96, has a more complete discussion of the armament and tactics at Janos.

20. Padilla to Comandante General, April 30, 1850; Padilla to Jefe Politíco, May 22, 1850, both in roll 33, JC; Edwin R. Sweeney, *Mangas Coloradas: Chief of the Chiricahua Apaches* (Norman: University of Oklahoma Press, 1998), 202–204.

21. Blyth, *Chiricahua and Janos*, 154; Griffen, *Apaches at War and Peace*, 237–39.

22. Griffen, *Apaches at War and Peace*, 237–40; Sweeney, *Mangas Coloradas*, 218–25; Edwin R. Sweeney, "'I Had Lost All:' Geronimo and the Carrasco Massacre of 1851," *Journal of Arizona History* 27 (Spring 1986): 35–52.

23. Relación de las prendas, Janos, April 1, 1851, roll 33, JC.

24. José María Zuloaga to Padilla, April 15, 1853, roll 34 [quotation]; Diario de Campaña, April 30, 1853, roll 34; Contrato del Clarin, Santiago Brito, Janos, October 1, 1849, roll 32, all in JC. See Morris Edward Opler, *An Apache Life-Way: The Economic, Social, and Religious Institutions of the Chiricahua Indians* (1941; repr., Lincoln: University of Nebraska Press, 1996), 356–58, for mescal harvesting practices.

25. Smith, "The Scalp Hunter in the Borderlands," 17; Julius Froebel, *Seven Years' Travel in Central America, Northern Mexico, and the Far West of the United States* (London: Richard Bentley, 1859), 354 [quotation]; Blyth, "Presidio of Janos," 211–12.

26. Blyth, "Presidio of Janos," 64–67, 230–34; Victor Orozco Orozco, *Las Guerras Indias en la Historia de Chihuahua: Antología* (Ciudad Juárez, Mex.: Universidad Autónoma de Ciudad Juárez, Instituto Chihuahense de la Cultura, 1992), 205 [first quotation]; Angel Frias to Padilla, August 2, 1853, roll 34, JC [second quotation].

27. Hoja de servicio, Capitán Don Baltasar Padilla, Janos, December 31, 1857, Folder 53, Section 1, JR; Comandante Militar to Ayudante Inspector, March 13, 1854; Diario de novedades, March 13, 1854; Comisario de Janos, Janos, June 3, 1854, all in roll 35, JC.

28. Contrato del Clarín, Santiago Brito, Janos, October 1, 1849, roll 32; Lista para revista, Janos, December 2, 1854; Estado de Fuerza, Janos, December 2, 1854; Relación que manifiesta los niños, Janos, December 1, 1854, roll 35, all in JC; Santiago Brito to Capitán de la Compañía, November 1, 1854, Folder 51, Section 1, JR.

29. Blyth, "Presidio of Janos," 121–35, 153–67.

30. Contrato del Clarín, Santiago Brito, Janos, October 1, 1849, roll 32; Comandante de Janos to Comandante General May 28, 1855, roll 36, both in JC; Sweeney, *Mangas Coloradas*, 317–18.

31. Hoja de servicio, Capitán Don Baltasar Padilla, Janos, December 31, 1857, Folder 53, Section 1, JR; Griswold del Castillo, *Treaty of Guadalupe Hidalgo*, 58–61; Joseph Richard Werne, *The Imaginary Line: A History of the United States and Mexican Boundary Survey, 1848–1857* (Fort Worth: Texas Christian University Press, 2007), 211–12; International Genealogical Index Individual Records "Santiago Brito" and "Ancelma Ruis," www.familysearch.org, (accessed December 24, 2003), courtesy BFA. Brito's obituary writer in 1908 likely confused this 1855 escort of the Mexican Commission of Limits with that of John Russell Bartlett's 1850 Boundary Commission. See "Old Pioneer of 1853 Dies at Pinos Altos: Santiago Brito Finally Crosses the Divide After a Long and Useful Career," *Silver City Independent*, November 3, 1908.

32. Estado de fuerza, Janos, March 1, 1856, roll 36; Contrato del Clarín, Santiago Brito, Janos, October 1, 1849, roll 32; Padilla to Michael Steck, November 3, 1856, roll 36, both in JC; Blyth, *Chiricahua and Janos*, 166–67; Brito, "Brito Family."

33. Blyth, *Chiricahua and Janos*, 167–69.

34. Lista y extracto de revista, Janos, February 1, 1857, roll 33; Contrato del Clarín, Santiago Brito, Janos, October 1, 1849, roll 32; José Merino to Capitán de San Elisario, October 22, 1856, roll 36 [first quotation]; Comandante de Janos to Don Esmergildo Quintana, April 3, 1857, roll 37; Merino to Capitán de Janos, April 27, 1857, roll 37 [second quotation], all in JC; Comandante Militar a la Frontera de Janos to Zuloaga, April 5, 1857, Folder 53, Section 1, JR.

35. Sweeney, *Mangas Coloradas*, 352–59; Casares to Padilla, March 21, 1857, Folder 53, Section 1, JR; Lista y extracto de la revista, Janos, April 1, 1858, roll 37, JC [quotations]; Brian R. Hamnett, "Wars of Reform (Three Years War)," in Michael S. Werner, ed., *Encyclopedia of Mexico: History, Society and Culture* (Chicago: Fitzroy Dearborn, 1997), 1601–1604.

36. Blyth, *Chiricahua and Janos*, 175–81, 188–96; Mark Wasserman, *Capitalist, Caciques, and Revolution: The Native Elite and Foreign Enterprise in Chihuahua, Mexico, 1854–1911* (Chapel Hill: University of North Carolina Press, 1984); Fernando Jordán, *Crónica de un País Bárbaro* (Chihuahua, Mex.: Centro Librero la Prensa, 1975), 250–60; Joaquín Terrazas, *Memorias* (Ciudad Juarez, Mex.: El Agricultor Mexicano, 1905).

37. *Twelfth Census of the United States*, New Mexico, Grant County, Precinct 2, Pinos Altos, June 11, 1900 (Washington, D.C.: U.S. Census Office, 1901); "Old Pioneer of 1853 Dies," *Silver City Independent*, November 3, 1908; Sweeney, *Mangas Coloradas*, 423–25; R. S. Allen, "A Summary of the History of Pinos Altos, Grant County, New Mexico," *Silver City Enterprise*, 1889, reprinted as "Pinos Altos, New Mexico," *New Mexico Historical Review* 23 (October 1948): 302–32 [quotation on 308]; Brito, "Brito Family."

38. Indian Depredation Claims Numbers 7070 and 7967, BFA.

39. Brito, "Brito Family"; "Old Pioneer of 1853 Dies," *Silver City Independent*, November 3, 1908 [quotations]; Frank Brito, "Frank Brito of the Rough Riders," http://www.spanamwar.com/Brito (accessed March 4, 2014); Santiago Brito to Francisco C. Brito, October 17, 1908, BFA.

2
Louis Geck

William S. Kiser

Following the arrival of Gen. Stephen W. Kearny's Army of the West in 1846, U.S. troops occupied New Mexico permanently, attempting to enforce that officer's impossible promise that the federal government would protect the mainly Hispanic residents from Apache, Comanche, and Navajo raiders, who regularly pilfered stock and abducted captives.[1] Although regiments of artillery, infantry, and dragoons participated in this occupation, the dragoons (mounted horse soldiers) bore the responsibility of campaigning in the field, skirmishing with enemies, and punishing parties that struck the Rio Grande settlements. The dragoons, then, saw the most active duty in antebellum New Mexico and frequently engaged in violent confrontations with independent Indians.

One man who experienced the rigors of borderlands military life was Pvt. Louis William Geck of Company H, First U.S. Dragoons, stationed at the village of Doña Ana in south-central New Mexico. Born in Warsaw, Poland, on June 4, 1818, Geck immigrated to the United States sometime in the early 1830s.[2] In 1841, the five-foot-six, dark-haired, twenty-three-year-old youth with a background in carpentry joined the dragoons at a Baltimore, Maryland, recruiting station. He spent his first five-year term of enlistment on the Southern Plains, where mounted troops campaigned against Cheyenne, Comanche, and Kiowa groups while watching over the Indian Territory. When his first tour of duty ended on January 12, 1846, Geck promptly reenlisted for another five years with the same company.[3] At that time, the unmarried Polish immigrant did not have any family obligations. For a bachelor, military service provided a reliable occupation, food and clothing, housing, and a source of income, however meager the eight-dollar monthly wage might have been.[4]

Geck's second term of enlistment began just four months before the United States opened hostilities with Mexico, a conflict he managed to

Louis William Geck, ca. 1880s. Courtesy Jess D. Weir, Jr.

avoid, as Company H remained at Dragoon Camp, Arkansas, and Fort Gibson, Indian Territory, for the duration of the U.S.-Mexican War. While at Fort Gibson in 1848, Geck married a German woman named Mamie—the first of his four wives—who perished shortly thereafter when she fell into a water well at the fort.[5] Not long after the tragedy, Geck's company transferred to New Mexico Territory to garrison a new post in the Mesilla Valley, where he would remain from July 1849 until his second, and final, discharge in January 1851. Geck's seventeen months of service in southern New Mexico placed him in the thick of the U.S. Army's conflict with Mescalero and Chiricahua Apaches in that region.

TO SOUTHERN NEW MEXICO

Geck served as a dragoon at a time when New Mexico's military department suffered from chronic shortages of soldiers and supplies. Although seven companies of mounted troops operated throughout the territory in 1850, officials believed that at least ten units—and preferably even more—would be necessary to effectively control Indian depredations, with one army inspector reporting that no less than 2,200 soldiers should patrol the vast southwestern domain.[6] Gen. Winfield Scott eventually dispatched 750 additional troops to augment the forces already stationed in New Mexico, but even with this added strength the army struggled to contain the Apaches, Comanches, and Navajos. A frustrated Col. Edwin Sumner wrote to Secretary of War Charles Conrad in 1852, opining that the occupation of the region was a waste of time, money, and manpower. He recommended that the military redirect its efforts and resources elsewhere and abandon New Mexico altogether, leaving the territory for the Hispanics and Indians to fight over.[7]

Whether they liked it or not, however, the troops were in New Mexico to stay. As the only land connection between Texas and California, the region became part and parcel to American aspirations of building a transcontinental railroad and establishing a coast-to-coast empire. The U.S. government had no intention of heeding Sumner's advice and abandoning the newly acquired Mexican Cession lands, and the dragoons would therefore be charged with controlling and chastising southwestern tribes, protecting government agents and civilians, and building infrastructure in advancement of American hegemony over the land.

For the final year and a half of his enlistment, Geck's permanent station would be the post at Doña Ana, a small Rio Grande farming village of several hundred Hispanic inhabitants at the northern terminus of the Mesilla Valley. The village not only was close to the new international border but also was squeezed between Mescalero and Chiricahua Apache homelands. Today the community is an unassuming (and still largely Hispanic) suburb of the much larger city of Las Cruces, but in the antebellum era—prior to the emergence of nearby municipalities as alternative political seats and population centers—Doña Ana dominated the regional landscape as the valley's first trail stop and place of commerce. The town's importance can be gleaned from the fact that it is mentioned or described in many firsthand accounts of 1850s New Mexico, providing a glimpse of the village that Geck called home for over forty years.

John Russell Bartlett of the International Boundary Commission spent the night at Doña Ana on January 13, 1851—the day after Geck mustered out of the service. Clearly unimpressed by what he saw, Bartlett—who previously managed a bookstore in New York City's Astor House and considered himself socially and intellectually sophisticated—wrote simply, "Its houses are mostly of a class called *jacals*, i.e., built of upright sticks [and] filled with mud." He also mentioned that "a better class of adobe buildings have just been erected along the main street, for occupation of the military," although these structures also seemed deficient to newcomers. Lt. Henry Lazelle of the Eighth Infantry visited for a single night on April 23, 1857, and left with an even more pessimistic opinion of the community, where Geck was living as a civilian merchant by that time. The young lieutenant wrote that he "passed through the miserably wretched village," which he prejudicially called a "Mexican collection of hovels, in perfect keeping, with their squalid filth and poverty."[8]

Capt. Randolph B. Marcy, who as early as 1849 understood Doña Ana to be an important crossroads and point of reference, offered a less cynical view when describing the citizens as hardworking subsistence farmers who relied upon the dragoons to protect them from "those brigands of the mountains, the Apaches, who were in the habit of coming down from their mountain retreats [and] stampeding and driving off cattle and horses." As British traveler George Ruxton pointed out during the U.S-Mexican War, the wood and mud huts offered residents little protection from Apaches, who had "already paid them several visits and carried off or destroyed their stock."[9] Prior to the arrival of U.S. troops in 1849, the residents of Doña Ana had seemed so vulnerable to Apache raiding that the sympathetic Col. Alexander Doniphan left behind a surplus cannon for their use against the Indians when he passed through with his Missouri Volunteers in December 1846.[10]

Like most other military posts in the territory at that time, the troops at Doña Ana occupied rented quarters in adobe dwellings located within town limits, a trend that created discipline and logistical problems until Colonel Sumner began relocating the soldiers away from settlements in September 1851.[11] Unlike many other units at that time, Geck's Company H was at full strength with fifty-four dragoons available for duty, along with forty-three men of Company B, Third Infantry.[12] In fact, the number of troops stationed at Doña Ana remained remarkably constant for the duration of its time as a post. A total of 123 men occupied the town in December 1849, a year later the garrison boasted 121 soldiers, and, when the department abandoned it in September 1851 to establish Fort Fillmore, 122 troops relocated there.[13]

One army inspector expressed satisfaction with the dragoons, writing, "They are fine riders, are expert in the use of their arms, and well drilled," going so far as to praise Company H for being "in better order than any I have seen in this department." He also observed that the dragoons at Doña Ana did a commendable job maintaining their horses in serviceable condition, a necessity for mounted troops who might be (and often were) called upon to chase Apaches into their homelands at a moment's notice.[14]

Although Geck himself did not leave behind any diaries or memoirs, several of his contemporary soldiers did, providing a glimpse of the many hardships—a long list that included torrential downpours, immobilizing snow storms, precarious river crossings, exhausting summertime heat, waterless camps, and exposure to Indian attack—that characterized military service at many borderlands garrisons in the 1850s.[15] On her journey with a military escort across the Santa Fe Trail to New Mexico, Lydia Spencer Lane, the wife of an officer in the Regiment of Mounted Rifles, recalled nights when her tent "rocked and shook" from deafening thunder and heavy rains, after which "everything and everybody were soaking wet and felt as dreary as they looked." As she followed her husband from one post to another, Lane shared many of the experiences of enlisted men accompanying their command and occupied living quarters at the same "dreary and uninviting" forts as dragoons like Geck.[16]

Pvt. James A. Bennett of Company I, First Dragoons chronicled comparable experiences in a diary that he kept from 1849 to 1856. After arriving in New Mexico, Bennett studied Spanish on his free time but frequently campaigned against Apache, Navajo, and Ute Indians, at one point receiving a serious gunshot wound that left him debilitated and bedridden for months in the Cantonment Burgwin hospital. Of one winter expedition, he lamented, "uncomfortable travelling as the snow is two feet deep. . . . Mules were dying from starvation and the men almost frozen to death," while a summertime expedition left him "almost eaten up by mosquitos."[17] Another dragoon, William Drown, recalled a 1855 campaign in the Sacramento Mountains of southeastern New Mexico, during which he found himself knee-deep in mud and snow, hardly ideal conditions for the ensuing skirmish with Mescalero Apaches that resulted in three men of his company wounded and one soldier killed by an arrow lodged nearly three inches deep in his skull. Similar violence characterized Bennett's term of service in New Mexico. He witnessed an Indian murder a captive white woman, saw the parched unburied bones of four men that Navajos killed at a military hay camp, looked on as a Mexican guide was shot through the hip during Maj. Marshall Howe's 1852 campaign against the Apaches, and watched as the wife of Capt. Henry Stanton mourned his death at the hands of Mescaleros in January 1855—all ominous signs of the fate that might befall anybody in the violent southwestern borderlands.[18]

CHASING APACHES

As an enlisted man, Geck participated in the numerous excursions that Company H undertook in pursuit of Mescalero and Gila (Chihennes, a subgroup of the Chiricahuas) Apaches on both sides of the Rio Grande.[19] On September 28, 1849—just one month after a skirmish against a group of Gila Apaches had left Maj. Enoch Steen, Geck's commanding officer, injured and a dragoon corporal dead—a band of Mescaleros swept through Doña Ana, killing a civilian herder and driving away eleven oxen.[20] The following morning, Steen ordered a detachment of twelve dragoons and ten Mexican guides to follow the Apaches' trail eastward into the Sacramento Mountains, but they eventually halted their pursuit and returned to the post without overtaking the Indians. The fact that Steen himself did not partake in this foray likely owed to his having been injured the month prior, which would have impeded his ability to effectively command troops in the field. It is not known whether Geck was among the dozen troopers assigned to this mission.[21]

Shortly afterward, a group of twenty-four Mescaleros entered Doña Ana to negotiate a treaty and exchange three captive Mexican boys taken during raids. Having recently suffered casualties at the hands of Gila Apaches, and failing to confront the Mescaleros in the brief September chase, a frustrated Steen gave these Apaches a cool reception. He immediately imprisoned the two headmen, Santos and Buffalo, and ordered the remainder of the group to return all livestock recently taken from Doña Ana. Geck looked on as the Mescaleros fled, leaving their incarcerated leaders behind. A week later, on December 16, 1849, they returned to the post and surrendered two captives but failed to produce the pilfered animals. In response, Steen threatened to hang Santos unless the band brought in a third Mexican captive and all stolen property. The Mescaleros dispersed, and Buffalo—once he was released

Enoch Steen, ca. 1850s. Courtesy William Kiser c/o Mary Maguire and Neta Pope.

from the guardhouse—promptly induced his followers to turn over the last captive in fulfillment of Steen's demands.[22]

Later the department commander in Santa Fe rebuked Steen for his petulant attitude toward the Mescaleros, lecturing that "when these people visit our posts peaceably it is important that they be received with kindness" and treated as friends.[23] The military's objective in retrieving captives from the Apaches accorded with Article XI of the 1848 Treaty of Guadalupe Hidalgo, which mandated that U.S. officials prevent Indians who resided on American soil from raiding into Mexico and repatriate captives taken during raids south of the border. Steen's undiplomatic actions, however, went beyond this obligation and risked violent retribution on American citizens, which the government hoped to avoid.[24]

As Geck knew from firsthand experience, the proclivities of various Mescalero and Gila communities to raid some settlements, seek trade and peace at neighboring places, and then strike again made it difficult for post commanders to act amicably toward any Apache group wishing to parley. Nonetheless, the young private was gaining firsthand knowledge of borderlands violence and diplomacy from these interactions between his superior and the Mescaleros. These lessons would prove invaluable, not only during Geck's term of enlistment, but throughout his ensuing forty years of civilian residency among the Hispanic villages of the Southwest.

Because Doña Ana sat directly between the homelands of the Mescalero and Gila Apaches, troops there focused their attention in two separate directions, adversely forcing them to divide resources and manpower. Furthermore, the necessity of dealing with two separate indigenous communities that lacked centralized leadership and identifying the culprits following raids caused considerable consternation among the troops and their officers. Many times, in fact, proper identification was something of an impossibility.[25] While Steen troubled himself with the peace-seeking Mescaleros, he also became discouraged with the more westerly Gila Apaches, who continued to raid in the vicinity of the Rio Grande despite Steen's recent heavy-handed diplomatic and militaristic overtures toward some of their kinsmen.

If the dragoons had been upset with their inability to identify, catch, and chastise the Apaches up to that point, events in 1850 would push the men and their commanding officer to new levels of frustration. In December 1849, just as a group of Mescaleros under Santos and Buffalo had approached the town to discuss peace, the Gila Apaches began raiding wagon trains along the Jornada del Muerto, a ninety-mile stretch of the Camino Real north of Doña Ana. Leaving many of the infantrymen behind, Geck's entire Company H rode out in response, hoping to strike the trail of the Apaches as they headed westward into their homelands along the Mimbres River and Black Range of southwestern New Mexico. Dividing his command, each column of approximately twenty-five dragoons galloped more than sixty miles in pursuit but came up empty-handed and walked back to Doña Ana alongside their broken-down horses. For Geck and his comrades, the thrill of the chase must have been exhilarating, but their failure to apprehend the Apaches, coupled with the fatigue of sauntering home on foot, would have been disappointing indeed.[26]

The recent success of stock-stealing incursions in the Mesilla Valley, and their subsequent evasion of Steen's dragoons, induced the Gila Apaches to become even more daring in their raiding practices. On February 2, 1850, a group of warriors swept through the fields directly below Doña Ana, driving off the village herd, taking a boy captive, and shooting four civilian herders before striking northward with their plunder in hopes of dodging the troops.[27] When news of the raid reached Steen, he and his entire command, including Geck, saddled their horses and commenced the chase. Having failed to overtake the Apache raiders in December, Steen chose a different strategic approach on this occasion. He designated twenty-five of his most reliable dragoons, mounted on the company's fleetest horses, to ride ahead in rapid pursuit, while the remainder of the column followed as reinforcements in the event of an engagement. Although the dragoons rode at full speed for forty miles, this improvised tactic nonetheless proved futile, as the Apaches escaped unscathed into the mountains.[28]

As they rode back toward Doña Ana, Geck and his cohorts noticed two Indians standing on a nearby peak, both of whom fled when the dragoons approached. As the troops arrived astride their already-exhausted horses, they discovered that the two warriors had merely been a ruse to entice them into an ambush on the other side of the mountain, where several dozen Apaches lurked in preparation for attack. According to Steen, the Indians cursed the soldiers "in bad Spanish and [called] us to come over and fight them."[29] With only twenty-five dragoons present, Steen realized that his men faced dire odds in a lopsided confrontation with the well-armed Indians. The commander stalled briefly, hoping that the second detachment might return in time to buttress his manpower, but ultimately returned to the post lest his outnumbered company suffer heavy casualties in a violent clash.

While Steen anxiously considered his options, his counterpart, Lt. Laurence O'Bannon (who commanded the other detachment), overtook another small group of Apaches. During a running fight, one dragoon, Private Teagarden, wounded one Indian warrior, the only casualty inflicted on either side during the entire affair. This outcome mirrored that of most engagements between the two groups, inasmuch as Apache tactics involved stealthy raids that primarily targeted livestock, provisions, and captives, thus avoiding armed confrontation with troops if possible. In the hot pursuit that followed, O'Bannon's dragoons rode to within a half mile of the Apaches, drawing closer and closer as the Indians tossed excess items aside to lighten the load on their horses. Their mounts held out long enough to enable their escape, although much of their stolen booty lay strewn over the desert for many miles.[30] The disappointment that accompanied these failures, however, paled in comparison to the debacle that awaited Steen and O'Bannon once they trudged back into the post.

Although Steen acted strategically during the maneuver by dividing his forces and sending his most distinguished dragoons ahead on well-rested horses, he made a critical mistake when he withdrew all of the troops from Doña Ana. With the village unprotected, a second band of Apaches had waited for the soldiers to disappear over the horizon before sweeping through the community without fear of military opposition. The Indians had successfully baited the dragoons away from the village by sending a small raiding party in first, allowing a larger group to plunder the unsuspecting residents with impunity. Duped and embarrassed, Steen wrote to the department commander in Santa Fe and begged permission to lead a destructive, unrelenting campaign into the Apache homelands, an offensive tactic that would carry the war to their camps, where the presence of less mobile women and children would make escape more difficult. Urging his commander to approve such an expedition, Steen explained that the Apaches had become "so bold [they] will come in broad daylight within a mile of a U.S. garrison where dragoons are stationed and drive off stock and murder the defenseless herders." Having failed to apprehend the depredators on several occasions, the major had learned that, "when these Indians start on a marauding expedition they come mounted on their best horses . . . and at the same time have relays waiting for them at 25 or 30 miles distant . . . and thus are mounted on fresh animals and can snap their fingers at us whose animals are broken down by the long chase; thus it is nearly impossible for any dragoons to overtake them." The only solution, Steen believed, was to organize a large foray into Gila Apache homes, the country flanked by the Black Range and the Mogollon Mountains, and establish a satellite post there for permanent military occupation. This would allow troops to monitor the Indians in their homelands and hopefully discourage them from raiding the settlements along the Rio Grande.[31] Steen's plan, however, would not be implemented until 1852, when the department established Fort Webster.

One can only wonder what Geck and his fellow enlisted men thought of these developments; surely they must have been disappointed by the fruitlessness of their exertions, and indeed many of them might have welcomed the change in tactics that a lengthy campaign in the field promised. It would break the monotonous routine of daily life at Doña Ana and offer a chance for military glory and redemption.

TO APACHE HOMES

One month later, Steen's dragoons rode out on a reconnaissance mission to the Santa Rita copper mines of southwestern New Mexico, where he hoped to establish a new post.[32] With thinly veiled exuberance, he reported to the territory's department commander that the site would be ideal for a fort. Not only could troops occupy preexisting buildings at the abandoned mines and thus save the time and expense of constructing new quarters or paying rent, but plenty of forage and other resources necessary to sustain a large group of men could also be found in close proximity. Moreover, troop morale might be raised if the soldiers relocated away from the Hispanics at Doña Ana (with whom they frequently quarreled), and the location would have a profound psychological effect on the Gila Apaches by housing a military force within striking distance of their homes and families.[33]

Before receiving any definitive word from headquarters about these recommendations, Steen again encountered troubles with the Mescalero Apaches to the east, a stark reminder that the dragoons faced two separate enemies and could not afford to direct too much attention to one or the other group. In June 1850, Geck and his comrades followed their commander on yet another campaign into the rugged Sacramento Mountains, where most of the tribesmen responsible for recent raiding along the Rio Grande resided with their families. Although his guides determined that Mescalero camps could be found in the immediate vicinity, a needlessly intimidated Steen ordered an about-face and led his dragoons home without engaging any Apaches. He justified the retreat by claiming that the Mescaleros boasted two thousand fighting men, a grossly exaggerated estimate, as reliable accounts during the antebellum period placed tribal strength at a mere two hundred warriors.[34]

On August 2, 1850, Col. John Munroe acknowledged Steen's suggestions for a new installation at Santa Rita and authorized him to conduct another reconnaissance in the vicinity of the Mimbres and Gila Rivers.[35] Private Geck would have been among the sixty-man force—which included all available troops of Company H—that Steen led on the campaign. When the column reached the copper mines, the men parleyed with a group of Apaches, including Delgadito and Josecito, as well as prominent headman Mangas Coloradas. Like most others who met this venerable leader, Geck and his fellow dragoons were impressed by the man's large physical stature, level-headed leadership and diplomacy, and amity toward the majority of American newcomers whom he encountered. Because this was the first time that Steen ever met with any Gila Apaches in person, it may also have been Geck's first experience with the tribe in a non-hostile setting.[36]

Based on their experiences with Apache violence toward the Hispanic inhabitants of the Mesilla Valley over the preceding year, neither Geck nor his commanding officer should have been surprised when Mangas Coloradas informed them that, although willing to pursue peace with the Americans, he and his followers "would swear eternal hatred to the Mexicans; that while the Americans could pass where they wished through their country, and could eat and sleep with them as safely as if he was by his own friends; with the Mexicans it was and ever would be 'War to the Knife.'" Despite this profession of enmity toward regional civilians (most of whom had been Mexican citizens prior to ratification of the Treaty of Guadalupe Hidalgo in 1848), Steen and his men felt somewhat assuaged after the conference, for the first time seeing their Apache foes within the light of humanity. Steen retracted his recommendation for a destructive campaign of total warfare when he later opined, "An agent with a few thousand dollars worth of presents, can without doubt conclude a lasting peace with this powerful band who have hitherto given us so much trouble."[37]

In the years immediately following this visit, a number of important developments occurred that impacted relations between Anglos and Apaches. In 1852, the army established Fort Webster at the Santa Rita mines, the first permanent military installation in Chiricahua Apache homelands, and thus fulfilled Steen's recommendations. The government negotiated numerous treaties with the Apaches, first in 1852 at Acoma Pueblo and again in 1855 at Fort Thorn, but the provisions of these pacts went mostly unfulfilled and the violence continued virtually unabated. In 1854, the army established Fort Thorn along the Rio Grande about thirty miles north of Doña Ana, where a new Indian Department official, Dr. Michael Steck, established his Southern Apache Agency and began issuing rations to both the Gila and

Mescalero Apaches. Despite these policy initiatives, raiding and killing continued, and by 1857 a frustrated military department dispatched a campaign of nearly one thousand troops into the field to flush the Apaches out of their southwestern New Mexico homes. By the time of the Civil War, relations had deteriorated even further, exacerbated when U.S. troops killed a number of Cochise's family members in the infamous Bascom Affair of 1861 and then executed Mangas Coloradas at Fort McLane, near the Santa Rita mines, in 1863. In essence, the activities of Steen's dragoons in the late 1840s and early 1850s laid the groundwork for a borderlands rife with violence that remained perilous into the 1880s.[38]

Before any further action was taken toward the Gila or Mescalero Apaches, however, both Geck and Steen would be removed from active participation. After two five-year enlistments, Geck received an honorable discharge on January 12, 1851. In the end, the Polish immigrant did not have much to show in the way of battles, victories, or personal glory, as Apaches still enjoyed a high level of independence and remained a powerful force throughout southern New Mexico. What Geck could claim, however, was the typical dragoon experience of exhaustion and frustration. Many U.S. troopers who followed Geck to the borderlands would share his experiences and emotions. Although he is not known to have personally killed any Apaches, Geck's role as a soldier forced him to witness and participate in a violent southwestern world. Steen, on the other hand, became embroiled in a local controversy involving landownership and Texas boundary claims, forcing his temporary transfer to another department.[39] By the time he returned to southern New Mexico several years later to resume command of Company H, the troops had relocated from Doña Ana to Fort Fillmore, about ten miles south on the east bank of the Rio Grande. Moreover, his former subordinate Geck had remarried, found acceptance in the local community, and was earning a living as a civilian businessman.

FROM DRAGOON TO MERCHANT

Geck's dragoon comrades remained at Doña Ana for several months following his January 1851 discharge, but in September Colonel Sumner removed troops from New Mexico villages to more rural forts.[40] This action doubtless disappointed Geck, as it not only transferred his friends away but also deprived the new merchant of their business. Residents of Doña Ana shared Geck's dismay and immediately sent a petition "to the illustrious governor" of the territory, James S. Calhoun, hoping that he might convince Sumner to reverse the order. The removal of the dragoons, the citizens explained, "would bring imminent peril to us, to the extent that our lives and families might be sacrificed and the little we have to live upon will be exposed to the fury of the bloody hands of the Apaches, just as we have been in past years."[41] Calhoun could do nothing to countermand a military order, and some officials found it difficult to sympathize with such concerns because they saw that the citizens often brought the trouble upon themselves. In 1855, for example, Gov. David Meriwether wrote, "I regret to learn that the people of Doña Ana are disposed to gamble with and sell whiskey to the Indians," actions that frequently resulted in conflict.[42] Realizing that the petitioners would mail a copy of their appeal to federal authorities in Washington, D.C., Colonel Sumner wrote preemptively to Secretary of War Conrad and informed him that, should the complaint reach his desk, he ought to ignore it. Such protests, the colonel wrote, came "directly or indirectly from those who have hitherto managed to live, in some way, from the extravagant expenditures of the Government."[43]

Sumner's allusion to regional inhabitants profiting from the army's presence did not apply just to civilians. While the primary undertaking of military men in the Southwest involved Indian fighting, some of them, including both Geck and his commanding officer, eyed personal interests during their time of service. The two respective dragoons, however, approached these endeavors in very different ways. Prior to the settlement of the Texas–New Mexico boundary dispute as a condition of the Compromise of 1850, Hispanics feared that a Texan invasion might assert sovereignty over the eastern portion of New Mexico. This became an especially worrisome issue at Doña Ana, which lies on the eastern bank of the Rio Grande and therefore would become part of Texas in the event of a new boundary being established. Opportunists seized the occasion to claim parcels within the 1839 Doña Ana Bend Colony grant, recognizing the potential ambiguity of prior landownership following the Treaty of Guadalupe Hidalgo.[44] This tactic met with direct opposition from local residents, who until 1848 had been citizens of Mexico and had no desire to become Texans.

U.S. troops stationed at Doña Ana inevitably became embroiled in this conflict. Like many other antebellum officers, Steen looked to pursue personal economic interests during his forays in the New Mexico countryside. On campaigns into Apache country, he collected ore samples and sent them to a Saint Louis assayer, hoping to locate a profitable mining claim and attract settlers. When conversing with easterners during a trip to Missouri, Steen beamed about the prospects for development in New Mexico, claiming, "The whole country is abounding in mines . . . and only requiring the aid of capital and enterprise to make it the most productive section of the continent."[45]

Steen's efforts to capitalize on New Mexico's potential growth went beyond collecting rocks in hopes that they might contain gold or silver. When Texas commissioner William Cockburn arrived in Doña Ana at the height of the Texas–New Mexico boundary dispute, he discovered the major to be "a perfect Texan in principle, and the strongest advocate of our [land] claims I have found in this territory." Cockburn had little difficulty convincing the officer to purchase a nefarious 640-acre headright claim that included the entire village of Doña Ana.[46] When local residents learned of the transaction, they protested to Colonel Munroe, the military commander and interim governor, condemning the deal between Cockburn and Steen as "contrary to all natural right and to that of the people" and demanding corrective action to halt the transfer of property.[47] Wary of inflaming the ongoing Texas–New Mexico boundary dispute before Congress could settle it, Munroe reprimanded Steen for purchasing the headright claim and reminded him that the recent Treaty of Guadalupe Hidalgo protected preexisting Mexican land grants, including the Doña Ana Bend Colony. To pacify residents and avoid direct punishment of Steen through court-martial, which Munroe perceived as overly harsh for such circumstances, the War Department opted simply to transfer the major out of New Mexico until tensions eased.[48]

As an enlisted man serving under Steen while all of this transpired, Geck must have watched his commander's land speculation with cautioned interest. In 1850, with just a few months remaining in his second five-year tour of duty, Geck faced an uncertain future as a civilian in a dangerous borderlands landscape. His Polish ancestry made him an ethnic outsider to the Hispanics among whom he lived, and, even more daunting, his service in the U.S. Army rendered Geck an invader and occupier of both the former Mexican province as well as the Apache homelands. Although military service in the antebellum Apache wars brought him to the region, it was landownership and marriage that would enable the now middle-aged serviceman to bridge these cultural and ethnic divides in pursuit of a prosperous livelihood in southern New Mexico.

In his first undertaking as a civilian, Geck followed in the footsteps of Steen, but he did so legally and without controversy. Following his honorable discharge in 1851, Geck immediately filed a bounty land claim with the U.S. pension office, a practice with origins in the eighteenth century. The Continental Congress approved the first land warrants for ex-soldiers in 1775; thirteen years later, an initial bounty land act enabled veterans of the Revolutionary War to stake claims that ranged from 100 acres for a private to 1,100 acres for a major general. The law remained on the books until 1855, by which time it had become a pivotal component of the American nation-building project in frontier regions. Geck claimed a small parcel of land near the southeastern edge of Doña Ana, where the dragoons sometimes camped outside their rented adobe barracks.[49] The pension office approved his warrant in June 1851, and Geck, having recently naturalized as an American citizen, constructed a general store and house on his new holding. While it is not known whether Geck ever traded with any Apaches, or if they in turn raided his business at any time, the store nonetheless flourished, enabling him to purchase additional property in the Mesilla Valley. In so doing, this former enlisted man succeeded where his commanding officer failed: he established himself economically and profited from increasing Anglo settlement. The final step to ensure Geck's permanent success—cultural adaptation and acceptance in the local community—would come through marriage.

Geck remarried three times after mustering out of the dragoons. On April 24, 1851, he wed Margarita Severiana de Jesus Barrio, a fourteen-year-old girl from nearby Paso del Norte, who died two years later during childbirth. In 1854, shortly after Barrio's death, Geck married Beatriz Aguirre, who also perished when giving birth to their son in 1856. Just three years later, on December 31, 1859, the former dragoon married for a fourth and final time, to Sarah Aguirre, who was just thirteen years old. The fact that two of Geck's three Hispanic wives were so young suggests that some type of marital arrangement must have been negotiated between the white merchant and the two girls' fathers. Despite the untimely deaths of Margarita and Beatriz, Geck's three marriages established kinship linkages to two separate Hispanic families and, coupled with the birth of seven multiethnic children, cemented his communal standing.[50]

In the summer of 1861, Geck's adoptive community was thrust into the Civil War when a battalion of Texas Confederates under Lt. Col. John R. Baylor invaded the Mesilla Valley, defeating the nearby Fort Fillmore garrison. Baylor immediately established the Confederate Territory of Arizona (with Mesilla as the capital), proclaimed himself governor, and readied his troops for the ensuing march northward toward Albuquerque and Santa Fe. It is not known whether Geck actually harbored pro-Southern or proslavery sentiments, or whether he simply did what he perceived most logical for the well-being of his business and family, but in the latter months of 1861 he mimicked many of his friends and neighbors in supporting the Confederate occupiers.

As the military commander and governor of Confederate Arizona, Baylor not only commanded his troops but also administered civil policy, which included the selection of judicial officers. Shortly after the invasion, Geck accepted an appointment as justice of the peace for Doña Ana, and also conducted business with the occupying Confederates.[51] On October 31, 1861, Baylor signed a contract to rent Geck's buildings for quartermaster storage, two of his corrals, and another structure to be occupied as soldiers' quarters, all at a rate of $106 per month. From October 1861 through January 1862, Geck also sold provisions to Baylor's men, including lemon syrup, sugar, soap, tea, and candles.[52] Although the contracts lasted only four months, the nature of the business that he conducted—including the quartering of enemy troops—situated Geck in the crosshairs of Union officers when they reclaimed southern New Mexico in 1862 and began identifying and punishing Confederate supporters. Once the Confederate forces retreated to Texas, federal soldiers confiscated Geck's store and inventory, valued at $21,675, and a court of inquiry charged him with treason. He later sued the government to regain his property and received an acquittal, but not without considerable hardship and financial expense.[53]

Despite this controversy, the former dragoon's activities following his discharge from the army set an example that many soldiers followed before and after the Civil War. A number of ex-troopers from both the California Column and the regular U.S. Army opened businesses or became professionals in southern New Mexico (and Arizona). Several of them acculturated themselves to the local Hispanic communities, following the strategy that Geck pioneered in that region.[54]

Louis William Geck died at Doña Ana on June 9, 1890, five days after his seventy-second birthday.[55] His gravestone, bearing an inscription that reads "Company H, 1st U.S. Dragoons," lies just east of the plot of land that he obtained through his bounty claim in 1851. It is worth noting that the memorial refers specifically to his military service, perhaps the most formative experience in his life, as it not only inculcated the discipline that would make him a successful businessman but also brought him to New Mexico, where he spent the remaining four decades of his life in a multicultural environment that he openly embraced.

NOTES

1. Ross Calvin, ed., *Lieutenant Emory Reports: Notes of a Military Reconnaissance* (Albuquerque: University of New Mexico Press, 1951), 50; Philip St. George Cooke, *The Conquest of New Mexico and California: An Historical and Personal Narrative* (Albuquerque: Horn and Wallace, 1964), 34–38. On Kearny's conquest generally, see William A. Keleher, *Turmoil in New Mexico, 1846–1868* (Santa Fe: Rydal Press, 1952), 1–20; and William S. Kiser, *Dragoons in Apacheland: Conquest and Resistance in Southern New Mexico, 1846–1861* (Norman: University of Oklahoma Press, 2012), 13–18.

2. Francis C. Kajencki, "Louis William Geck: Soldier, Merchant, and Patriarch of Territorial New Mexico," *Polish American Studies* 39 (Autumn 1982): 5n2.

3. Louis William Geck File, Enlistment Documents, January 12, 1841 and February 6, 1846, Adjutant General's Office, Record Group (RG) 94, National Archives and Records Administration, Washington, D.C. (NARA).

4. Kiser, *Dragoons in Apacheland*, 27.

5. Kajencki, "Louis William Geck," 7–8.

6. George Archibald McCall, *New Mexico in 1850: A Military View*, ed. Robert W. Frazer (Norman: University of Oklahoma Press, 1968), 180–84; John Munroe to George McCall, March 1, 1850, Letters Sent (LS), Department of New Mexico (DNM), M1072, roll 1, RG 393, NARA. At the time, only about one thousand troops were stationed in New Mexico.

7. Winfield Scott to Munroe, August 6, 1850, in Annie H. Abel, ed., *The Official Correspondence of James S. Calhoun while Indian Agent at Santa Fe and Superintendent of Indian Affairs in New Mexico, 1849–1852* (Washington, D.C.: Government Printing Office, 1915), 164–65; Edwin Sumner to Charles Conrad, May 27, 1852, in U.S. War Department, *Annual Report of the Secretary of War* (*ARSW*), 1852 (Washington, D.C.: Government Printing Office, 1852), 23–25; Durwood Ball, "The U.S. Army in New Mexico,

1846–1886," in *Telling New Mexico: A New History*, ed. Marta Weigle (Santa Fe: Museum of New Mexico Press, 2009), 178–79.

8. John Russell Bartlett, *Personal Narrative of Explorations and Incidents in Texas, New Mexico, California, Sonora and Chihuahua, Connected with the United States and Mexican Boundary Commission during the Years 1850, '51, '52, and '53*, (New York: Appleton, 1854), 1:212; Lazelle quote in Frank D. Reeve, ed., "Puritan and Apache: A Diary," *New Mexico Historical Review* 23 (October 1948): 280. On the role of Doña Ana in the boundary surveys and ensuing controversies, see Joseph Richard Werne, *The Imaginary Line: A History of the United States and Mexican Boundary Survey, 1848–1857* (Fort Worth: Texas Christian University Press, 2007), 157–71.

9. Grant Foreman, ed., *Marcy and the Gold Seekers: The Journal of Captain R. B. Marcy, with an Account of the Gold Rush over the Southern Route* (Norman: University of Oklahoma Press, 1939), 342–43; George F. Ruxton, *Adventures in Mexico and the Rocky Mountains* (New York: Harper and Brothers, 1848), 171.

10. Susan Shelby Magoffin, *Down the Santa Fe Trail and into Mexico: The Diary of Susan Shelby Magoffin, 1846–1847*, ed. Stella M. Drumm (Lincoln: University of Nebraska Press, 1926), 201; William W. H. Davis, *El Gringo, or, New Mexico and Her People* (New York: Arno Press, 1973), 373; Bartlett, *Personal Narrative*, 1:211.

11. Beginning in 1848, the army paid $170 per month to rent the privately owned buildings in Doña Ana, an amount that doubled over the next two years before the post was finally relocated in September 1851. Thomas Swords to Thomas Jesup, October 25, 1851, in *ARSW*, 1851 (Washington, D.C.: Government Printing Office, 1851), 246; McCall, *New Mexico in 1850*, 168; Robert W. Frazer, *Forts and Supplies: The Role of the Army in the Economy of the Southwest, 1846–1861* (Albuquerque: University of New Mexico Press, 1983), 55.

12. As of 1850, the legislated strength of a dragoon company was fifty men plus officers, but that number increased to seventy-four in 1855. S. Cooper to Scott, November 27, 1855, in *ARSW*, 1856 (Washington, D.C.: Government Printing Office, 1856), 127; Durwood Ball, *Army Regulars on the Western Frontier, 1848–1861* (Norman: University of Oklahoma Press, 2001), xxii–xxiii; Bvt. Maj. Gen. Emory Upton, *The Military Policy of the United States* (Washington, D.C.: Government Printing Office, 1907), 223–24.

13. Doña Ana, December 1849, December 1850, and September 1851, Returns from U.S. Military Posts, 1800–1916, M617, roll 320, NARA.

14. McCall, *New Mexico in 1850*, 167–69.

15. See, for example, Percival G. Lowe, *Five Years A Dragoon ('49 to '54) and Other Adventures on the Great Plains* (Norman: University of Oklahoma Press, 1965).

16. Lydia Spencer Lane, *I Married a Soldier, or, Old Days in the Old Army* (Albuquerque: Horn and Wallace, 1964), 59–60, 99.

17. James A. Bennett, *Forts and Forays: A Dragoon in New Mexico, 1850–1856*, ed. Clinton E. Brooks and Frank D. Reeve (Albuquerque: University of New Mexico Press, 1996), 17, 38.

18. Theophilus F. Rodenbough, comp., *From Everglade to Canon with the Second Dragoons: An Authentic Account of Service in Florida, Mexico, Virginia, and the Indian*

Country (New York: D. Van Nostrand, 1875), 195–203; Samuel D. Sturgis to Lorenzo Thomas, January 17, 1855, Letters Received (LR), DNM, M1120, roll 4, RG 393, NARA; Bennett, *Forts and Forays*, 23–25, 30, 34, 63.

19. Chihenne is the ethnohistorical term for the subgroup of Chiricahua Apaches living in southwestern New Mexico, although historically numerous other names, including "Gila Apaches" and "Mimbres" or "Mimbreño Apaches," have been used to identify the Apache communities who resided in this area. I use "Gila Apaches" because that is the term that U.S. military officers and enlisted men used to describe these Apaches in the antebellum era.

20. Enoch Steen, a Kentuckian, joined the First Dragoons in 1833, the same year that Congress founded the regiment. He fought meritoriously in the U.S.-Mexican War and earned the rank of brevet major for his commendable performance during the Battle of Buena Vista. By the time Steen commanded the troops at Doña Ana, he boasted almost twenty years of military experience and would go on to retire as a lieutenant colonel in 1863. One observer wrote of Steen in the *Santa Fe Weekly Gazette* that, "although well advanced in years he still exhibits the enthusiasm of youth," an important trait for an officer charged with maintaining a frontier military garrison and pursuing Apaches through the dangerous southwestern terrain. *Santa Fe Weekly Gazette*, April 5, 1856; Constance Wynn Altshuler, *Cavalry Yellow and Infantry Blue: Army Officers in Arizona Between 1851 and 1886* (Tucson: Arizona Historical Society, 1991) 316–17. On the Apache skirmish during which Steen was wounded, see Enoch Steen to John H. Dickinson, September 1, 1849, Folder 1548, Albert H. Schroeder Collection, New Mexico State Records Center and Archives, Santa Fe.

21. Steen to Lafayette McLaws, December 9, 1849, LR, DNM, M1102, roll 2, RG 393, NARA.

22. Ibid; McLaws to Steen, January 28, 1850, LS, DNM, M1072, roll 1, RG 393, NARA.

23. Munroe to Steen, June 15, 1850, LS, DNM, M1072, roll 1, RG 393, NARA.

24. On the eleventh article of the treaty, see Brian DeLay, *War of a Thousand Deserts: Indian Raids and the U.S.-Mexican War* (New Haven: Yale University Press, 2008).

25. See, for example, Sumner to William Carr Lane, June 15, 1853, LS, DNM, M1072, roll 1, RG 393, NARA.

26. Steen to McLaws, December 1849, LR, DNM, M1102, roll 1, RG 393, NARA.

27. See *Claims for Depredations by Indians in the Territory of New Mexico*, S. Doc. No. 55, 35th Cong., 1st Sess., Serial No. 929, 33.

28. Steen to McLaws, February 5, 1850, LR, DNM, M1102, roll 2, RG 393, NARA.

29. Ibid.

30. Ibid.

31. Ibid.

32. Steen to McLaws, March 26, 1850, LR, DNM, M1102, roll 2, RG 393, NARA.

33. Ibid; Swords to Jesup, October 25, 1851, in *ARSW*, 1851, 241–48.

34. Steen to McLaws, July 8, 1850, LR, DNM, M1102, roll 2, RG 393, NARA; Unsigned report of June 28, 1852, Series 1, roll 1; Michael Steck, Quarterly Report, December 10, 1856, Series 1, roll 2, both in Microcopy E93, Michael Steck Papers, Center for Southwest

Research, University of New Mexico (Steck Papers); Dan L. Thrapp, *Victorio and the Mimbres Apaches* (Norman: University of Oklahoma Press, 1974), 46.

35. McLaws to Steen, August 2, 1850, LS, DNM, M1072, roll 1, RG 393, NARA.

36. Steen to McLaws, Sept. 4, 1850, LR, DNM, M1102, roll 2, RG 393, NARA. For the details of this meeting, see *El Sonorense*, April 23, 1850; and Edwin R. Sweeney, *Mangas Coloradas: Chief of the Chiricahua Apaches* (Norman: University of Oklahoma Press, 1998), 205–206.

37. Steen to McLaws, September 4, 1850, LR, DNM, M1102, roll 2, RG 393, NARA.

38. Kiser, *Dragoons in Apacheland*; Sweeney, *Mangas Coloradas*; Dan L. Thrapp, *The Conquest of Apacheria* (Norman: University of Oklahoma Press, 1967).

39. See Mark J. Stegmaier, *Texas, New Mexico, and the Compromise of 1850: Boundary Dispute and Sectional Crisis* (Kent, Ohio: Kent State University Press, 1996), 71–83.

40. Conrad to Sumner, April 1, 1851, in Abel, *Official Correspondence*, 383. On Sumner's reorganization generally, see Chris Emmett, *Fort Union and the Winning of the Southwest* (Norman: University of Oklahoma Press, 1965), 101–53. On Sumner's economic impacts, see Frazer, *Forts and Supplies*, 61–85.

41. Citizens of Doña Ana to James S. Calhoun, August 8, 1851, in Abel, *Official Correspondence*, 402–403. Geck's signature does not appear on the petition.

42. David Meriwether to Michael Steck, August 28, 1855, Series 2, roll 1, Steck Papers.

43. Sumner to Charles Conrad, October 24, 1851, LS, DNM, M1072, roll 1, RG 393, NARA.

44. Bartlett, *Personal Narrative*, 2:212–14.

45. *St. Louis Daily Missouri Republican*, January 16, 1854. See also McLaws to Steen, April 13, 1850, LS, DNM, M1072, roll 1, RG 393, NARA; *St. Louis Daily Missouri Republican*, January 26, 1854; and *Santa Fe Weekly Gazette*, February 26, 1853.

46. Stegmaier, *Texas, New Mexico, and the Compromise of 1850*, 71–73, 132–33 [first quotation on 71]; Kenneth Franklin Neighbours, *Robert Simpson Neighbors and the Texas Frontier, 1836–1859* (Waco, Tex.: Texian Press, 1975), 89–93 [second quotation on 91].

47. Munroe to Jones, May 20, 1850, LS, DNM, M1072, roll 1, RG 393, NARA; Mark J. Stegmaier, "The Guadalupe Hidalgo Treaty as a Factor in the New Mexico–Texas Boundary Dispute," in *The Treaty of Guadalupe Hidalgo, 1848: Papers of the Sesquicentennial Symposium, 1848–1998*, ed. John Porter Bloom (Las Cruces, N.Mex.: Doña Ana County Historical Society, 1999), 48.

48. Munroe to Steen, April 15, 1850; McLaws to Steen, September 5, 1850, both in LS, DNM, M1072, roll 1, RG 393, NARA.

49. A three-acre portion of this claim is still in the possession of Geck's descendants. See RG 15, NARA, for a historical overview as well as the actual land bounty claims.

50. Kajencki, "Louis William Geck," 11–12.

51. Ibid., 13–16.

52. Entry for Louis William Geck, War Department Collection of Confederate Records, "Citizens File 1861–1865," M346, roll 342, RG 109, NARA.

53. Louis William Geck Papers, Folders 31–32, New Mexico State Records Center and Archives, Santa Fe. A number of Mesilla Valley citizens issued formal complaints,

alleging that the Union commander Gen. James Carleton had "taken away our property without just compensation and refused to restore it." See Certificate of the Clerk of the Third Judicial District of Doña Ana County, June 10, 1864, Series 2, roll 3, Steck Papers.

54. Darlis A. Miller, *The California Column in New Mexico* (Albuquerque: University of New Mexico Press, 1982); Laura Graves, *Thomas Varker Keam: Indian Trader* (Norman: University of Oklahoma Press, 1998).

55. Kajencki, "Louis William Geck," 18.

3
Homobono Carabajal

Jerry D. Thompson

As early as May 11, 1861, Caleb Blood Smith, Abraham Lincoln's secretary of the Interior, asked for a vigorous defense of New Mexico and urged Secretary of War Simon Cameron to authorize the recruitment of volunteers in the territory.[1] With the U.S. Army pulling its troops to the East, New Mexico governor Henry Connelly and the territory's military commander, Col. Edward Canby, also realized that a volunteer force had to be recruited as fast as possible, not only to defend the territory from Texas expansionists, but also to deter the increasingly frequent and daring raids by Navajos and Mescalero and Chiricahua Apaches. Canby and Connelly aimed to take quick action, issuing commissions, starting enlistment, and designating rendezvous sites for the troops.[2]

Every community of any size in the vast New Mexico Territory was asked to raise volunteers. As soon as fifty men had been enrolled, they were to be designated as a company and officially mustered. In all, New Mexico would send 6,561 of its men—the vast majority of them Hispanic—to the Civil War. This number far eclipsed the number of recruits from North and South Dakota, Washington, Montana, Idaho, Wyoming, and Colorado combined.[3] Volunteers were to be between the ages of eighteen and forty-five. If possible, recruits were to provide their own horses and equipment. In rare instances, company commanders outfitted entire companies at their own expense, even providing horses and mules for the men. As was the case elsewhere, recruits received a bounty of one hundred dollars, provided they would enlist for three years; privates were paid thirteen dollars per month and sergeants between seventeen and twenty-one dollars.[4] The would-be enlistees were inspected by military surgeons and had to be "free from all malformation, defects of sight, hearing, ulcers, piles, rupture, fracture, dislocation, and disease of any kind."[5] Although the first regiments were designated as infantry, many of the companies were mounted. In theory, recruits were to be treated as if they were part of the regular army.

One of the fresh enlistees was Mexican-born twenty-two-year-old Homobono Molino Carabajal. He enrolled at Albuquerque in Company F of the Second New Mexico Volunteer Infantry, commanded by Miguel Estanislado Pino, a wealthy farmer, merchant, and popular political figure from Galisteo and La Ciénega. Enlistment papers list the five-feet-five Carabajal as having light skin, brown hair, and hazel eyes. Young Carabajal was largely illiterate and reported that he was born in Chihuahua, Mexico. Carabajal said that he had been a laborer, but enrolling officers frequently heard the Spanish word "labrador," meaning a farm laborer, and simply recorded the men as being "laborers."[6] Unlike information on other men in Company F, there is no indication that Carabajal was married. His company commander was Capt. Ethan Wayne Eaton, a wealthy sawmiller, rancher, and merchant from Santa Fe and Galisteo. Although consistently struggling with alcohol, Eaton proved to be able and popular with his men. By the end of the war, although briefly dismissed, he had risen to the rank of lieutenant colonel.[7]

With little proficiency in Spanish, many of the enrolling officers and clerks at military headquarters in Santa Fe and posts throughout the territory had a tendency to spell Spanish names phonetically, and "Homobono Molino" may not have been the young recruit's correct name. In the records of the New Mexico Volunteers, Carabajal's name was spelled in a plethora of different ways.[8]

Scapegoated for the Union defeat at the bloody Battle of Valverde on February 21, 1862, many Hispanic New Mexicans, nuevomexicanos, despite the prevailing and biting racism that existed in the army at the time, took great pride in their Civil War service. Today their white marble tombstones are scattered across a vast swath of the arid Southwest. Their overlooked and misunderstood role in the turbulent years of the Civil War is memorable and worthy of recollection.

BLOODY VALVERDE

After being enrolled at Albuquerque, Private Carabajal and Company F, along with three other companies, in all 252 men, marched down the Rio Grande, past and through the small villages of the Rio Abajo, to Fort Craig, where they arrived on August 14, 1861. At Fort Craig, the men were ceremoniously mustered into the army for three years. On post records, the nuevomexicanos were always listed last, almost as an afterthought.[9] Many regular army officers in the borderlands, including Canby, possessed deeply ingrained ideas of racial superiority. Canby never trusted the nuevomexicanos, and his insistence on having an "American" officer in every volunteer company had as much to do with his ethnocentricity as with the desire to enhance communications. Canby was also concerned about the tardiness of enlistment, not wanting the regulars to leave until the volunteer units were complete. He also expressed reservations about the "inexperience of the volunteers," as well as numerous "ignorant" officers who were enlisting. Such men would have to be "posted" in small bodies in detached villages, Canby was sure, and, unless they were "under the supervision of an officer of the army," they would be largely ineffective.[10]

Carabajal's first action came on the night of September 25, 1861. Volunteer soldiers from Peñasco, led by Capt. John Henry Mink, were overrun at Cañada Alamosa, a post on the west bank of the Rio Grande, thirty-eight miles downriver from Fort Craig. Company F was immediately dispatched as part of the reinforcements that went in pursuit of the Confederate raiders. Three days after arriving at Cañada Alamosa, with the enemy retreating back into the Mesilla Valley, the men were ordered back to Fort Craig, where they remained for the next three months.[11]

By Christmas 1861, as new recruits continued to arrive at Fort Craig, the area upriver from the post became a sea of white tents, endless small campfires, hundreds of wagons, and thousands of tethered horses and mules. The largest force New Mexico had ever seen was being assembled at Fort Craig, and the young Carabajal found himself in the midst of all the excitement. Besides the 4,350 soldiers at and near the fort, 100 civilians, including herders, wagon masters, spies, guides, blacksmiths, couriers, laborers, clerks, interpreters, seventeen packers, and seventy-two teamsters, all scurried about in anxious anticipation of what was certain to be a massive, at least on borderlands scales, confrontation with a Texan army that was reported to be moving north out of the Mesilla Valley.[12]

By February 1862, the Texans, numbering over three thousand men, were at the gates of the fort. With a battle imminent, the Confederates abruptly pivoted, crossed the Rio Grande, and moved north in an attempt to gain control of the Rio Grande above Fort Craig. On February 20, Carabajal and Company F were ordered across the frigid waters of the river as skirmishers. After several hours, they had gained a position within eight hundred yards of the enemy lines, just south of a large volcanic-topped Mesa de la Contadera, which jutted out into the valley from the east. It is amazing that Canby, who later claimed that he had not wanted to place the volunteers in a position where they would be forced to maneuver under enemy artillery fire, thrust them into the crux of battle. Suddenly, the tension was broken by exploding shells. Many of the explosions did little more than send a cloud of sand and dust into the cold February sky as the bulk of the Union forces scurried to find cover behind large sand hills. Canby, whose prejudice toward the volunteers seemed to grow exponentially during and after the Battle of Valverde, wrote that Pino's regiment was "thrown into such utter confusion by a few harmless cannon shots that it was impossible to restore them to any kind of order."[13]

As the Texans reached the river north of Mesa de la Contadera on the cold dawn of February 21, Canby ordered Carabajal and all of Pino's men on the east bank of the river, south of the mesa, as a rear guard. Once Canby became convinced that the enemy had no intention of attacking Fort Craig, he recalled Pino's regiment and sent several of its companies to escort the ammunition train. By midafternoon, with a battle raging for control of Valverde Ford, the regiment was in total disarray, according to Canby. There was "the wildest confusion and no efforts of their own officers or of my staff could restore any kind of order," Canby reported. Large numbers of men were reported to have deserted from the regiment during and shortly after the battle. Several volunteers even cut the mules loose from a supply wagon and galloped bareback into the mountains.[14]

In his brief report, Pino mentioned having been stationed on the east bank of the river the day before the battle but said that his regiment was in the process of crossing the Rio Grande when the men were ordered back to the west bank, where they took position and "fired upon the enemy." He made no mention of any panic, of entire companies refusing to cross the river, of men disobeying orders, or of the 147 men charged with desertion.[15]

A VAST AND UNFORGIVING LAND

Only days after the Battle of Valverde, Canby issued orders consolidating and reorganizing the Second New Mexico Infantry into six companies.[16]

Carabajal's old Company F became a new Company B, but within months most of the troopers and officers were discharged. Private Carabajal was retained and found himself in Company D of the new First New Mexico Cavalry to be commanded by the famed trapper and explorer, and now colonel, Christopher "Kit" Carson. He remained at Fort Craig as the war raged in the northern part of the territory. Following the Texans' defeat at Glorieta and their disastrous mountain retreat back into the Mesilla Valley, Carabajal, possibly still shaken by the enormity of the violence at Valverde, found himself on a patrol approaching the rough rock and adobe village of Cubero on the edge of the Navajo country.[17] Still on foot, the company left Albuquerque on May 12, 1862, arriving at Cubero five days later. Within days, the men marched north to the village of Seboyeta, a haven for bandits and Indian slave traders, where it was reported that several deserters from the volunteers were in hiding. Captain Eaton estimated that there were as many as one hundred deserters and "thieves" in and around Cubero and Seboyeta, many of them participating in the Indian slave trade. In fact, he felt that the "entire population" of the area was hostile to the U.S. troops. Eaton also thought that the army was pitting such men as Carabajal against "their own people" in a futile, disagreeable mission that was bound to produce few results and even less glory, no matter how dedicated the troops appeared to be in the fulfillment of their duties.[18]

After two days of finding no deserters, the men returned via Cubero and began the long, dusty march across the Rio Puerco and back to Albuquerque, where they arrived on May 30. Leaving Albuquerque the next day, they turned upriver for a four-day march to Fort Marcy at Santa Fe. Including the Seboyeta excursion, Carabajal marched 263 miles in three weeks.[19] On July 17, 1862, Carabajal and his colleagues learned that they were being sent north to the remote San Luis Valley in southern Colorado. Leaving Fort Marcy in the heat of mid-summer on July 17, the men marched another 160 miles across the mountains to Taos and then on to Fort Garland, where they arrived two weeks later. Fort Garland was still part of the Department of New Mexico, and the new department commander, Gen. James H. Carleton, was forced to direct more and more attention to the post.

At the base of 14,345-foot Blanca Peak in the northern Sangre de Cristo Mountains, Fort Garland helped to guard La Veta Pass and the eastern entrances to the valley, as well as the small settlements that were referred to at the time as simply *placitas*. Built of adobe around a parade ground, the

Fort Garland, Colorado, 1874. Courtesy National Archives and Records Administration.

post was often neglected, and was viewed by many of the soldiers as downright forlorn. Not long after Carabajal arrived, the inspector general for the department, Maj. Henry Davies Wallen, visited the garrison. He immediately felt that the post was constructed too close to some nearby hills and was therefore indefensible. While he found housing adequate for the cold climate, Wallen had much to complain about concerning uncleanliness. He noticed that the prevailing winds in the valley were out of the west and southwest and that the post latrines had been dug on that side of the fort. Wallen not only declared the latrines to be in a "very filthy state" but also insisted that they be removed to a location east of the post and inspected daily by the officer of the day to ensure their cleanliness. As Wallen watched Eaton's ninety-five-man company drill, he reported that the men were "neatly and comfortably clad" and, overall, they made "quite a military appearance." At target practice, however, Wallen pronounced Carabajal and his comrades "sadly deficient," citing one of the reasons as the men's lack of ammunition with which to practice. More exciting for Company D was the fact that on November 1, 1862, the men were given horses. To be on horseback was far more honorable and manly than to be on foot, and Carabajal and others must have taken great pride in their new status.[20]

Still, morale and discipline plummeted, and there is no indication that Carabajal was an exception. While at Fort Garland, Eaton complained that his men had not received "a cent of pay" in the fifteen months since they had enlisted, and many of the families of the soldiers were in "absolute want." Canby had earlier warned that the inability of the army to pay the New Mexico Volunteers was likely to "produce an unfortunate effect upon the volunteers." Little could be done, although orders went out to issue the "indigent Mexican families" rations at several of the military posts.[21] Army records indicate that Carabajal became indebted to the post sutler, Frederick William Posthoff, and each month the amount of his debt increased. By April 1863, he owed Posthoff $15.88, a considerable amount of money at the time.[22]

Meanwhile, Eaton protested vociferously that his company was discriminated against because it was composed of nuevomexicanos. The captain fumed at the degree of "distrust" toward his men "on account of their being Mexicans." His men had consistently been given the worst assignments and sent only to the most remote and isolated posts, such as Cubero and Fort Garland. The men, Eaton assured Carleton, "are as true to the government as any soldiers in the territory." Moreover, he claimed, "The policy generally used towards the Mexican people by Americans [was] wrong" and not in "the best interest of the country." The Americans had done nothing but "keep them back . . . continually st[i]rring up a feeling of jealousy & animosity between the two people." Eaton wanted his men "treated properly," for they have "feelings as well as ourselves."[23]

As was the case at many borderlands posts, the "sale of whiskey" proved to be a serious problem at Fort Garland, and orders were issued to stop Posthoff and others from selling intoxicating beverages to the soldiers. Guards were posted near the post to watch for any whiskey peddlers. Yet the men at the post were frequently drunk. Convinced that the whiskey was originating from individuals in nearby Conejos, who were also selling liquor to the Ute Indians, the army offered a twenty-dollar reward for the detention of any person caught selling alcohol to the garrison.[24]

The men at Fort Garland were also used to combat a spike of banditry. In early September, Eaton was sent with a sixty-five-man force that included several Colorado Volunteers and probably Carabajal, to either apprehend or kill bandits or Confederate guerillas hiding in the mountains. Sure that any movement from the post would be signaled to the outlaws, Eaton, with "utmost secrecy," led the patrol out of Fort Garland after dark on September 5, 1862, heading due west. Out of sight of the post, the column abruptly turned east out of the San Luis Valley and into the Sangre de Cristo Mountains before camping for the evening. By using an old Indian trail away from the main Sangre de Cristo Pass to the north, and with a spy and guide in the lead, Eaton again took his men through the night, across the towering heights of the snow-shrouded mountains into the headwaters of the Cucharas River, and then along the eastern slopes of the Spanish Peaks.[25] After reaching the Apishapa River, Eaton examined the area where the Confederates were thought to be camped, all the way to the Denver to Fort Union road.

Short on rations, with five of his men contracting measles, and still not finding any signs of bandits or Confederates, Eaton opted to head back across the mountains to Fort Garland. The captain calculated that his men traveled 242 miles, much of the time with short rations, over one of the most difficult mountainous regions in the United States.[26]

In the winter of 1862–63, tensions between the settlers and the military in the San Luis Valley reached a breaking point and boiled over into violence. The violence began when authorities tried to arrest two brothers from the small village of San Rafael (Paisaje), west of Conejos, Felipe Nerio Espinosa and José Vivian Espinosa, who were said to have robbed a wagon between Santa Fe and Galisteo in December 1862.

The Espinosa brothers resented the intrusion of the military and Colorado civil officials into their lives. They were not alone. Culturally and religiously, the people in the valley were more closely tied to the nuevomexicano cousins than to the Anglos, the '59ers who had started to arrive in masses in search of gold in places such as Denver, Cañon City, and Fairplay, in the newly established Colorado Territory. Many resented outsiders squatting on their lands and the legal chicanery they were seeing these interlopers use to acquire land grants in the area. They worried about becoming second-class citizens in their own homes, and of being conscripted into the military.

Upon receiving Carleton's orders, Eaton sent Lt. Nicolas Hodt and ten men from Fort Garland to apprehend the brothers and other individuals who had resisted the arrest warrant. Riding sixty miles to San Rafael,

Hodt promptly arrested the two Espinosa brothers and confined them in a small log cabin and posted a sergeant to guard the men while he chased after several other men who had fled into the nearby hills to the east. In the meantime, the Espinosas broke through a wall of the room where they were being guarded and somehow acquired, probably from sympathetic villagers, an array of weapons, including rifles, pistols, and even bows and arrows. Hodt soon found himself under siege, with pistol shots and arrows flying across the small, barren plaza. In response, the lieutenant ordered the cabin from where the Espinosas were shooting set on fire. As the Espinosas rushed out of the burning building, unleashing a shower of arrows as they ran, Hodt emptied one pistol, only to find a second pistol jammed. After he tossed the weapon to the ground, the pistol discharged a bullet that scraped his forehead, exited through his hat, and ultimately knocked him down.[27]

Although badly wounded, Hodt was able to send an express to Fort Garland asking for the acting assistant surgeon, Dr. Lewis B. McLain, before sending what remained of his command in pursuit of the Espinosas, who had fled into the hills just west of the village. A squad of soldiers followed the brothers and their friends into the mountains but lost the trail. After several hours, however, Cpl. Desiderio Abeita succeeded in finding a set of tracks in the snow. Just as he turned to call out the news to the other soldiers, the sudden reverberation of a rifle shot echoed through the hills and Abeita fell dead, shot through the head. According to official records, the young corporal was "killed by rifle shot from escaped criminals while attempting to arrest them." Abeita, who worked as a cook and lumberjack in the military, was taken back to Fort Garland and buried nearby.[28]

Captain Eaton and Dr. McLain arrived on the scene at nine o'clock in the evening, and the pursuit of the Espinosas continued through the night and into the next day, but without success.[29] Eaton and a detachment later returned to San Rafael, where they confiscated all the personal property of the "Conejos murderers." The items were then auctioned off and the money used to "pay the expenses" incurred during the manhunt, the wages of a guide, and the burial of Corporal Abeita.[30]

What happened at the small village of San Rafael in the cold winter of 1862–63 only deepened the Espinosas' hatred of all things gringo. "They ruined our families—they took everything in our home; first our beds and blankets, then our provisions. Seeing this we said: 'We would rather be dead than see such infamies committed on our families,'" Felipe Espinosa wrote in his diary.[31] Before they were finally killed, the Espinosas ranged across the San Luis Valley into the Sangre de Cristos and north to the Arkansas River valley, then through south-central Colorado, committing murder after murder and offering the blood of their victims to the Virgin Mary.[32]

Although he was probably appalled and angered by the cowardly shooting of Abeita, Carabajal may have been apprehensive with the army's perceived persecution of a large part of the Hispanic population of the San Luis Valley. He may have even identified with the plight of the Espinosas. Judging by what followed, he was undoubtedly sick of all the violence he had encountered and of the discrimination in the army at the time, and certain that his manliness was being challenged.

ACUTE HOMICIDAL MANIA

For Private Carabajal, the problems at Fort Garland came to a climax on the night of May 21, 1863. Officers at the post blamed what happened on "Mexican whiskey peddlers," who congregated near the post following the arrival of the paymaster, and who were selling the men whiskey at three dollars a canteen.[33] Carabajal was one of the men who consumed too much alcohol and was reported to have been "very drunk" when he became involved in an angry argument with several men from his company. Carabajal was said to have rushed into the squad room at the post and commenced to curse Pvt. Francisco Martinez and Pvt. Francisco Luján. Moments later a scuffle ensued, at which time the lights of the barracks went out. Several men, including Luján, dragged Carabajal outside just as someone struck him over the head with a club, violently knocking him to the ground, while other men in the company began to beat him.[34]

The following evening, long after taps sounded and the men lay sleeping in their barracks, the badly beaten Carabajal entered the darkened barracks, calmly crawled up to where eighteen-year-old Luján lay sleeping face down on his cot, placed a revolver to the back of his head, and blew his brains out, the bullet exiting just above the left eye. As men excitedly scrambled out of their beds, the sergeant of the guard rushed into the barracks. "I done it," Carabajal was heard to say. So incensed were many of the men in the company upon viewing Luján's blood-splattered remains, that it took considerable effort to prevent them from lynching Carabajal.[35]

Capt. Joseph B. Davidson of the First Colorado Cavalry, commanding the post at the time, excitedly wrote department headquarters that "the most diabolic murder ever perpetrated" had "been committed at the post" and noted that both the victim and the perpetrator were "Mexicans."[36] Carabajal was placed in double irons, hands and feet, and confined in the guardhouse on the northeastern edge of the fort. Court-martial convened only a few days after the crime was committed. Carabajal, it was charged, had shot Luján in the head "with a pistol loaded with powder and ball." Every officer at the post except for Eaton, who had returned from leave and who served as interpreter for the court, and Second Lt. H. Ford Horrell, who was named as judge advocate, were assigned to the court.[37]

In the gut-wrenching case of the *United States vs. Homobono Carabajal*, the facts seemed indisputable. Carabajal had killed Luján with malice and in cold blood. Although Carabajal pleaded guilty, he did call individuals to testify in hopes that they would shed light to the events that led to the shooting and thus somehow elicit sympathy and save him from the death penalty. The first witness, Pvt. Guadalupe Bernal, a grey-eyed twenty-eight-year-old recruit from Chihuahua, Mexico, said that he had been in the squad room when he heard someone being beaten outside, but he was not absolutely sure that Luján was to blame.[38] Twenty-three-year-old Pvt. Francisco Martinez, a recruit from Taos, said that on the night before the murder Carabajal had cursed Luján, "using very bad language." Moreover, Carabajal had come into the squad room very drunk, intent on killing Martinez. It appeared at the time "as though he had a dag[g]er in his hand," Martinez went on to say. Fearful of being stabbed, Martinez retreated to the corner of the room and grabbed a stick to defend himself only to learn that Carabajal was unarmed. On the orders of the sergeant of the guard, Martinez helped to drag Carabajal outside into a moonlit night. Twenty-two-year-old Cpl. Daniel Sandoval testified that, although the door to the barracks had been slammed shut, he could hear the blows striking Carabajal. "Poor fellow, how they are pounding him," he remembered Private Martinez remarking.[39]

On May 26, 1863, a statement Carabajal dictated to Eaton was read to the court. He offered no explanation, only that he regretted having "the misfortune to touch in an ugly manner one of my own kind." Carabajal said that at the time he was under the influence of the devil and that he was one of the "weakest and most fe[e]ble of God's creatures on Earth." The private went on to say that he expected no leniency from the court, only from the

"God of heaven." Appearing remorseful, Carabajal asked for forgiveness, nevertheless, saying that if he were forgiven he would serve in the military for an additional five years and he would give all his pay to Luján's widow, Benigna, back in Valencia, until she could "take another husband."[40]

With little hesitation, the court, two-thirds of the members agreeing—as was required for conviction in capital cases—found Carabajal guilty, and he was ordered to be hung by the neck until dead.

As Carabajal waited in the guardhouse for transportation to Denver and his execution, the First New Mexico Volunteers marched away, leaving Fort Garland in the hands of the Colorado Volunteers. Four days after leaving Fort Garland, the New Mexico troops were already at Taos, and by June 28, after a march of 275 miles, the men arrived at Los Pinos. Then they were sent west for the war against the Navajos. By destroying crops, animals, and villages of the Dinés, and by driving the survivors on the Long Walk to the utterly desolate Bosque Redondo on the Pecos River, they brought unprecedented levels of violence, destruction, and misery to Navajo lives.[41]

Carabajal did not have to fight the Navajos or witness any more violence resulting from military campaigns. Borderlands violence had already done him in. His compiled service record indicates that Carabajal was executed at Denver on November 17, 1863, by General Order No. 104 of the Department of Missouri. Regimental records document his death by execution at Denver on October 10, 1863.[42] However, several documents in Carabajal's compiled military service record, even a "Casualty Sheet" signed in 1865, indicate that he was hanged for murder in Denver on November 27, 1863. An official "List of U.S. Soldiers Executed by United States Military Authorities during the Late War," published shortly after the end of the conflict but kept confidential for many years, reveals that "Homoboma Carrabojol," a private in Company D of the First New Mexico Cavalry, was hanged by General Order No. 104.[43] In reality, Carabajal remained in the small post guardhouse at Fort Garland, "awaiting execution," throughout 1863 and into the cold Colorado winter.

As Carabajal remained chained in the guardhouse at Fort Garland awaiting transportation to Denver to be hanged, the post surgeon, Dr. Lewis B. McLain, a civilian who had been contracted as an acting assistant surgeon, became convinced that the private was mentally ill and "not in a fit condition" to be executed. McLain was described at the time as "competent and attentive to his duties" and the only physician in the entire department who was said to be qualified. According to the doctor, to take Carabajal the 220 miles to Denver in chains in the middle of the winter would only make his condition worse.[44] Col. John M. Chivington, commanding the District of Colorado and a year away from his role in the infamous Sand Creek Massacre, had no doubt that the "man is crazy," but he agreed that the hanging should be postponed.[45]

There is little doubt that Carabajal was caught in the never-ending web of military bureaucracy. Letters flew up and down the chain of command between Fort Garland, Denver, Saint Louis, and Washington, D.C. When Col. Samuel M. Tappan came to command Fort Garland, he agreed that Carabajal was mentally ill. Tappan appears to have taken a personal interest in Carabajal, writing department headquarters from Fort Garland on January 5, 1864, that there was no doubt that the private was "guilty of a cruel and cowardly assassination of a fellow soldier" but that to hang Carabajal "in his present apparent condition of mind would be inhumane and unjust in the extreme." Moreover, the "exigencies of the public service do not require the execution of an insane man." Carabajal was securely confined at Fort Garland, Tappan continued, and every care was being taken to prevent him from committing suicide. The colonel had not set a date for Carabajal's transfer to Denver and felt nothing was lost by a "further postponement of his execution." Of course, "the execution must not take place until he is mentally restored, and it may be that the case at that time will present some reason for suspension of the sentence altogether," Col. N. P. Chipman, chief of staff at department headquarters for the Department of Kansas, who mistakenly thought that Carabajal was to be executed by firing squad, wrote from Fort Leavenworth, Kansas, on February 9, 1864. Chivington was to investigate the case of Carabajal, "a bad character," further and notify the commanding general when, if at all, Carabajal became "mentally restored."[46]

By April 1864, Carabajal's fate fell under the jurisdiction of the Department of Kansas, and it was decided that "the execution must not take place" until Carabajal was "mentally restored" and there was "some reason for suspension of the sentence entirely."[47] Well into 1865, however, the army continued efforts to hang Private Carabajal. On February 18, 1865, Maj. Gen. Grenville Mellen Dodge, fresh from Gen. William T. Sherman's Atlanta Campaign and of future transcontinental railroad fame, issued special orders for the private's execution, as was originally ordered in 1863.[48]

On April 5, 1865, only days before events at Appomattox Court House, Virginia, brought the Civil War to an end, military authorities in Denver were still proceeding with plans for Carabajal's hanging. Friday, April 14, 1865, 2:00 P.M., was set as the time and date for his execution. A scaffold was to be erected at a suitable place in the "suburbs or vicinity of Denver." A grave was to be dug in a place set aside by city authorities where other criminals lay buried, and proper arrangements were to be made for the interment of the body. Three days after the order for his execution was issued, a reprieve came from the general commanding the District of the Plains.[49]

In April 1865 in Denver, where the young private was then held in irons in the local jail, the medical director of the District of Colorado, Dr. John F. Hamilton, examined Carabajal and pronounced him of "unsound mind and not in a present condition to have the death penalty inflicted."[50] The thirty-three-year-old Hamilton, a native of Litchfield, Connecticut, came west in a wagon train in hopes of improving his health. He had received his medical license from the prestigious Rush Medical College in Chicago in 1854 and probably knew as much about medicine and the pioneering field of psychiatry as anyone in Colorado Territory at the time.

Along with Acting Assistant Surgeon C. P. Yates, Hamilton continued to carefully examine Carabajal, and both doctors found him mentally disturbed. Then Gen. Edward Patrick Conner, commanding the recently created District of the Plains, forwarded Hamilton's conclusions to the headquarters of the Department of Missouri in Saint Louis, Missouri, saying that the provost marshal and guards also agreed that Carabajal was of "unsound mind" and should not be executed. Conner finally recommend Carabajal's sentence be commuted to life in prison.[51] As citizens in the territorial capital watched with great interest, Carabajal's execution was again delayed.

In May 1865, the recently appointed commander of the Department of Missouri, General Dodge, telegraphed General Conner at Julesburg, Colorado, to have a board of surgeons examine Carabajal, and if they found him to be "crazy beyond doubt," he was to be sent to the Government Asylum for the Insane in Washington, D.C.[52] Dr. Hamilton responded that it was difficult to judge Carabajal since he had been confined, usually in chains, for so long and that he should be placed on fatigue duty in the open where he could receive some exercise and hopefully become sane. The board could then better judge him.[53] But the surgeons continued to pronounce Carabajal mentally ill, and it was finally decided to send the private to the Government Asylum for the Insane (or what inmates called Saint Elizabeth's Hospital, in hopes of avoiding the stigma of being held in an "insane asylum") in Washington, D.C.

Starting on September 8, 1865, and traveling first by stage and then by train through the heart of the Midwest, the small entourage—a corporal, a private, and Carabajal, still in chains—made it to Washington. Carabajal was admitted to the hospital on September 25, 1865, nearly two-and-a-half years after he had murdered Private Luján and nearly two years after he was supposedly hanged. What little that remains of the Saint Elizabeth's Hospital records at the National Archives list Carabajal as "white" and his place of birth as Mexico. Within days of his arrival, he was diagnosed with "acute homicidal mania."[54]

A FREE MAN

Overlooking a green, sloping expanse along the gently flowing Anacostia River, in red brick buildings at Saint Elizabeth's, just east of the capitol, it is likely that Carabajal came under the caring eye of Dorothea Dix, the leading mental health reformer of the era. Here the most humane and enlightened curative treatment proved to be in stark contrast to the rough and cruel Colorado imprisonment he had received at Fort Garland and the dark Denver jail where he had spent many long and weary days and months. Finally, on March 13, 1866, after five months and nineteen days at Saint Elizabeth's, Carabajal was said to have "recovered." Although he was technically still in the army and subject to execution, there is no evidence that the military attempted to retain him. Carabajal evidently walked out of Saint Elizabeth's a free man.[55]

Perhaps he made his way back to New Mexico Territory although the census for New Mexico Territory and the United States in the decades that followed fail to show a Homobono Carabajal or anyone with a name that remotely resembled his. Perhaps Carabajal, who was certain to have learned some English since he had shot Luján that fateful, moonlit night in distant Colorado Territory, stayed in the East. Or did he somehow make his way back to Mexico? A Homobono Carabajal, who was approximately the same age, fathered three children in the 1870s with a Felipa Lopez at the village of

San Agustin, Tlapa de Comonfort, Guerrero, Mexico, but this would have been far from his native Chihuahua.[56] His whereabouts before and after the war remain an intriguing mystery.

Although technically Carabajal did not ask that he be declared innocent by reason of insanity, his mental illness was what saved him from execution. Had Dr. Lewis B. McLain and Dr. John F. Hamilton and other military physicians not intervened, it is certain that the military would have executed Carabajal. Although there is little scholarly study of the use of the insanity defense within the military judicial system in the nineteenth century, it is almost certain that Pvt. Homobono Molino Carabajal was one of the first individuals in the United States to escape the death penalty by reason of insanity.[57]

Whether the borderlands violence he had participated in triggered Carabajal to insanity and murder or not, it would seem plausible to suggest that his ordeals as a borderlands soldier at least contributed to the decline of his mental state. If he had shown signs of mental illness in 1861, he probably would not have been accepted into the army. For most nuevomexicanos, Apache and Navajo raiding and counter-raids represented the norm of collective violence. The scale of mayhem at Valverde represented a degree of violence unfamiliar to Carabajal, and indeed beyond his conception, while the ugliness of duty at Cubero and Fort Garland did little to boost his self-esteem or sense of righteousness or manliness. Nevertheless, by 1866 the young soldier and his incredible case had already been lost to the tides of time.

NOTES

1. Caleb B. Smith to [Simon Cameron], May 11, 1861, *The War of the Rebellion: A Compilation of the Official Records of the Union and Confederate Armies* (*OR*) (Washington, D.C.: Government Printing Office, 1880–1901), series 1, vol. 53, 490. See also Jerry D. Thompson, *A Civil War History of the New Mexico Volunteers and Militia* (Albuquerque: University of New Mexico Press, 2015), from which much of this chapter is drawn.

2. Circular, August 20, 1861, General Orders (GO), Special Orders (SO), and Circulars Received (CR) from the Department of New Mexico (DNM) and District of New Mexico, 1855–1869, Adjutant General's Office (AGO), Record Group (RG) 393, National Archives and Records Administration, Washington D.C. (NARA); GO No. 38, September 18, 1861, *General Orders 1861*, DNM, AGO, RG 393, NARA; Edward Canby to Assistant Adjutant General (AAG), June 20, 1861, *OR*, series 1, vol. 4, 41.

3. During the war, the more populated territories of Nebraska, Oregon, and Nevada only contributed 6,047 men combined. *Governor's Annual Report to the Department of the Interior* (1892). Courtesy of Mike Scarborough.

4. GO No. 42, September 25, 1861, Orders Received, Southern District of New Mexico, DNM, AGO, RG 393, NARA; Circular, July 16, 1861, GO, SO, and CR from the DNM and District of New Mexico, AGO, RG 393, NARA; GO No. 20, July 23, 1863, *General Orders 1863*, DNM, AGO, RG 393, NARA. In addition, recruits were provided a clothing allowance of $3.50 a month. Anyone furnishing a horse or mule would be given forty cents per day for the animal's use and risk. GO No. 16, June 27, 1861, "District of New Mexico," Consolidated Files (CF), Quartermaster General's Office (QGO), RG 92, NARA.

5. GO No. 21, July 17, 1861, *General Orders 1861*, DNM, AGO, RG 393, NARA. For an account of the training of the New Mexico Volunteers at Fort Union, see Leo E. Oliva, "Fort Union: Historic Resource Study," https://www.nps.gov/foun/learn/management/upload/FOUNandFrontierArmyOfSW-2.pdf (accessed June 24, 2016).

6. Homobono Carabajal Compiled Military Service Record (CMSR) (Second New Mexico Infantry and First New Mexico Cavalry), RG 94, NARA. On Pino, see GO No. 18, July 13, 1861, "District of New Mexico," CF, QGO, RG 92, NARA.

7. Ethan W. Eaton CMSR, RG 94, NARA; 8th Census (1860) and 9th Census (1870), Santa Fe County, New Mexico, NARA; Thompson, *Civil War History*, 42, 97; Jerry D. Thompson, ed., *New Mexico Territory in the Civil War: Wallen and Evans Inspection Reports, 1862–1863* (Albuquerque: University of New Mexico Press, 2008), 204–205.

8. Carabajal's name is variously given as "Carvajal," "Carrabal," "Carrabyal," "Carbajal," "Carbojol," "Carrvajal," "Carrejabel," and "Carrobajal." His given names are recorded as "H. Molino," "Hombres," "Homoborne," "Humbres," "Homobo," but generally as "Homobono Molino." Carabajal CMSR.

9. Fort Craig, September 1861–March 1862, Returns from U.S. Military Posts, 1800–1916, M617, roll 261, NARA.

10. Canby to Benjamin Roberts, July 21, 1861, Letters Received (LR), DNM, AGO, RG 393, NARA.

11. Regimental Returns (RR), Second New Mexico Infantry, August, 1861–February, 1862, AGO, RG 94, NARA. See also Thompson, *Civil War History*, 35, 103–106.

12. RR, Second New Mexico Infantry, December 1861, AGO, RG 94, NARA.

13. Canby to Adjutant General (AG), March 1, 1862, *OR*, series 1, vol. 9, 489. See also James L. Collins to Wm. P. Dole, March 1, 1862, in Jerry Thompson, ed., "Indian Agent at Valverde: The Civil War Journal and Letters of James L. Collins," *Southwestern Historical Quarterly* 103 (October 1999): 223.

14. Canby to AG, March 1, 1862, *OR*, series 1, vol. 9, 491 [quotation], 493.

15. Miguel E. Pino to W. J. L. Nicodemus, February 26, 1862, *OR*, series 1, vol. 9, 503. For a list of those who were charged with desertion, see John Taylor, *Bloody Valverde: A Civil War Battle on the Rio Grande* (Albuquerque: University of New Mexico Press, 1995), 167–68.

16. L. Thomas to Canby, April 4, 1862, LR, DNM, AGO, RG 393, NARA.

17. GO No. 44, May 10, 1862, *General Orders 1862*, DNM, AGO, RG 393, NARA.

18. Ethan Eaton to Gurdin Chapin, August 18, 1862, Eaton CMSR.

19. RR, Second New Mexico Infantry, May–June, 1862, AGO, RG 94, NARA.

20. Ibid. Wallen's report is in Thompson, *New Mexico Territory*, 39–50.

21. Eaton to Ben Cutler, November 30, 1862, Eaton CMSR [first quotation]; Chapin to AAG, February 1, 1862, LR, DNM, AGO, RG 393, NARA [Canby quoted].

22. Carabajal CMSR.

23. Eaton to Chapin, August 18, 1862, LR, DNM, AGO, RG 393, NARA.

24. Ibid.

25. Eaton to Adolph H. Mayer, September 5, 1862, LR, DNM, AGO, RG 393, NARA.

26. Ibid.; Nicolas Hodt to Eaton, September 24, 1862, LR, DNM, AGO, RG 393, NARA.

27. *Denver Rocky Mountain Weekly News*, February 12, 1863.

28. Desiderio Abeytia [*sic*] CMSR, RG 94, NARA. Far to the south in Socorro, New Mexico, Abeita's grief-stricken and poverty-plagued widow, Clementa Baca de Abeita, asked the army to forward her husband's possessions and any pay he might be due. Clementa Baca de Abeita to Cutler, March 10, 1863, Desiderio Abeytia CMSR.

29. Eaton to Cutler, February 7, 1863, LR, DNM, AGO, RG 393, NARA.

30. Eaton to Acting Assistant Adjutant General (AAAG), April 14, 1863, Mauro Montoya Papers, Museum of New Mexico, Santa Fe. See also Charles F. Price, "Espinosas Scapegoating Goes Awry: The Strange Case of Capt. E. Wayne Eaton," pt. 2, *CoZine.com: Colorado Central Magazine*, May 1, 2009, http://cozine.com/2009-may/espinosas-scapegoating-goes-awry/ (accessed December 24, 2014). The items sold at auction included a steer, an ox, a trunk, and four fanegas of wheat. Items confiscated by the territorial martial included eight cows and oxen, four beds complete with bedding, a beaver trap, and two water buckets. (A fanega is equivalent to 1.575 bushels.)

31. *Denver Weekly Commonwealth and Republican*, October 28, 1863.

32. For a comprehensive study of the Espinosas and their crimes, see, Charles F. Price, *Season of Terror: The Espinosas in Central Colorado, March–October 1863* (Boulder: University of Colorado Press, 2013). José Vivian Espinosa was mortally wounded by a posse out of Park County in May 9, 1863, not far from Cañon City. Felipe Nerio Espinosa was killed high in the Sangre de Cristo Mountains, northeast of Fort Garland, on October 15, 1863, by a group of men led by the well-known tracker and frontiersman Tom Tobin. He was beheaded and his head taken back to Fort Garland as a trophy of war.

33. Joseph B. Davidson to AAAG, May 31, 1863, Carabajal CMSR.

34. Testimony of Guadalupe Bernal, Daniel Sandoval, and Francisco Martinez, Humberto Carabajal Court-Martial, Case No. NN 382, Judge Advocate General's Office (JAGO), RG 153, NARA.

35. Davidson to AAAG, May 21, 1863, Carabajal CMSR; Certificate, May 21, 1863, Francisco Luján CMSR, RG 94, NARA. Luján, who was born at the village of Valencia, downriver from Albuquerque, was a diminutive man—barely five feet four inches tall—with a light complexion. He had enlisted in the New Mexico Volunteers at Albuquerque in late July 1861, about the same time as had Carabajal, and Luján, too, had been at Valverde. Today, Luján's ghost is said to haunt Fort Garland.

36. Davidson to AAAG, May 21, 1863, Carabajal CMSR.

37. Capt. W. A. Van Vliet was presiding since he was the highest-ranking officer at the post at the time. Second Lt. Nicolas Hodt was the only officer from the New Mexico Cavalry on the court.

38. Testimony of Guadalupe Bernal, Carabajal Court-Martial, JAGO, RG 153, NARA. Bernal and Carabajal had much in common in that they were both born in the state of Chihuahua, both had enlisted at Albuquerque, and both had listed their occupation as laborer. When ordered back to New Mexico, Bernal committed suicide by shooting himself in the head with a pistol at Taos on June 25, 1863. Joseph Berney to AAG, June 30, 1863, Guadalupe Bernal CMSR, RG 94, NARA.

39. Testimony of Francisco Martinez and Daniel Sandoval, Carabajal Court-Martial, JAGO, RG 153, NARA.

40. Carabajal Statement, JAGO, RG 153, NARA.

41. RR, First New Mexico Cavalry, June, 1863, AGO, RG 94, NARA; Lawrence C. Kelly ed., *Navajo Roundup: Selected Correspondence of Kit Carson's Expedition against the Navajo, 1863–1865* (Boulder, Colo.: Pruett, 1970); Gerald Thompson, *The Army and the Navajo: The Bosque Redondo Reservation Experiment, 1863–1868* (Tucson: University of Arizona Press, 1976).

42. Carabajal CMSR.

43. Casualty Sheet, October 5, 1865, Carabajal CMSR; "List of U.S. Soldiers Executed by United States Military Authorities during the Late War," AGO, NARA. Thompson, *New Mexico Territory*, makes the same mistake.

44. Lewis B. McLain to Samuel M. Tappan, October 26, 1863, Carabajal CMSR; Thompson, *New Mexico Territory*, 44, 57.

45. John M. Chivington to AG, November 27, 1863, Carabajal CMSR.

46. Tappan to G. H. Stillwell, January 5, 1864; Norton P. Chipman to Chivington, February 9, 1864, both in Carabajal CMSR.

47. H. P. Chapin to Chief of Staff, April 9, 1864, Carabajal CMSR.

48. SO No. 11, February 18, 1865, Carabajal CMSR.

49. AAAG to Silas S. Soule, April 18, 1865, Carabajal CMSR.

50. John F. Hamilton to AAAG, April 13, 1865, Carabajal CMSR.

51. Edward Conner to J. W. Barnes, April 17, 1865, Carabajal CMSR.

52. Barnes to Conner, May 3, 1865, Carabajal CMSR.

53. Hamilton endorsement, n.d., Carabajal CMSR.

54. SO No. 48, September 8, 1865, Carabajal CMSR.; Register of Patients, St. Elizabeth's Hospital, RG 418, NARA. Unfortunately, the case file for Homobono Carabajal was one of the many files that were destroyed after the war. Records for the Government Asylum for the Insane indicate that Carabajal was given a pair of pants, two flannel shirts, two pairs of drawers, one blouse, two pairs of socks, one pair of shoes, and a blanket upon arrival. The Carabajal case is summarized in Edward C. Johnson, Gail R. Johnson, and Melissa Johnson Williams, *All Were Not Heroes: A Study of the List of U.S. Soldiers Executed by U.S. Military Authorities during the Late War* (Chicago: privately printed, 1997), 122–25.

55. Register of Patients, Saint Elizabeth's Hospital, RG 418, NARA.

56. "Mexico Baptisms, 1860–1950," https://familysearch.org/search/collection/1473011 (accessed March 28, 2015). In 1839, a José Gregorio Homobono Carabajal, who appears to have been the same age as the troubled Private Carabajal, was born at the village of San Agustín, Chiautla de Tapia, in the state of Puebla.

57. Meredith L. Mona, Carroll J. Diebold, and Ava B. Walton, "Update on the Disposition Military Insanity Acquittees," *Journal of the American Academy of Psychiatry and the Law* 34 (December 2006): 538–44; Raymond G. Lande, "The Military Insanity Defense," *Bulletin of the American Academy of Psychiatry Law* 19 (1991): 193–201. At the time of the Civil War, the military appears to have been reliant on the M'Naghten rule that dated back to 1843 when Daniel M'Naghten, a paranoid sailor, shot and killed the secretary to British prime minister Robert Peel, who was the intended victim. The presiding judge in the case provided an option for a verdict of "not guilty on the ground of insanity." Case law came to state that an individual could be declared innocent, providing the "accused was laboring under such a defect of reason, from disease of the mind, as not to know the nature and quality of the act he was doing"; Mona, Diebold, and Walton, "Update," 539. It is likely that Drs. McLain and Hamilton were both familiar with the M'Naghten case. They were certain to have been familiar with the sensationalized 1859 case of Daniel E. Sickles, a well-known New York congressman who shot and killed Philip Barton Key II, son of Francis Scott Key and district attorney for the District of Columbia, in Lafayette Square, only blocks from the White House, who he discovered was having an affair with his young wife. Sickles was found innocent when he and his prominent attorneys successfully argued that he was driven temporarily insane by his wife's infidelity. It was the first use of temporary insanity as a legal defense. In 1921, a varation of the M'Naghten test was included in the U.S. Military's *Manual for Courts-Martial*.

4
Alonzo Ickis

Megan Kate Nelson

In 1861, Alonzo Ickis was young (twenty-five years old) and unmarried. He saw war as an opportunity to do his duty and have adventures. At times his desire for action, danger, and excitement seemed foolhardy and reckless. But he wanted to measure up, to prove his manliness to himself and to his peers in combat. When he joined the Union Army, he was already seasoned to a life of risk, privation, and violence. He had come to what he called "the Far West" in 1859 to seek his fortune in the Rocky Mountain gold mines. Life in the diggings prepared him for the arduous conditions of military life. During the Civil War, Ickis fought in one major battle but spent most of his time marching and garrisoning forts. The marches he participated in were long ones, beginning with a three-hundred-mile journey from the tiny mining town of Cañon City in Colorado Territory to Santa Fe, the capital of New Mexico Territory.[1] When the action in one theater subsided, Ickis and his company were transferred to another in these borderlands, where the vagaries of nature shaped collective violence as did the built environments: ranches, towns, and forts, and the trails and roads that covered the vast distances between them. Ickis was wounded once (taking a bullet in the thigh) but survived his three-year term of service. When he mustered out of the Union Army in 1864, Ickis left the borderlands for good and returned home to his family and his life as a farmer in Iowa.

Ickis served in a Union army that was multiethnic and multinational. He fought alongside Native Americans and Hispanic New Mexicans in the Battle of Valverde, and he perceived himself to be fighting for the United States but outside of its borders. For Ickis, the Southwest borderlands were foreign places to be conquered in the name of the Union, and thus defended from Confederate invasion. He described these places and experiences in

Alonzo Ferdinand Ickis, ca. 1864. Published in Ickis, *Bloody Trails along the Rio Grande: The Diary of Alonzo Ferdinand Ickis*, ed. Nolie Mumey (Denver: Old West Publishing, 1958). Image courtesy Harvard University Libraries.

his diary and in sporadic letters he wrote to his family in 1861 and 1862. These records, along with those penned by his fellow Union soldiers and military reports from the field, reveal to us not only Ickis's personal experiences of war but also the ways that natural forces shaped violence, in this case the Civil War, in the Southwest borderlands.

THE ROAD TO COLORADO TERRITORY

Alonzo Ferdinand Ickis's family had been farming in western Iowa in the 1850s when a series of misfortunes—a drought, crop failures, and falling land prices—brought hard times. And then the panic of '57, as historian Elliott West has put it, "reverberated out onto the prairie" and "thousands of young men were shaken loose from their roots."[2] So when the reports of gold strikes in the Rocky Mountains began to filter into Iowa in the fall of '58, Alonzo (twenty-two years old and eager to make his own way in the world) was ready to go. He and his eldest brother, Johnathan, left Creston for the gold mines in the spring of 1859.[3]

If Ickis wrote a diary of his journey westward, it has disappeared. Any letters that he or Johnathan wrote to their family after they left for the mines have also been lost. It is probable that they took the most straightforward route to the Rockies: Creston to Council Bluffs, and then on to Nebraska via the Northern Route, a trail moving along the Platte River and then cutting south to Denver. In late March and early April of 1859, this route was thronged with Argonauts, traveling alone or with their families, pulling carts or driving wagons full of provisions and personal belongings. Along this road, the Ickises would have passed a string of tiny towns and a mail station or two. Alonzo and Johnathan likely saw Indians for the first time in Nebraska, in and around the Pawnee, Cheyenne, and Arapaho villages that were perched near the trading posts of the plains.[4]

About five weeks after they left Council Bluffs, the brothers arrived in Denver. They did not stay there long. The mining frontier had already expanded westward (and upward) from the diggings in the foothills of the Rockies, and so the Ickises left immediately for Leadville, a mining boomtown ten thousand feet up in Lake County.[5] There they built themselves rudimentary shelters, panned in streams, and looked for signs of gold in outcroppings. They worked around Leadville for a year but then moved on to the Blue River near Breckenridge. The Ickis brothers did not have much luck striking veins. But they did figure out another way to make money in the diggings.[6] They bought and sold cattle, and they loaned money to men who needed to buy pans, axes, and food.[7] These schemes did not make the brothers rich, however. By the summer of 1861, their parents needed them back on the farm. Johnathan left for Iowa on October 1, but Alonzo stayed, thinking he might prospect in the mountains through the winter. He quite liked Colorado (which had achieved territorial status, courtesy of the Union Congress, in February 1861). He was determined to stick it out.

VOLUNTEERS WANTED!

A few weeks after Johnathan left for home, a notice appeared in the local paper: "VOLUNTEERS WANTED! For C. D. Hendren's Company of Colorado Volunteers, to serve for three years, or during the war."[8] The war news from the East had trickled in over the past year, but now there was an opportunity to serve in the Union Army from where he was. So Ickis and his friend Simon Motz headed south and joined almost one hundred other men in Cañon City, where C. D. Hendren and Lieutenant J. C. W. Hall had set up a recruiting station. All of the new recruits were gold miners, and Ickis knew at least twenty of them personally.

All of the new recruits were coming off of disappointing prospecting seasons and facing a winter of deep snows and inactivity. They were adventurers who thought nothing of changing their plans on the fly. Spending the winter "in the Service of our Uncle" seemed like a pretty good deal. They would have plenty of food and earn regular wages, and maybe they would get to fight a few Texans. It was not all about survival, though; it was about doing what was right and honorable. After he signed up, Alonzo wrote to Johnathan, "I hope you will not think I have done wrong for I do think it is the duty of every single man to enlist and do all in his power to end this war."[9]

For almost two months, Ickis and his fellow miners-turned-soldiers lived in a hotel in Cañon City and received uniforms, weapons, and training. They drilled during the day and caroused by night, "determined to spend the time as pleasantly as possible."[10] In early December, Hendren's company received word that they were to march to Fort Garland in southern Colorado. They would garrison the fort and defend it against incursions while the U.S. Army regulars currently serving there went down to New Mexico to defend Santa Fe against the Texans, who were heading that way from San Antonio.[11]

On December 6, 1861, Hendren's Independent Company—ninety-one men strong—left Cañon City and made its way down the Arkansas River past the Indian trading town of Pueblo, turning south along the Huerfano River toward the Sangre de Cristo Mountains. The southern Rockies were blanketed with snow and the temperatures had plummeted; the men barely made it up Sangre de Cristo Pass, hauling the wagons and yanking the cattle up the slope with their bare hands. This was the first in a series of extensive marches that the company undertook, most of them crossing vast stretches of deserts, and moving up and over high mountain passes. The Civil War in the desert Southwest was characterized by such long hauls. The terrain and the weather tested soldiers on both sides throughout the winter and spring of 1862, and highlighted how reliant they were on their own wagon trains.[12]

Hendren's company arrived at Fort Garland on December 12. For several weeks, the men camped outside the fort's adobe walls, drilled every morning, wrote letters home every evening, and tried—but failed—to catch trout in Ute Creek. On December 22, they lost their captain. Hendren had gotten in a drunken fistfight with some U.S. Army regulars the night before, and Maj. Charles Whiting, in charge of Fort Garland, relieved him from duty and replaced him with Theodore H. Dodd, a big man from Ohio with a degree from West Point. Ickis approved of Dodd, and he had high hopes for the company, for he judged it was "the best that was ever raised in any country."[13]

After this change in command, Ickis and his comrades were mustered into the Union Army; from this point on they were referred to interchangeably as "Dodd's Independent Company" or "Company B, Second Colorado Volunteers." They spent Christmas and New Year's at Fort Garland. Celebrating the holidays so far from home depressed the men. They "longed for active service" and "hoped to go to Santa Fe soon." And then, by some miracle, on January 3, 1862, they got their wish and left the confines of Fort Garland to march into New Mexico Territory.[14] On the 150-mile traders' path to Santa Fe, they faced a new set of challenges: pelting snowstorms; nearly constant crossings of icy creeks and *acequias* (irrigation ditches); and, in the towns they passed along the way, the seductions of Taos Lightning (a hard liquor distilled from wheat) and fandangos.

After almost two weeks of dancing and drinking their way through northern New Mexico, Ickis and his comrades arrived in Santa Fe. They bunked down outside Fort Marcy and received their Union uniforms; the new kits and good grub lifted their spirits. Ickis and the boys stayed in Santa Fe for eight days, drilling every morning and marching on dress parade every evening.[15] Meanwhile, rumors swirled through town: the Texans were approaching, closer every day. Marching up the Rio Grande. Sneaking up the Pecos River with their Apache allies. Coming down the Santa Fe Trail with giant wagon trains in their wake.[16] Some officers said that the Colorado boys might go to join Col. Edward Canby's Union troops south of Albuquerque. But nothing happened. So Ickis and the boys rambled around town, gambling and drinking and dancing. They had "good times in these quarters plenty of grub a F[andango] every night." They marched to the plaza for a grand review on January 22, and the next day, they received their orders. The Second Colorado was going to join Canby at Fort Craig, and the men were going to fight the Texans for control of the West.[17]

VALVERDE

The march from Santa Fe to Fort Craig was another 150-mile slog. The roads swallowed wagon wheels, and the Rio Grande was choked with ice. "It makes a man catch for breath when in the ice water five feet deep," Ickis wrote in his diary. By the time the men set up tents on the undulating ground between Fort Craig and the Rio Grande on January 31, Company B had lost twenty of its men to illness—most to smallpox, which had spread through their camps in Santa Fe. But the healthy men were strong and eager to fight.[18]

The Union camp they joined at Fort Craig was a multiethnic one. Alongside the Second Colorado and the regulars of the U.S. Fifth and Seventh Infantries were camped two regiments of New Mexico Volunteers, Hispanic soldiers recruited from the territory and commanded by Christopher "Kit" Carson and Miguel Pino. There were also New Mexicans serving under James "Paddy" Graydon as spies and irregulars. Ickis, like most of his Anglo contemporaries, did not hold the Hispanics in high esteem. He refused to see them as brave men, and he did not hesitate to describe New Mexican soldiers and civilians as "greasers" and "carajos."[19]

While all of these soldiers drilled and cleaned their weapons and speculated on the movements of the Texans, hundreds more began to arrive at Fort Craig. Their wagon trains lagged behind, and Canby sent an entire company of soldiers to go and meet it. "There is great danger in bringing a train from [Fort] Union as the Navajoes [*sic*] are very troublesome," Ickis noted.[20] To move a wagon train loaded with food and weapons more than two hundred miles in one haul from Fort Union to Fort Craig was difficult not only from a logistics standpoint—wagon wheels became mired in sand or splintered due to the aridity, and mules and oxen became jaded and gave out by the side of the road—but also because long trains on a single road through an open landscape were tempting targets for Navajo and Apache raiders.

Ickis's thoughts soon turned from food to fighting. Canby's scouts had spied enemy troops several miles south of the fort on the west bank of the Rio Grande, and Dodd's men were ordered to march down to Bosque Bonita with Company B of the Fifth Infantry, to scout the Texans' position. They marched for two hours, excited by the prospect of battle. As they crested a ravine, they saw an advance guard of Gen. Henry H. Sibley's mounted Confederate troops, and dropped back below the rise, taking up a defensive position and sending word to Canby at Fort Craig. As the Union main force gathered and moved southward to face the Confederates, Sibley's men stayed where they were. Ickis crouched in that ravine, rifle at the ready, until 9:00 P.M., when it became evident that the Texans, seeing that this particular field of battle would not favor them, had retreated back to their camp. Dodd's men marched quickly back to Fort Craig to prevent a Confederate flanking maneuver to the west and arrived at 11:00 P.M. "Laid on our arms expecting an attack," Ickis wrote in his diary, "morning came but Texans did not."[21]

For the next two days, snow and sleet bombarded Ickis's tent outside Fort Craig while the Confederates moved closer; Canby sent out pickets and the Texans drove them in. "I believe the instruments are well strung," Ickis wrote, "and the ball will open soon." He was cheered by the arrival of the long-awaited wagon train, "laden with grub which we need 'you bet.'" The Navajos had not attacked it after all.[22]

When Ickis awakened on February 16, the storms had cleared and the soldiers were ready. Paddy Graydon's spies had reported that the Texans were moving en masse toward Fort Craig. If Ickis had been able to stand on one of the fort's exterior walls (made of adobe and shored up with dirt, looped for musketry every three or four feet), he would have seen the Texans advancing in a line of battle with their right flank anchored on the riverbank and their left on the high ground to the west.[23] When the Confederates drew within a half mile of Fort Craig, Ickis and the rest of Dodd's men left the post to meet them. But Canby did not order them to charge. Instead, he sent some cavalry to poke and prod the Texans, trying to get them to leave the arroyo that protected them and attempt a frontal assault on Fort Craig. However, Sibley quickly determined that a fight on open ground favored the Union troops and he called off the attack, ordering his men to retreat to their campsite a few miles to the south.[24]

The ball did not open for the next few days, either. A sandstorm set in and both armies stayed put. But on the 19th the Texans made their move, crossing the Rio Grande and marching up its eastern bank. Ickis was scornful of this strategy. "They passed by the Ft and were endeavoring to get to Albuquerque," he wrote to his brother Thomas, "without giving us a fight." Ickis and his comrades—along with several regiments of New Mexico Volunteers—were called out at four that morning and ordered to cross over to intercept the enemy in their progress up the Rio. But the Texans had taken a northbound road that wound its way up to higher ground. Ickis reported, "The enemy is on a high divide 4 m from the Rio. We cannot get a position where our battery can do any execution."[25] The next day, the situation became untenable as the Texans unlimbered some of their artillery. "[The] Enemy has a position where their guns can throw round shot among us," Ickis noted in his diary. "We cannot return the fire as we are far below them." The Union men retreated to the fort later that evening, again frustrated in their desire to have a fight.[26]

The next day—February 21, 1862—Ickis and his mates got their wish. In the morning, with the Texans on the move up the east side of the Rio Grande, Dodd's men moved up the west side, skirting the edge of the towering Mesa de la Contadera, a volcanic formation jutting up from the river valley. At this point in its course, the mesa forced the Rio Grande to meander; the force of the water flow carved out curves and then cut them off, changing the river's course over time. As the Texans came around the northeast side of the mesa, they found protection in the sand ridges of one of the river's former beds. Ickis and his comrades faced them more than half a mile away, on the Rio Grande's west bank. Ickis was jubilant: "The enemy will have to come to the Rio for water they have not had any water for 24 hours." They planted a battery on the water's edge, and when the Texans, as Ickis predicted, came across the Valverde plain to quench their own and their horses' thirst, "our battery of 8 guns opened upon them sending forth a volley of grape & canister which provide too many for the enemy they retreated."[27]

For Alonzo Ickis, the war had now truly, and finally, commenced. All the marching, or the chasing and raiding, that seemed so prevalent in the borderlands was nothing better than banditry. It was in a battle that men were measured and things decided.

In the early afternoon, Ickis splashed across the Rio Grande, up to his armpits in icy water, and then took up a position on the extreme left of the advancing Union line. Here the "the ball began in earnest between the skirmishers," Ickis described as he and his comrades moved quickly toward the Texans' position and peppered them with rifle and musket fire.[28] After coming within a few hundred yards of the Texans squatting in the old riverbed, as Confederate Alfred Peticolas put it, Dodd's men "began to pay dearly for getting so close to us."[29] Ickis and the others were stalled, taking cover wherever they could. The Texans, who had seen them clearly as they drew closer, were confused by their uniforms. Although Ickis and his comrades were wearing Union blues, they were clearly not U.S. Army regulars; the Texans therefore assumed they were New Mexico Volunteers. This case of mistaken identity resulted in one of the more unusual actions in the Civil War, with Ickis and the Second Colorado right in the center of it.

Because the Confederates "thought us Mexicans," Ickis wrote, "they then thought they had a soft snap." Confederate colonel Tom Green ordered a charge on Dodd's company. When Ickis and the others saw Willis Lang's cavalry trotting swiftly over the field toward them, they could not believe it. The seventy Texans were charging not with guns or sabers but with, as historian John Taylor has described them, "nine-foot lances, each tipped with twelve-inch blades and sporting red guidon banners, emblazoned with a single white star." Dodd overcame his befuddlement to assemble Ickis and the others into the classic hollow square formation. The Colorado boys waited "until they got within 40 yds of us" and then Dodd reportedly raised his sword and shouted, "They're Texans! Given 'em Hell!" Ickis "took deliberate aim and it was fun to see the Texans fall." The lancers wavered and the Second Colorado reloaded and shot again, giving the Confederates "the buck and ball after this second volley there were but few of them left and but one of them got away the others were shot." Ickis affixed his bayonet to his gun, and he and the others charged; according to Ickis, the Lancers "appeared bewildered did not appear to know how or what to do they were soon butchered (I can not call it else)."[30]

After this rather astonishing charge, the battle fell into a lull. Both sides rested, ate some of the rations they had cooked the day before, and cleaned their guns. Ickis and the Second Colorado were drawn back and to the right to support one section of the battery that had crossed over the river. A cannonade commenced, and lasted until late afternoon.[31] At this point, Ickis saw his second Confederate charge of the day; only this time, the Texans sent half of their men to take the Union battery at the center of their line. They succeeded. Ickis blamed this failure—which led to a Union retreat back across the Rio Grande and the loss of the Battle of Valverde—on the cowardice of the New Mexico Volunteers. "At the first sight of such a very large body of Texans," he wrote afterward to his brother, "[Miguel] Pinos men ran leaving us white men only 250 to hold the section or let it go and go it did we stood our ground against 1500 of the enemy."[32]

There was plenty of blame to go around, however. Ickis reported that Capt. Richard Lord and his company of dragoons disobeyed an order in not coming to their support at the time the enemy made the charge. Soldiers also blamed Canby for his late arrival at the battlefield and the mismanagement of troops in the afternoon, which created vulnerability at the center of the Union line, inviting the Texans to charge it. For his part, Canby reported that the Confederates possessed a great advantage, as they were all mounted. But Ickis always came back around again to the New Mexico Volunteers. Although historians have since proven that many of them served bravely at Valverde and during the engagements after it, Dodd's men were convinced that Pino's men were to blame. Ickis noted bitterly in his diary, "Those who ran off at the time of the Battle have not been seen since they were formally disbanded. We would have been a damn sight better off if they had all been in hell before we came in the Ter[ritory]."[33]

By his own reckoning, Ickis's company lost four killed and thirty-seven wounded—"the most from any one Co in the field," he wrote a letter to his brother. "We were the first in action the last from the field."[34] This was only a bit of an exaggeration. Ickis was clearly proud of his own and his company's performance at Valverde. His account emphasized their coolness under fire and their bravery in the face of overwhelming odds in the final charge of the day. This was how Ickis justified his regiment's actions and kept his morale up in the wake of a devastating loss.[35]

After a three-day truce and the burial of the dead, Sibley's army marched northward, taking Albuquerque and Santa Fe without opposition. Ickis and the Second Colorado did not join the Union troops who followed.[36] Instead, they stayed at Fort Craig to defend it against further attacks from Texans or Indians, and to prevent any Confederate supplies from reaching Sibley from points southward. On March 5, Ickis and several friends climbed Mesa de la Contadera and "enjoyed a splendid view of the Battle ground." They were able to see the extent of the sand ridges that protected the Texans; this gave them "a vivid impression of the great disadvantage we fought under on that day."[37] Like many of their compatriots in other theaters of the Civil War, Ickis and his comrades were battlefield tourists. They wanted to see where they had been fighting in order to make sense of the battle.

TRACKING ENEMIES, NEW AND OLD

Ickis stayed at Fort Craig under the command of Kit Carson until early April. Dodd's men heard only sporadic news from northern New Mexico as Sibley's troops had cut off their lines of communication. They spent their days drilling and fanning out across the Rio Grande valley to dig up hay the U.S. Army regulars and civilians had buried to protect it from Texans and Indians. There was little, too little, excitement to all this.

In mid-March, however, Ickis fought briefly against a different enemy. Navajos were "trying to run off our herd of mules," he reported excitedly in his diary. "We soon broke toward them at full speed every man 'on his own hook.'" They were unable to recover the herd—the Navajos had made it into the mountains and then scattered, making it difficult for the Union soldiers to follow. Ickis and his comrades likely never saw those mules again, but in a development typical for this region, ten days later Pueblo Indians brought to trade 250 mules, which they had stolen from the Texans. The presence of the Apaches, Navajos, and other independent Indians complicated the fight between the Union and Confederate armies. Native American groups traded with and raided both armies in mules, horses, cattle, and foodstuffs. These activities meant that in the Southwest borderlands, the Civil War was also an Indian war.[38]

This skirmish with the Navajos whetted Ickis's appetite. Although he had paled at the sight of so many dead and wounded friends on the Valverde battlefield, Ickis longed to get back into the fight. Garrison life was dull, and he wished that the First Colorado (which had marched south from Denver that month to meet the Texans at Glorieta Pass) would trade places with the Second so that it could get into the action.[39] On March 31, the men heard that the First Colorado had been successful and the Texans were on the run. Ickis and his comrades marched northward, hoping to intercept the Confederates as they retreated from Albuquerque. Outside of Socorro, the Union men stopped briefly to hear Canby read a dispatch out loud: there had been a "desperate fight at Apache Cañon between Col 1st and Sibley's army Col cleaned them out." Dodd's men cheered, proud of their fellow '59ers. The excitement made their meal of "transparent bacon & soda bread" taste better—but only slightly.[40]

When they arrived outside of Albuquerque on April 9—the same day that the Texans marched into that city in full retreat from Santa Fe—Ickis waited anxiously, hoping that he and the rest of Dodd's men would storm the town. Canby had refused to shell the Texans out of their trenches because there were still women and children in Albuquerque. Dodd had therefore volunteered his men to lead a charge against the trenches. But instead of charging into the city, Ickis and the others withdrew from Albuquerque at 9:00 P.M. Canby had received a dispatch saying that Sibley was on the move, marching southeast toward Fort Stanton.[41] This intelligence proved faulty, but it did give Canby's men the opportunity to unite with the First Colorado, which had been marching south from Fort Union since the battle of Glorieta Pass. Ickis was glad to see several old acquaintances from the mines and to discover a large wagon train loaded with grub.[42] Together they marched toward Albuquerque, only to find that the Texans had withdrawn southward, toward the town of Peralta.

When Ickis and the others arrived outside of Peralta on the evening of April 14, Sibley's men had already occupied the town and were dancing and drinking the night away. Canby could have attacked that night but he did not, as the town contained too many walls and acequias, both of which formed barriers to military charges. The next day, the armies traded cannon fire and skirmished along the lines. The battle of Peralta did not have a clear victor, but Ickis wrote triumphantly to his brother Thomas that the Texans "were in a hot place and had to come to our terms or retreat. They retreated after dark leaving their wounded in the town buried their dead in a seche [acequia]."[43]

For the next several days, Dodd's men shadowed Sibley's troops southward along the Rio Grande. Many soldiers complained about the tracking strategy—they wanted to cross the river and whip the Texans once and for all. But Canby knew that the greatest challenge in a war of this scale in the desert was provisioning the troops, and he did not want to have to subsist more than one thousand prisoners of war. So Ickis and the others continued to march down the river on the opposite bank, keeping Sibley's men always in sight. On the night of April 18, Ickis noted in his diary that in the middle of a sandstorm, the enemy troops were burning their wagons.[44] Although he did not know it at the time, the Texans had done so in in order to cut loose from the river and evade their pursuers in the Magdalena Mountains to the west.

Ickis and the Second Colorado kept on marching, reaching Fort Craig on April 23, 1862. There they found many of their wounded and sick compatriots on the mend.[45] Three weeks later, after Sibley's troops had emerged from the mountains south of Fort Craig but made no indication that they planned to fight rather than retreat, Ickis and the Second Colorado moved to Camp Mischler, a mile below Fort Craig. There, they spent the days "as best we can," that is by "lounging around camp [with] nothing to do nothing to read and no paper . . . to write upon."[46] They moved to another site nearby and named it Camp Dodd in honor of their gallant, mustachioed officer. Ickis still spoiled for a fight and was so bored that he rarely wrote in his diary during this time, noting only a brush with death on May 31 when he dove into the Rio Grande to try and save a comrade. They managed to survive by "keeping a 'stiff upper lip' and good swimming." In early June, the Texans were preparing to retreat back to San Antonio from Fort Bliss. From his camp farther north, Ickis reported that all was quiet and the men of the Second Colorado mostly slept the time away.[47]

A few weeks later, a party of Navajos did make an appearance, however, and Dodd's men went out to track them, ultimately killing four men and taking one thousand sheep. But this was one of their few forays during the summer of 1862. The more than 1,200 Union men who had marched from San Diego under Gen. James Carleton had reached the Rio Grande in mid-July; this meant that there was no need for the Coloradans to make an expedition into Arizona. So Ickis and the others spent most of the summer drilling and going out on fatigue duty on days that reached 100 degrees Fahrenheit. They subsisted on half rations. In early August, Dodd's men received good news. They were being sent to Santa Fe to operate as scouts and escorts in northern New Mexico. As they marched out of Fort Craig on August 12, Ickis hoped "never to return to this Ft again."[48]

For a man who had meticulously recorded his Civil War experiences so far, Ickis was not so detailed in describing his service in the fall and winter of 1862–63. Sporadic diary entries trace his movements from Santa Fe, where he lived in the confiscated house of Confederate sympathizers who had retreated with Sibley, and, of course, attended many fandangos; to Peralta, where he had acted as escort to a Union paymaster traveling through the territory paying off New Mexico Volunteers; and back to Santa Fe, where he was stationed at Fort Marcy and was probably deployed as part of small parties ordered to fight Indians in their own style: surprise attacks, slashing raids, and swift pursuits. He ended up hospitalized with a bullet in his thigh in October of 1862. How exactly he was injured, he did not say. It is likely that he was taking part in an expedition against Mescalero Apaches, several of which left from Santa Fe and points southward that month.[49]

Ickis next wrote from Fort Scott, Kansas, in June of 1863. Ickis and Companies A and B of the Second Colorado had spent the spring at Fort Lyon (previously called Fort Wise) in Bent County, Colorado, escorting wagon trains and chasing down Comanche raiders. After reaching Kansas, Ickis confessed that he was happy to be back "in America after a long tedious march of over 1000 miles."[50]

Ickis's diary ends abruptly mid-entry on June 7, 1863, as he left for Dry Wood Creek, Missouri. But we do know that afterward, Ickis and his comrades fought in anti-guerrilla campaigns, putting their experiences pursuing Navajo, Apache, and Comanche raiders in New Mexico and Colorado to good use. And in October 1863, they were combined with the Third Colorado, mounted, and reorganized as the Second Colorado Cavalry.[51] Gen. Sterling Price's invasion of Missouri in September diverted Ickis, and he fought Confederate soldiers throughout the fall of 1864, ultimately pushing Price's troops back to Arkansas. After these victories, Ickis and the Second Colorado Cavalry were transferred to Fort Leavenworth, Kansas. His three-year commitment to Uncle Sam having expired, Alonzo Ferdinand Ickis mustered out of the Union Army in eastern Kansas on December 19, 1864.

HOMEWARD BOUND

It took Ickis less than a week to make the 150-mile journey northeast to Creston. His family welcomed him back to the farm, where he worked for four years before marrying a local girl named Ella Pott and settling down on his own plot of land. Ickis did not return to Colorado until 1896, when he and his wife and two of his six sons traveled there on vacation. Ickis showed them the mining towns where he had once prospected—Leadville, Breckenridge—and probably regaled them with tales of miners' misdeeds. That trip sparked something in Ickis, and he and Ella moved to Colorado a few years later. They settled in the eastern plains, in a small ranching town called Wray. He and Ella moved to Denver in 1900, and Alonzo Ickis died there in 1917. He was buried back in Union County, Iowa, along with several of his family members—including Johnathan, who had died the year before.[52]

New Mexico was not the only theater in which Alonzo Ickis fought, but it was the theater in which he "saw the elephant" and became a soldier fighting a range of enemies. He came into the army seasoned to an itinerant, violent life, and this experience served him well between 1861 and 1863. He fought alongside or against gold miners from the Midwest, West Point–trained professional soldiers, and New Mexicans and Native Americans whose relationships with the United States and the Union Army were complicated and often unpredictable. In so doing, he helped to secure the borderlands for the Union. Alonzo Ickis's Civil War was a war fought in a region where identities shifted rapidly and the most powerful people were those who knew the landscape most intimately and could navigate its dangers most successfully.

NOTES

1. For the duration of the war, both Colorado and New Mexico were American territories; from this point on in the chapter, however, I will refer to them as "Colorado" and "New Mexico" to avoid excessive verbiage.

2. Elliott West, *The Contested Plains: Indians, Goldseekers, and the Rush to Colorado* (Lawrence: University Press of Kansas, 1998), 115.

3. For accounts of the 1858 gold rush and the journey across the Great Plains to the Rocky Mountains, see Ovando J. Hollister, *The Mines of Colorado* (Springfield, Mass.:

Samuel Bowles, 1867); E. H. N. Patterson Diary, in LeRoy R. Hafen, ed., *Overland Routes to the Gold Fields, 1859, from Contemporary Diaries* (Glendale, Calif.: Arthur H. Clark, 1942).

4. Patterson Diary, April 6, 1859, in Hafen, *Overland Routes*, 86; West, *Contested Plains*, 134, 148–49.

5. Carl Abbott, Stephen J. Leonard, and Thomas J. Noel, *Colorado: A History of the Centennial State*, 5th ed. (Boulder: University Press of Colorado, 2013), 50; Horace Greeley to *New York Tribune*, June 21, 1859, in Horace Greeley, *An Overland Journey, from New York to San Francisco in the Summer of 1859* (New York: C. M. Saxton, Barker, 1860), 160, 163.

6. Ickis to Cass Ickis (his sister), July 7, 1861, in Ickis, *Bloody Trails along the Rio Grande: The Diary of Alonzo Ferdinand Ickis*, ed. Nolie Mumey (Denver: Old West Publishing, 1958), 25; Abbott, Leonard, and Noel, *Colorado*, 53; West, *Contested Plains*, 227; Duane A. Smith, *The Trail of Gold and Silver: Mining in Colorado, 1859–2009* (Boulder: University Press of Colorado, 2011), 50.

7. On promissory notes in mining communities and the problem of debt collection, see Gordon Bakken, *Practicing Law in Frontier California* (Lincoln: University of Nebraska Press, 2006).

8. *Cañon City Times*, October 7, 1861 [quotation]; Edward Canby to William Gilpin, October 11, 1861, in *The War of the Rebellion: A Compilation of the Official Records of the Union and Confederate Armies* (*OR*) (Washington, D.C.: Government Printing Office, 1880–1901), series 1, vol. 4, 72.

9. Ickis Diary, October 27, 1867, in Ickis, *Bloody Trails*, 48 [first quotation]; Ickis to Johnathan F. Ickis, October 25, 1861, in Ickis, *Bloody Trails*, 27, 28 [second quotation]; Robert M. Utley, *Frontiersmen in Blue: The United States Army and the Indian, 1848–1865* (New York: Macmillan, 1967), 217.

10. Ickis Diary, October 27, 1861 [quotation], Alonzo Ferdinand Ickis Diary (1861–1863), Western History Collection, Denver Public Library, Denver, Colorado (AFID); Canby to Adjutant General (AG), December 8, 1861, *OR*, series 1, vol. 4, 78–79.

11. The order bringing Ickis's company to Fort Garland in early December has not been located, but, by the end of the year, Col. Edward Canby reported the arrival of Hendren's company of Colorado Volunteers and the departure of U.S. Army Regulars to Santa Fe in "Abstract from Field Return of the Department of New Mexico, commanded by Col. E.R. S. Canby, Nineteenth U.S. Infantry, for December 31, 1861," *OR*, series 1, vol. 4, 81.

12. Ickis Diary, December 7–8, 1861, AFID.

13. Ibid., December 12, 13, 21, 22, and 23 [quotation], 1861; Ickis to Thomas Ickis, May 14, 1862, in Ickis, *Bloody Trails*, 29–30.

14. Ickis Diary, December 25, 1861, and January 1, 1862 [quotation], AFID; Special Orders No. 228, December 26, 1861, reprinted in John P. Wilson, ed., *When the Texans Came: Missing Records from the Civil War in the Southwest* (Albuquerque: University of New Mexico Press, 2001), 141.

15. Ickis Diary, January 16, 1862, AFID; John Clark Diary, January 18, 1862, John Clark Diary #2 (December 9, 1861–February 17, 1862), Box 1, John A. Clark Papers, Fray Angélico Chávez History Library, New Mexico History Museum, Santa Fe.

16. B. S. Roberts to Canby, November 10, 1861; R. S. C. Lord to [Canby], December 25, 1861; Canby to Major Donaldson, December 26, 1862, all in Wilson, *When the Texans Came*, 134, 140, 141.

17. Ickis Diary, January 18, 1862 [quotation], AFID; Clark Diary, January 22, 1862; Ickis to Thomas, May 14, 1862, in Ickis, *Bloody Trails*, 30; Canby to Donaldson January 20 and 23, 1861, in Wilson, *When The Texans Came*, 215, 218.

18. Ickis Diary, January 27, 1862, AFID.

19. Ibid., January 31 and February 6, 1862; Roberts to Canby, September 17, 1861, in Wilson, *When the Texans Came*, 128; Canby to AG, March 1, 1862, *OR*, series 1, vol. 9, 488.

20. Ickis Diary, February 10, 1862, AFID.

21. Ibid., February 13, 1862; John Taylor, *Bloody Valverde: A Civil War Battle on the Rio Grande* (Albuquerque: University of New Mexico Press, 1995), 22.

22. Ickis Diary, February 14–15, 1862, AFID.

23. Taylor, *Bloody Valverde*, 26; Roberts to Assistant Adjutant General, October 21, 1861, in Wilson, *When the Texans Came*, 132.

24. Ickis Diary, February 16, 1862, AFID; Taylor, *Bloody Valverde*, 25–29.

25. Ickis to Thomas, May 14, 1862, in Ickis, *Bloody Trails*, 30–34; Canby to AG, March 1, 1862, *OR*, series 1, vol. 9, 488; Ickis Diary, February 19, 1862, AFID.

26. Ickis Diary, February 20, 1862, AFID.

27. Ibid., February 21, 1862 [first quotation]; Ickis to Thomas, May 14, 1862, in Ickis, *Bloody Trails*, 30–34 [second quotation]; Canby to AG, March 1, 1862, *OR*, series 1, vol. 9, 489.

28. Taylor, *Bloody Valverde*, 57, 61; Ickis Diary, February 21, 1862, AFID; P. W. L. Plympton to H. R. Selden, February 24, 1862, in Wilson, *When the Texans Came*, 242.

29. Peticolas quoted in Taylor, *Bloody Valverde*, 62.

30. Ickis Diary, February 21, 1862 [first, third, fifth, and sixth quotations], AFID; Taylor, *Bloody Valverde* [second and fourth quotations], 67–68; Ickis to Thomas, May 14, 1862 [seventh quotation], in Ickis, *Bloody Trails*, 30–34; Canby to AG, March 1, 1862, *OR*, series 1, vol. 9, 490; Ray C. Colton, *The Civil War in the Western Territories: Arizona, Colorado, New Mexico, and Utah* (Norman: University of Oklahoma Press, 1959), 30.

31. Ickis Diary, February 21, 1862, AFID; Joseph Bell to Charles Newbold, February 26, 186[2], in Wilson, *When the Texans Came*, 245.

32. Ickis to Thomas, May 14, 1862, in Ickis, *Bloody Trails*, 30–34; Plympton to Selden, February 24, 1862, in Wilson, *When the Texans Came*, 243.

33. Ickis Diary, February 21, 1862, AFID; Louis Felsenthal to Eben Everett, February 25, 1862, in Wilson, *When the Texans Came*, 247; Canby to AG, February 22 and March 1, 1862, *OR* series 1, vol. 9, 487–93; Canby to G. R. Paul, March 16, 1862, *OR*, series 1, vol. 9, 653.

34. Ickis to Thomas, May 14, 1862, in Ickis, *Bloody Trails*, 30–34. Official records list the Dodd's company casualties as two killed, twenty-eight wounded, and nine missing. "Official List of the Killed, Wounded, and Missing at the Battle of Valverde, February 21, 1862," in Wilson, *When the Texans Came*, 249, 252–53; "Return of Casualties in the United States Troops, commanded by Col. Edward R.S. Canby at the battle of Valverde, February 21, 1862," *OR*, series 1, vol. 9, 493.

35. Ickis to Thomas, May 14, 1862, in Ickis, *Bloody Trails*, 30–34; Ickis Diary, February 21, 1862, AFID.

36. Canby to AG, February 23, 1862, *OR*, series 1, vol. 9, 633.

37. Ickis Diary, March 5, 1862, AFID.

38. Ibid., March 17 and 26, 1862. On Native Americans and the various roles they played in the Civil War, see Megan Kate Nelson, "Indians Make the Best Guerrillas: Native Americans and the War for the Desert Southwest, 1861–1862," in *The Civil War Guerrilla: Unfolding the Black Flag in History, Memory, and Myth*, ed. Joseph M. Beilein, Jr., and Matthew C. Hulbert (Lexington: University Press of Kentucky, 2015), 99–122.

39. Ickis Diary, March 22, 1862, AFID.

40. Ibid., April 2–3, 1862.

41. Ibid., April 9–10, 1862.

42. Canby to AG, April 11 and 23, 1862, *OR*, series 1, vol. 9, 549–50; Ickis Diary, April 13, 1862, AFID.

43. Ickis to Thomas, May 14, 1862, in Ickis, *Bloody Trails*, 35; G. R. Paul to William J. L. Nicodemus, April 16, 1862, in Wilson, *When the Texans Came*, 277–78; Canby to AG, April 23, 1862, *OR*, series 1, vol. 9, 551; Donald S. Frazier, *Blood and Treasure: Confederate Empire in the Southwest* (College Station: Texas A&M Press, 1995), 247.

44. Canby to AG, April 23, 1862, *OR*, series 1, vol. 9, 551; Paul to AG, May 1, 1862, *OR*, series 1, vol. 9, 552; Ickis Diary, April 18, 1862, AFID; Ickis to Thomas, May 14, 1862, in Ickis, *Bloody Trails*, 35.

45. Ickis Diary, April 23–24, 1862, AFID.

46. Ibid., May 1 and 11 [quotation], 1862; Ickis to Thomas, May 14, 1862, in Ickis, *Bloody Trails*, 35.

47. Ickis Diary, May 31, and June 5, 1862, AFID; John M. Chivington to Canby, June 6, 1862, in Wilson, *When the Texans Came*, 285.

48. Ickis Diary, June 20 and 22, and August 12, 1862 [quotation], AFID; Canby to AG, July 20, 1862, *OR*, series 1, vol. 9, 686–87. The plan to send Ickis and Dodd's regiment northward to Fort Union and Santa Fe first appears in Canby to AG, August 6, 1862, *OR*, series 1, vol. 9, 688–89.

49. "Abstract from Return of the Department of New Mexico, Brig. Gen. J. H. Carleton commanding, for the month of September, 1862," and James Carleton to Joseph R. West, October 11, 1862, both in *OR*, series 1, vol. 15, 574, 580–81; Ickis Diary, August 25, September 4 and 8, and October 22, 1862, AFID; Utley, *Frontiersmen in Blue*, 234.

50. Ickis Diary, June 4, 1863, AFID. The Second Colorado does not appear in James Carleton's command records in May 1863, suggesting that it had already been transferred to Fort Wise. "Abstract from Tri-Monthly Return of the Department of New Mexico, Brig. Gen. James H. Carleton Commanding, for May 10, 1863," *OR*, series 1, vol. 15, 725.

51. Special Orders No. 278, October 11, 1863, Department of Missouri, in *The Union Army: A History of Military Affairs in the Loyal States 1861–65—Records of the Regiments in the Union Army—Cyclopedia of Battles—Memories of Commanders and Soldiers* (Madison, Wis.: Federal, 1908), 4:451.

52. Ickis, *Bloody Trails*, 42.

5

Alonzo Davis

Andrew E. Masich

Though not by nature a violent man, Alonzo E. Davis sought military service during the Civil War—the most violent time in American history. While seeking his fortune in California, far from the seat of war, he was drawn to the profession of arms for patriotic reasons, hoping to do battle with traitors in the eastern theater of the conflict. Ordered instead to the Southwest, when Arizona Territory was new, he soldiered in the desert just as an unprecedented wave of violence swept the region. His story is representative of many Anglo-Americans who found themselves thrust into a war that they had neither imagined nor wanted but which changed their lives, the lives of the indigenous peoples they encountered, and the course of empire in the Southwest borderlands.

It was altogether fitting and proper that Alonzo Davis chose to enlist as a California Volunteer. His great-grandfather and grandfather had served as commissioned officers in the Continental Army during the American Revolution. As a young drummer boy during the War of 1812, his father had also seen military service. Thus born, on June 30, 1839, into a military family, young Alonzo was steeped in the tradition of service inculcated by his fiercely patriotic forebears in upstate New York. Following the death of his wife, Alonzo's father, Thomas Davis, left the "frontier farm" and log house in the Mohawk valley that he had helped hew from the wilderness with his "pioneer" father.[1]

Seeking new opportunities to support his eleven children, Thomas headed his family west in 1847. He packed eight-year-old "Lon," along with his twin brother and other siblings and all their belongings, and made it to Wisconsin, where they built and operated a hotel. A disastrous fire two years later sent them destitute back to New York, but the lure of the West had begun to seep into young Alonzo's consciousness just as news of the California Gold Rush captured the imagination of many Americans.[2]

CALIFORNIA

In 1857, Alonzo completed his public school education, and at the age of seventeen announced to family and friends that he intended to follow his older brother Robert (who loaned him $150 for passage) to the California goldfields to make his fortune. He reveled in the admiration and fame heaped upon him by schoolmates, especially the girls, who "fairly lionized" him for his heroic determination to go west.[3] On Valentine's Day, Alonzo set out alone. He piled his meager possessions into a bag, took the train to New York City, boarded the steamer *Illinois*, and, lodged in a steerage berth, shipped off for Panama. While there were many notable incidents, one that disturbed his sense of fairness and stood out in his memory occurred when the ship lay over at Kingston, Jamaica. There he witnessed the second mate mistreat "a negro agent for a laundry." Davis remembered that for no apparent reason, "this bully struck the colored man full in the face" and knocked him down an open hatch, injuring him badly. The horrified young traveler was relieved when red-coated British soldiers arrested the antagonist, and Davis thought justice served when the local magistrate fined the cruel officer. "Any attacks made on defenseless persons," he wrote of this episode, "be they white, negro or Indian," should not be meekly tolerated.[4] Alonzo's journey continued as he crossed the Isthmus of Panama on rail cars then boarded the steamer *Golden Gate* bound for San Francisco.

The voyage from New York had taken more than three weeks, but Davis stopped in San Francisco only long enough to be unimpressed by the cheap houses and unpaved streets of the small town that proud westerners called the "Queen City of the Pacific."[5] He booked passage on steam-powered riverboats that carried him to Sacramento, Marysville, and then on to Oroville, where he quickly found employment with brother Robert. Unwilling to burden Robert's family and eager to make it on his own, Alonzo decided to try his luck in the booming mines of the Mother Lode country. As soon as he repaid his brother, he struck out for the goldfields. Constructing five-foot-long wooden "cradles" with a partner, they rocked and washed the gravels for placer gold alongside thousands of Chinese, Mexican, and Anglo miners. Wet, dirty, and brutal conditions soon broke the health and spirits of even the hardiest workers.

As Alonzo sifted his paltry earnings of gold dust through his blistered hands, he realized that the rough and dangerous life of a miner was not the quickest path to wealth and happiness. He next tried his hand at freighting and even taught school for a term but found the routine too tame and the accommodations in the little country schoolhouse too confining. He then turned to cowboying, riding the range, and breaking horses. Independent and unafraid of manual labor, he surveyed his own 160-acre ranch in nearby Butte County, building a house and tending livestock in the summer and, in the winter, cutting timber in the mountains and hauling lumber for posts and fencing needed to improve his property.[6]

By now Civil War news came in daily from the East. Letters from his twin brother Edwin, who had early in 1861 joined a regiment of New York Volunteers and even participated in the fighting at Bull Run, stirred Alonzo's imagination. He devoured the stories of great battles and momentous events reported by San Francisco's *Daily Alta California* and *Evening Bulletin* and followed the news of the regiments of California Volunteers organized to stop the Confederates then threatening the Southwest borderlands and California itself. Thousands of able-bodied young men, inured to the hardships of frontier mining camps and full of fight, sprang to the call. They eagerly filled the ranks of the volunteer regiments as regular troops in the West gathered on the coast to board eastbound ships or rallied on the Rio Grande to resist the Confederate advance from Texas.[7]

Within a year of the Civil War's opening guns at Fort Sumter, Davis saw more than eight thousand Californians enlist. By the war's end, the state of California would contribute more than 16,000 troops—a higher enlistment rate, based on population, than any other state—serving in twelve distinct battalions or regiments. These units of cavalry, artillery, and infantry constituted a fighting force larger than the entire prewar regular army. Although enlistments flagged as the war dragged on, causing California authorities to offer cash bounties to spur recruitment efforts, there appeared to be more than enough manpower to meet federal quotas. California never implemented a draft, as did other states, and even sent excess enlistees north to Washington Territory and eastward to augment other states' underfilled levies. Though "jealous of his [brother's] glory" and sorely tempted to "join the fray" in the rush of 1861, the twenty-two-year-old Davis was tolerably successful by California standards and prudently resisted the patriotic pull.[8]

Though most Californians were loyal to the Union, secessionists from the Southern states were well-represented in the goldfields. Davis had a flair for oratory and could not resist ascending a soapbox in Lynchburg, just a few miles from his ranch, to lambast the rebels. The pro-Confederate audience tolerated his speech for a time, until he cast aspersions on Southern womanhood by defending Gen. Ben Butler's infamous New Orleans "Woman Order," which suggested that disloyal ladies might be treated as "common" women. During the uproar that ensued, Davis's friends spirited him out of town and urged him to lay low. Incensed by the open display of disunion sentiment, he gathered a half dozen of his loyal friends and rode to Oroville. On October 9, 1862, the group enlisted in Capt. Charles Atchisson's Company I, Fourth California Volunteer Infantry. The recruiting officer led the young men to believe that the regiment would be sent east to fight and would soon see action against the Confederates.[9]

Driven by a sense of patriotic duty and desire for adventure, Davis and his partners were typical of the hardy young men who undertook the massive voluntary migration to California in the 1850s. They were intelligent, above average in height and weight, adaptable, and had, by the very fact of emigrating across the continent, already demonstrated a willingness to take risks. Many regular army officers thought the California men represented the finest material for soldiers, a much higher caliber than the enlisted men found in the regular ranks. The army would discover that the volunteers' propensity for independent action could be both a blessing and a curse, as the trait also led to a profound lack of respect for authority.[10]

ARIZONA

Davis and the other new recruits were transported by steamboat to San Francisco. At Benicia Barracks, located at the U.S. arsenal and principal ordnance depot on the West Coast, they received blue wool uniforms emblazoned with brass buttons bearing Uncle Sam's eagle coat of arms, slept in army bunks, and drilled. Captain Atchisson and Lt. Robert Nason memorized passages from Hardee's infantry manual while the men performed close order drill. Davis graduated from the "awkward squad" in a week or two, then practiced marching four abreast by squad, platoon, and then with the entire one-hundred-man company. The men drilled four hours each day, and once a week each soldier was expected to perform guard duty. When Davis stood inspection before the guard was mounted, he had "his shoes polished, his brasses bright, his clothes spotless, and his gun faultlessly clean inside and out." The onetime miner began to feel more like a soldier.[11]

After being issued .58 caliber Springfield rifle muskets, the men loaded and fired blanks. They practiced firing by company—by rank, by file, and in double-ranked "line-of-battle" all at once in crashing volleys. The officers drilled their company in compact linear formations, modeled on Napoleonic tactics, and then dispersed in open order as skirmishers. The men believed they were ready to face the rebels in Texas or in the fighting farther east. Secession sentiment still ran high in California's southern counties, however, so the Fourth Infantry companies were gathered at Camp Drum near New San Pedro (Los Angeles) for additional training and as a show of force to quell civil unrest.[12]

At first, the independent-spirited young men resisted regimentation. The soldiers in the ranks growled about most everything, but the deplorable quality of their army rations incited their special dissatisfaction. In early April, 1863, the enlisted men conspired to hold a military funeral for the ox that the commissary had designated for their dinner. The disgruntled soldiers contended that since the ancient animal (just short of its one hundredth birthday, they claimed) had died of natural causes it deserved an honorable send-off. Several companies paraded with considerable pomp and mock solemnity, bearing the coffined ox to the burial ground for ceremonial interment complete with muffled drums, fifes, and a gun salute.

Outraged by this egregious breach of etiquette and discipline, Maj. Henry Hancock called out the guard, with muskets loaded, and demanded an end to the farce. Fearing that their superior had lost control of the situation and that bloodshed might ensue, the company commanders took a quick vote and immediately relieved Hancock of command. Company A's Capt. Converse Rowell, the next senior officer, put Hancock under arrest and restored order, but only after the ox was laid to rest and a fitting epitaph inscribed on its headboard.[13]

The week following the ox incident, the quartermaster advertised for "fresh beef, good and wholesome" for the troops at Camp Drum.[14] The entire drama would have been a comedy had not Hancock, a Harvard-trained lawyer, convinced Army of the Pacific commander, Gen. George Wright, to cashier Rowell and the other officers for "mutinous conduct." Though Davis considered Hancock a "martinet" and believed that Rowell had acted in the men's best interest, the army could brook no threat to its time-honored command structure. Just a year before, similar disciplinary infractions by unruly volunteers had been harshly dealt with by officers at Fort Yuma as Colonel—soon General—James H. Carleton, commanding the California troops headed for Arizona and New Mexico, prepared to enter the borderlands. Officers had placed their headstrong soldiers in irons and even ordered their summary execution by firing squad in an effort to quash mutiny.[15]

Things settled down once Davis and the men of the Fourth California were detailed to their duty stations in California and the territories. On the last day of April, 1863, Capt. J. Ives Fitch's and Capt. Charles Atchisson's Companies B and I marched three hundred miles overland to Fort Mojave, Arizona, on the Colorado River. Other companies went to Fort Yuma, two hundred miles downstream at the confluence of the Gila River. The Colorado served as a water transportation and supply corridor to Arizona and southern New Mexico. Oceangoing steamers carried food and ordnance from the Pacific coast, up the Gulf of California, then transferred to shallow-draft riverboats to supply Forts Yuma and Mojave, as well as other posts in Arizona.

As Davis and his comrades tramped along the Mojave Road, carrying their ten-pound Springfield rifle muskets and fourteen pounds of gear in tarred canvas knapsacks, they learned about marching in the desert. The 240-man command split into two sections so as to not overtax the wells along the route. Even so, the water was alkaline and the twenty- to thirty-mile daily marches were hard. To relieve the stress, the soldiers resorted to grumbling about not being sent east to fight the rebels and wondering what the government, in its wisdom, had in store for them at the isolated post located in the heart of Mojave Indian country, where three years earlier Capt. Lewis Armistead's regulars had engaged powerful warriors in battle.[16] Now the Californians were ordered to "cultivate the most friendly relations with the Indians, at the same time to prevent them from committing depredations upon the whites."[17]

LA PAZ

Alonzo Davis knew as well as anyone that sympathy for the Confederate cause on the Pacific coast had been high in the months following the fall of

Fort Sumter in 1861. Those first shots signaled an exodus of heavily armed and well-organized outfits that traveled overland from southern California through Arizona or Mexico to the East. In November 1861, some of the California Volunteers ordered to suppress secessionists surrounded and captured eighteen rebels traveling with Dan Showalter, who had intended to head east by way of Fort Yuma and the Southern Overland Trail.[18] Wanting to clamp down on all Southern sympathizers bound to or from California on all of the routes near the Mexican border, Carleton required citizens and soldiers to carry passes when entering or leaving garrisoned towns and when traveling the roads in New Mexico and Arizona. He also ordered suspected secessionists arrested and imprisoned. Most of these political prisoners were eventually released after they signed loyalty oaths, but one rebel, captured with the Showalter party, launched an attack in Arizona Territory that some consider the westernmost engagement of the Civil War.[19]

On the night of May 20, 1863, just as Davis with Captain Atchisson's exhausted Company I approached the Colorado River, William "Frog" Edwards ambushed three soldiers belonging to the Fourth California's Companies H and K at La Paz. The placer mining boomtown, one hundred miles below the fort, was then the largest settlement in Arizona, having drawn thousands of gold rushers from Sonora, California, and elsewhere. After being captured with Showalter, Edwards seethed with resentment for nearly six months of imprisonment at Fort Yuma. When an escape attempt failed, Carleton had ordered him securely shackled in heavy irons. Edwards vowed revenge. After his release, the Frog bided his time for nearly a year, waiting for an opportunity to get even and strike a blow for the Confederacy in the Far West. When news of Gen. Robert E. Lee's victory at Chancellorsville, Virginia, reached the Colorado River, Edwards made his move.

The soldiers escorting the military cargo on the steamer *Cocopah* were on the return trip from Fort Mojave when several of the men stacked their muskets on the boat's deck and disembarked to purchase personal supplies. They had gathered in front of Cohn's Store when gunshots suddenly burst from the darkness. Witnesses heard Edwards curse the unarmed guards as he blazed away with his revolver. His first shot shattered the knee of Pvt. Thomas Gainor of Company H. Before he knew what hit him, Pvt. Truston Wentworth of Company K fell over with a mortal chest wound. Edward's next bullet passed completely through Pvt. Ferdinand Behn's abdomen and struck a nearby Mexican miner in the head. Then the shooting abruptly stopped. Lt. James A. Hale quickly organized a search of the town, but to no avail.[20]

A monthlong manhunt by a detachment of forty men from Fort Mojave under Captain Atchisson failed to bring the Frog to justice, but soon afterward his desiccated body was found south of the Gila near the mining settlement of Ajo, not far from the Sonoran border. Either in the company of others or alone Edwards had attempted to elude his pursuers, but, finding only dry waterholes, he died of exposure in the seemingly endless miles of scrub and 100-degree daytime temperatures. Davis and his comrades, who had vowed bloody revenge, believed that the Frog had received his just deserts. According to Lt. Col. James Curtis, "Edwards, alias Frog, the assassinator of two soldiers of our regiment, at La Paz, on the Colorado, has met his merited punishment," meted out by "an avenging God" and an unforgiving desert.[21]

The La Paz incident alerted federal authorities to other rebel movements. On May 28, Capt. Joseph Tuttle received orders in Tucson to intercept a party of fifteen to twenty Confederates, including the La Paz ambushers, heading for the Mexican border. Intelligence reports indicated that it might be possible to head off the rebels, along with the cattle and horses they had stolen in San Bernardino County. Tuttle commanded twenty men of the Fifth California Infantry and a "spy party," including Jackson H. Martin, deputy sheriff of San Bernardino County; Joseph Bridges; and a Mexican vaquero named Prefetto. Tuttle tracked the raiders and finally apprehended them in the Sonora village of Altar. The pursuers recovered the stolen livestock and prevented the California secessionists from uniting with Texas Confederates. Mission accomplished, Tuttle's worn-out command returned to Tucson nearly a month after the chase began.[22]

FORT MOJAVE

On the high banks of the Colorado River in the rude buildings fashioned from native rock, adobe mud, and the willows and cottonwoods that grew thick in the river bottoms of the Mojave valley, the volunteer soldiers stationed at Fort Mojave found far different wars than they had imagined. Davis and his comrades had all read the best-selling book *The Captivity of the Oatman Girls* or had heard stories of the warlike Mojaves. Olive Oatman, the most popular woman orator of the day, was even then touring eastern cities telling enthralled audiences of her captivity among these very Indians, who had marked her face with the blue tattoos common to Mojave women and men. Based on Oatman's much-publicized case and rumors of excesses perpetrated by her captors, most Anglos eyed the Mojaves suspiciously.[23]

But the soldiers soon discovered the Mojaves to be personable, eager to please, and willing to barter for food, tobacco, and other trade items. Some of the Indian men and women contracted to supply wood and hay for the military's needs. Finding new friends, Davis placed targets of hardtack crackers and coins in a split stick stuck in the ground and delighted in watching Mojave boys as young as six expertly shoot, with their bows and arrows, for the prize.[24] It seemed to him hard to believe that only a few years earlier Chief Iretaba and his men had, with only their bows, arrows, and ironwood or mesquite war clubs, attacked and nearly overwhelmed a well-disciplined force of the Sixth U.S. Infantry led by Captain Armistead. Davis noted admiringly that many of the Mojave men were powerfully built and stood six feet tall, but also concluded that the crushing defeat they had suffered at the hands of Armistead's two companies, armed with rifled muskets and fixed bayonets, seemed to have taken the fight out of them.[25]

Establishing the fort in 1859, Armistead's regulars had abandoned Fort Mojave when the Civil War forced their withdrawal, but miners drawn by the rich Colorado River gold deposits came in ever-increasing numbers and coexisted uneasily with the Indians, prompting the army to reoccupy the place. In truth, the Mojave leaders, especially the venerable Iretaba, had come to find the whites good allies against Chemehuevis to the south and Paiutes to the north and the related but unpredictable Yavapais to the east. The allied Quechans, connected by their Yuman language and customs, had made friends with the soldiers and white travelers who passed over the river at Yuma Crossing beginning with the California Gold Rush a decade earlier. Believing accommodation the best survival strategy, the Mojaves would also learn to live with the newcomers.[26]

The neighboring Hualapais were quite another matter. They too were peaceful people, but they resented the whites who now tramped their lands east and west of the river and killed or frightened away their game. The newcomers helped themselves to grass for their stock and cut timber to fuel their voracious steamboat boilers, as well as for charcoal, cooking, and building construction. The Hualapais and many of their neighboring indigenous communities reasoned that the miners and soldiers surely owed them something for what they took. As mining activity increased, the wood disappeared even faster, needed for steam engines that drove pumps and stamp mills, shoring timbers, and other mine-related construction. Davis thought the Hualapais reckoned correctly—the white "invaders" were in fact "trespassers" who should pay with flour, sugar, tobacco, and other articles equal to the value of that which was taken. The appropriation of Indian land constituted an implicit contract, but disagreements over payment would occasionally turn violent. A killing would result in retaliation and war. Davis believed that he and his fellow soldiers served as a frontier constabulary, keeping the peace between the white freighters, miners, and emigrants and the Indian peoples they came in contact with—and sometimes between the different Indian tribes. Even after the signing of a treaty and the establishment of a Colorado River Reservation in 1865, peace was not assured.[27]

Iretaba counseled his Mojave warriors against making war and kept them in check by recounting stories of the "white father's" might. From November 1863 until June 1864, the chief traveled at government expense first to San Francisco and then by sea to Washington, D.C., accompanied by Pima chief Antonio Azul and escorted by Indian agent John Moss. Though longtime enemies, the Arizona Indian leaders put their differences aside, spending weeks together aboard steamships and railroad cars. They witnessed the firing of great cannons, participated in reviews of regiments of well-armed soldiers, and slept in fancy hotels in cities teeming with white men and women too numerous to count. In New York, Iretaba met Olive Oatman, then on a speaking tour, and although reporters expected recriminations against the chief of her captors, the two spoke only of mutual friends in the Mojave valley.[28]

Iretaba returned to his people gaudily outfitted in the dress uniform of a general, convinced that resisting the whites would be futile. The goodwill tour and propaganda campaign worked where military action might have failed. Davis saw the Mojave headman address his people, comparing the whites to the leaves of a cottonwood stand—beyond counting—and, as his people gathered around him, scooping a palmful of sand representing the Mojaves and then pointing to a great sandbar in the river saying dolefully, "Americans." Davis and most Arizonans considered such trips and gifts well worth the expense, reasoning that it was more cost effective in both lives and treasure to awe the Indians and inspire loyalty in their leaders than it was to fight them.[29]

While the Mojaves remained nonviolent, Davis reported that Paiutes and Chemehuevis threatened Colorado River steamboat refueling stops and waylaid Anglo and Hispanic miners, freighters, and travelers on the Fort Mojave–Prescott road across central Arizona. Lieutenant Nason and the men of Company I retaliated, though with limited success. Unprepared for the hit-and-run style of warfare, Davis observed that the Indians "were too fleet of foot for infantrymen and gave us wide berth when we got after them." Close order tactics and volley firing were useless in this kind of campaigning. Indeed, California soldiers in these sections of the borderlands never fired their weapons in anger or even saw their indigenous enemies on the battlefield.[30]

Frustrated by their inability to track down elusive Chemehuevi warriors, the soldiers arrested innocent chiefs and held them hostage until depredations ceased or guilty raiders were apprehended. Davis and his comrades also knew and felt the impacts that an all-out offensive against the Western Apaches by Carleton's troops, taking place in central Arizona and coordinated with attacks by Mexican troops from Sonora and Chihuahua, had on the Colorado River region. The Yavapais were caught in the cross fire. As their old Papago and Pima enemies allied themselves with Anglo soldiers and civilians, many of the Western Apaches and Yavapais found little refuge from incessant forays into their once secure mountain retreats. The Mojaves, once on trading terms with the Yavapais, now scouted for the army along the road to Prescott.[31]

By 1865, the Hualapais were drawn into the fighting. Davis believed that this war began with the killing of a respected Hualapai headman who regularly contracted with freighters to provide native gramma and galleta grasses. Like the Mojaves, most of the Hualapais could no longer subsist by agriculture and hunting alone. They sought employment as laborers and had become, as Davis observed, "hewers of wood and drawers of water" for the whites. Chief Hitche-Hitche's Hualapai band had been successful in securing food by providing fodder for the teamsters' draft animals and sometimes herding mules to pasturage. One day, a mule from a train laying over at Hitche-Hitche's Cottonwood Spring encampment went missing. A liquored-up wagon master held the chief responsible and saw fit to chain him to a wagon wheel until the Hualapais returned the lost mule. Somehow,

Hitche-Hitche managed to retrieve his bow and quiver and sent an arrow into his tormenter. One of the teamsters instantly drew a revolver and fired a fatal bullet into the chief's chest just as another well-aimed arrow went through the gunman's heart. Two weeks later, Hitche-Hitche's young son killed two settlers in their beds and set their cabins ablaze. Soon after this incident, the unarmed Wauba Yuma, the Hualapai head chief, was shot down when he approached a freight train to parlay. Numerous confrontations and skirmishes followed. The men of a wagon train waiting at Hardyville for a steamer shipment decided they would go to Cottonwood in search of scalps and a measure of revenge for the white victims of the violence. Unable to find the perpetrator, the heavily armed "scouting party" fell upon a Hualapai family returning from a visit to the Mojaves. Davis remembered it as a "massacre" that left two men, one woman, and five children dead. Only a woman who managed to hide herself in a nearby thicket survived the vicious attack. Mojave scouts assisted the soldiers as Yavapai and Havasupai warriors allied themselves with the Hualapais and the violence escalated. "From this time on," Davis lamented, "it was relentless war, and we were, of course, all in it."[32]

However unsettled the peace, the garrison troops spent the majority of their time combatting the oppressive heat, short rations, and boredom. Most of the California men were practical miners, and their interests naturally turned to the region's mineral resources. Davis's glowing accounts of the richness of the area encouraged California soldiers and civilians to prospect along the Colorado and its tributaries. The men of the Fourth California Infantry established entire mining districts. In fact, they dominated the mining in the Cerbat Mountains near Fort Mojave to the extent that citizen prospectors complained of a soldier monopoly. As the La Paz placers began to play out in 1863, new gold strikes at Walker's diggings at Lynx Creek near Prescott, the newly designated Arizona capital, drew miners from the territories, California, and Mexico. By 1864, Arizona prospecting fever was in full swing. As with Carleton's command near Fort Whipple in central Arizona and elsewhere in the territory, officers at Fort Mojave gave their men leave and provided them with rations, encouraging them to prospect the mountain ranges flanking the Colorado River.[33]

Davis understated the amount of soldier prospecting around Fort Mojave when he remembered, "A few of us boys went out on prospecting trips into the mountains. We would get a pass and, taking ten days rations of hardtack, pork and beans, we would explore the region for mining wealth." Promoted corporal then sergeant, Davis was called upon to lead prospecting parties and organize soldier-run mining districts modeled on those in northern California. In 1864 the soldiers from Fort Mojave filed 22 percent of the claims in the Sacramento and San Francisco mining districts of Mohave County. Davis and others purchased town lots in Mohave City, situated on a bluff overlooking the river about a mile north of the fort, and planned to return after the war to construct houses. Though most would never get rich, the returning veterans did establish new businesses and communities. They led the economic development of the territory, and doomed the Indian peoples whose land they had usurped.[34]

None of the soldiers spent more time and energy prospecting, promoting, and staking claims than Davis. When explorer and writer J. Ross Browne came to Fort Mojave in search of a guide to help him scout the region for his book *Resources of the Pacific Slope*, Captain Atchisson recommended Sergeant Davis. Browne was so impressed with his guide's knowledge that he used his reports verbatim in the final publication.[35] Davis understood that the key to unlocking the region's mineral wealth was the eastern capital that would bring stamp mills for ore reduction and the men and equipment needed to operate the hard rock gold, silver, and lead mines. Writing letters touting the richness of the mines to the *Daily Alta California* and other newspapers, he became one of Arizona's leading boosters. Through these efforts, he unknowingly contributed to more violence than he could have dreamed of as the Colorado River tribes suffered malnutrition and sickness resulting from the flood of whites who competed for resources and brought diseases.[36]

Though the Mojaves remained at peace, the soldier-miners continued to engage in clashes with Chemehuevis, Yavapais, and Hualapais. Civilian miners now searched the mountains from the Colorado River all the way to Prescott. The steamboat business boomed as Captains Isaac Polhamus, Jack Mellon, and Thomas Trueworthy added barges to their boats to increase capacity and then added more and bigger boats to accommodate the increasing demand. Freighters made enormous profits as all the goods for Arizona had to be offloaded at La Paz and then hauled overland. Entrepreneurs like W. H. Hardy cut and improved roads for ever-larger freight wagons carrying massive loads that included mining machinery, food, and all kinds of merchandise. Mojave and Hualapai Indian laborers worked alongside Hispanics and Anglos, but as the traffic increased so too did deadly encounters.[37]

The soldier-miners valued Davis's good sense in avoiding hostilities while prospecting, and his knowledge of the mining districts, trails, and peoples of the Mojave valley made him the logical choice for escorting visiting entrepreneurs and dignitaries. In the fall of 1863, the French photographer Rudolph d'Heureuse lugged his cumbersome glass plate camera equipment to Fort Mojave to record the fort and the surrounding geological features for eastern investors. He also documented the people, especially the soldiers and the Mojaves. In all, d'Heureuse made forty-four glass plate images, some of the earliest outdoor photographs of the territories and the only images ever made of soldiers in the field in Arizona during the Civil War. It just so happened that he also captured the likeness of Alonzo Davis, standing as the company orderly beside Captain Atchisson.[38] In d'Heureuse's photo, Davis's face is deeply bronzed, and, rather than wearing his forage cap, he sports his black dress uniform hat, stripped of its regulation ostrich feather and brass trimmings, with the brim turned down to protect him from the sun. He is otherwise neatly attired in his fatigue uniform but with shined brass and even white gloves, ready for inspection. Atchisson was a spit-and-polish officer, and the fastidious Davis was always interested in getting out of guard duty by competing for the cleanest outfit, which was sure to win him the easy orderly job.[39]

Early in the war, commanders fearing intelligence breaches forbade soldiers from writing for newspapers, so Davis wrote under several pseudonyms during the war years. His nom de plume included the thinly disguised "SIVAD" and even less imaginative "California Volunteer." After mustering out of the service, Davis returned to Arizona and continued as an "occasional correspondent" for California's most popular paper, the *Daily Alta California*.[40] During and after the war, he wrote of everyday occurrences—weddings, balls, July Fourth celebrations, and even natural wonders. He reported hearing the boom and seeing meteors flash across Arizona's night sky and hunting for the meteorites that fell to earth.[41] Invariably his articles cast Arizona in a favorable light, pointing out investment opportunities for capitalists and promising prospects for miners. In 1864, as many soldiers' enlistments expired, he wrote that most of the men "intend to stick to the country, for they feel confident they have got their 'golden-egged goose' cooped, sure." As the California soldiers increased awareness

Capt. Atchisson, his orderly, and clerk in the rear of his dwelling, Ft. Mojave. Photograph by Rudolph d'Heureuse. Cpl. Alonzo E. Davis (*center*), Capt. Charles Atchisson (*right*), and the clerk of Company I, Fourth Infantry, California Volunteers (*left*) at Fort Mojave's commanding officer's quarters in 1863. This is among the earliest images of Arizona and the only one known depicting an identified enlisted man in the field in Arizona during the Civil War. Courtesy Bancroft Library, University of California, Berkeley. Photographic Views of the Mojave Route, El Dorado Canyon, and Fort Mojave, 1863, BANC PIC 1905.16894–A.

of the territory, they also provided information-hungry Arizonans with news from the states by sharing incoming letters and newspapers.[42]

Davis's writings never got him in trouble with his superiors, who actually valued his reporting of their activities and his ability to boost the value of their own business investments in the territory. His opinions on the mistreatment of the Native Americans by "whiskied white braves" and the "savagery" perpetrated by his fellow citizens and soldiers earned him the enmity of some of his former friends.[43] One letter he wrote as a soldier correspondent for the *Daily Alta California* almost got him killed. He had criticized the massacre of the Hualapai family by the teamsters following the slaying of the settlers by Hitche-Hitche's son. Confronted by a man associated with the affair who had been pressured by peers to prove his manliness, as he had been reluctant to take scalps, Davis was forced to defend himself with his fists. When his "ginned up" assailant pulled a pistol, local businessmen rushed in to stop the fight.[44]

CALIFORNIA THEN BACK TO ARIZONA

Many of the Fourth California Infantry soldiers stationed at Fort Mojave did not want to return to Drum Barracks for their discharges because they hoped to remain with their profitable claims. Carleton, who had served as military governor of Arizona and New Mexico, saw to it that many California soldiers were mustered out in the territories. He believed that a "military colony" of miners would be the surest way of subduing the indigenous tribes and "civilizing" the borderlands.[45] But army headquarters in San Francisco determined, as the war wound down in the East, that it was time for the volunteer troops to come home.

On their return to California, Davis and his companions were pressed into service as mounted infantry. They chased Paiutes who had captured a boy from a Mexican immigrant train, but the soldiers turned back after their five-day supply of rations ran out. They also attempted, without success, to intercept diehard Confederate "guerillas" heading to the territories via Yuma Crossing.[46] Sergeant Davis commanded the rear guard of the column. Laying over with the supply wagons to allow the wells to refill as the main body marched on, he ordered his men to shoot rabbits and quail to supplement their monotonous army rations. Little did the soldiers comprehend that they were taking food from the mouths of the Paiutes and other peoples of the mountains and desert. On April 16, 1865, a lone rider on a lathered horse brought the news of President Lincoln's assassination. The veteran soldiers of the Fourth California openly wept as the messenger read aloud the dispatch from Captain Atchisson. Arriving in San Bernardino, the men were in no mood to meekly tolerate the noisy secession celebration then in progress and quickly hauled down the Confederate flag raised in renewed hope for what most now knew was a lost cause.[47]

Davis stayed in Los Angeles only long enough to fit out a stock of sutler store goods for his return to the Colorado River. He also took time to propose marriage to Emily Matthew, the daughter of a Hardyville businessman, whom he had met at the Fort Mojave New Year's ball in 1864.[48] Upon his return to Arizona, he wrote the editors of the *Daily Alta California*: "Now 'the cruel war is over,' 'Cal. Volunteer' has doffed the blue and brass of our good Uncle, and returned to the Frontier, and in the garb of a humble citizen would again contribute his mite towards bringing to notice and advancing the mighty mineral resources of our young Territory."[49]

During the war years, Captain Atchisson had encouraged his ambitious sergeant to "read law" in a window-darkened commissary supply room after lights-out. Soon after his return to Arizona, Davis passed the bar exam and was elected to Arizona's territorial legislature as the representative from Mohave County. After serving several terms in the territorial legislature, he received an appointment as Mohave County attorney. A tireless campaigner, Davis stumped across the territory and narrowly missed election as Arizona's representative to Congress.[50] He worked timbering, freighting, and running a Hardyville hotel.[51] He sold his mining interests for sizable profits, which he invested in general store merchandise for soldiers, miners, freighters, and settlers at Mojave City, Hardyville, and in the Prescott area. While serving in the legislature, Davis pushed to raise "minute men" to take the place of the disbanding battalions of California and Arizona (Pima, Papago, and Hispanic) Volunteers in order to combat the Yavapais and Western Apaches.

Frustrated by frequent robberies and killings committed by starving Indians along the Mojave-Prescott road and at remote mines, Davis hardened to the cruelty of the conflict, and his sympathy for the indigenous people began to fade. He now spoke frequently of the "murdering Pahutes" who "infested" the country and endorsed the use of Mojave scouts to scour the countryside for enemy war parties. He even supported the idea of poisoning Indians, who lay in wait for freighters and other travelers, with strychnine-laced sugar placed as if forgotten at campsites along the road. Though far from advocating "extermination," as did many of his contemporaries, he came to believe that progress demanded the elimination of all Indians proven to be "hostile."[52]

Though not a violent man, Alonzo Davis brought violence to the Colorado River. He had witnessed, contributed to, or participated in great change to Arizona's land and its inhabitants. He and his comrades fought Confederates and Indians, and survived the Civil War in the Southwest borderlands. The experience shaped his life. In Arizona he made his fortune, started a family, and became a lawyer, businessman, and legislator. He helped build the fledgling territory as a soldier and a settler. In the process, he learned much about people. Looking back, near the end of his days, he mused with lawyerly regret, "I was always sorry for the Indians. Their side of the question was always so inadequately represented or considered." He never fully understood the role that he, as an Arizona "pioneer," had played in their ruin. Davis had helped strip the native habitat of its grass and timber, blast mines from its mountains, and carve roads through virgin desert and high country. Unknowingly complicit in the violence, the aftereffects of his soldiering, boosterism, lawmaking, and settlement efforts had visited destruction on the land and disrupted the lifeways of the Mojaves—and their allies and enemies. Life along the Colorado River and neighboring mountains would be forever changed.[53]

NOTES

1. Alonzo E. Davis, "Pioneer Days in Arizona by One Who Was There," 1916, Tucson Manuscript Collection, 1–3, Arizona Historical Society, Tucson; James Miller Guinn, *A History of California and an Extended History of Los Angeles* (Los Angeles: Historic Record Co., 1915), 2:151.
2. Davis, "Pioneer Days in Arizona," 3, 6–7.
3. Ibid., 9.
4. From this time forward, Alonzo vowed to stand against those who would oppress the powerless and resolved that injustice would be "met with my strongest denunciations." Ibid., 15–16.

5. Ibid., 21; *San Francisco Daily Alta California*, June 7, 1862. Andrew E. Masich, *The Civil War in Arizona: The Story of the California Volunteers, 1861–1865* (Norman: University of Oklahoma Press, 2006), 173.

6. Davis and his partner earned only fifteen dollars after their first two weeks of placer mining—only half the prevailing wage for day laborers. Davis, "Pioneer Days in Arizona," 25–33.

7. Guinn, *History of California*, 2:152; Richard H. Orton, *Records of California Men in the War of the Rebellion, 1861 to 1867* (Sacramento: State Office, 1890), 6.

8. Davis described himself as "naturally and intensely patriotic." Davis, "Pioneer Days in Arizona," 32, 34.

9. Ibid., 37–38. Captain Atchisson had served under Col. Ferris Forman during the Mexican-American War. He stood 5'9" tall and had auburn hair, blue eyes, and a florid complexion. Charles Atchisson Compiled Military Service Record (CMSR), Record Group (RG) 94 and Mexican War Pension no. 9779, RG 15, National Archives and Records Administration, Washington D.C. (NARA).

10. Orton, *Records*, 68, 87. A survey of "Descriptive Lists" for California regiments shows that the height of the average California soldier was more than an inch taller than his 5'8" eastern counterpart. "California Volunteer Descriptive Lists and Clothing Accounts," RG 95, NARA. Quartermaster records indicate that the hat, coat, and shoe sizes were also larger. Lt. Colonel George H. Crosman, commanding the Philadelphia Depot, noted, "The tariff for boots and bootees has been in operation for twenty years, with slight variations, but I have discovered that it does not suit the men of the West and those of the East equally well. In the western departments larger sizes are needed than in the East. The men are generally larger and have larger feet in the West." *The War of the Rebellion: A Compilation of the Official Records of the Union and Confederate Armies* (*OR*) (Washington, D.C.: Government Printing Office, 1880–1901), series 1, vol. 19, pt. 2, 505. Davis's descriptive record shows him to be 5'11½" tall with a dark complexion, grey eyes, and brown hair. Alonzo E. Davis CMSR, RG 94, NARA.

11. The men of Company I received both dress (1858 pattern frock coat, black felt hat with ostrich plume, brass insignia, and blue worsted hat cords) and fatigue uniforms (1854 pattern blouse and 1858 forage cap). "Every evening," Davis remembered, "there was a dress parade where we had to doff the blouse and don the dress suit." Davis, "Pioneer Days in Arizona," 39.

12. Ibid., 39–41.

13. Epitaph:

> "Why should we mourn for this old ox or grieve for his poor beef?
> When he has caused us pain and woe and worn out all our teeth?
> His spirit has gone to other lands; we trust it's for the best.
> For when we had his bones to gnaw were we more cursed than blessed."

Ibid., 39–41, 46–47.

14. *Daily Alta*, April 10, 1863.

15. Davis, "Pioneer Days in Arizona," 46. For examples of mutinous conduct and the consequences, see Orton, *Records*, 89, 94, 124, 377, 871; *Mesilla Valley (N.Mex.) Independent*, October 6, 1877; George Pettis, *Frontier Service during the Rebellion, or, A History of Company K, First Infantry, California Volunteers*, Personal Narratives of Events in the War of the Rebellion no. 14 (Providence: Soldiers' and Sailors' Historical Society of Rhode Island, 1885), 34–37. Henry Hancock, a Democrat, served in the California General Assembly 1858–60. Commissioned major of the Fourth California Volunteer Infantry, he commanded Camp Drum, established to guard against pro-Confederate activities near Los Angeles. Though restored to rank and pay, his superiors saw fit to assign him to survey remote Catalina Island, where he spent the remainder of the war. After the war, he made a fortune selling the tar from his Rancho La Brea for asphalt paving.

16. Several Company I men deserted, traveled east, and reenlisted in Washington in order to fight as they had been promised. Davis, "Pioneer Days in Arizona," 42–52; Special Orders (SO) No. 89, April 6, 1863, Department of the Pacific, *OR*, series 1, vol. 50, pt. 2, 383.

17. Ferris Foreman to R. C. Drum, April 27, 1863, *OR*, series 1, vol. 50, pt. 2, 413. For the purpose of this chapter, tribal names as known to Davis and his contemporaries are used for consistency with quoted primary sources. Today, tribal members and scholars generally prefer using specific names that predate European contact. Mojaves are also known as "Pipa Aha Macavs," Chemehuevis as "Nuwus," Havasupais as "Havsuw' Baajas," Hualapais as "Hwalbáys," Paiutes as "Pah-Utes," Papagos as "Tohono O'odhams," Pimas as "Akimel O'odhams," and Quechans as "Yumas." Yavapai (aka Mojave-Apaches) western bands included the Đo:lkabaya, Yavbe', and Mađqwadabaya groups.

18. Edwin Rigg to James Carleton, November 30, 1861, *OR*, series 1, vol. 50, pt. 1, 33. See also L. Boyd Finch, "Arizona in Exile: Confederate Schemes to Recapture the Far Southwest," *Journal of Arizona History* 33 (Spring 1992): 57–84; Robert J. Chandler, "California's 1863 Loyalty Oaths: Another Look," *Arizona and the West* 21 (Autumn 1979): 215–34; and Robert J. Chandler, "The Velvet Glove: The Army during the Secession Crisis in California, 1860–1865," *Journal of the West* 20 (October 1981): 35–42.

19. SO No. 142, September 10, 1863, HQ Tucson, "Commands of J. R. West," RG 393, NARA.

20. *Los Angeles Tri-Weekly News*, June 1, 1863. Edwards may have acted alone, but there is evidence that he was acting in concert with other Confederates. Edward D. Tuttle, "River Colorado," *Arizona Historical Review* 1 (July 1928): 57; C. E. Bennett to Drum, May 28, 1863, *OR*, series 1, vol. 50, pt. 2, 459–61; William Ffrench to Joseph Tuttle, May 28, 1863, *OR*, series 1, vol. 50, pt. 2, 461. Wentworth died aboard the *Cocopah* the following day while Behn succumbed to his wounds by the time the boat reached Yuma on May 22. Orton, *Records*, 652–53, 667, 872, 883.

21. *Los Angeles Tri-Weekly News*, July 29, 1863.

22. George Pettis, *The California Column: Its Campaigns and Services in New Mexico, Arizona and Texas, during the Civil War* (Santa Fe: New Mexican Printing, 1908), 18; Ffrench to Tuttle, May 28, 1863, *OR*, series 1, vol. 50, pt. 2, 461.

23. Royal B. Stratton, *The Captivity of the Oatman Girls: Being an Interesting Narrative of Life among the Apache and Mohave Indians* (San Francisco: Whitton, Towne, 1857). See also Brian McGinty, *The Oatman Massacre: A Tale of Desert Captivity and Survival* (Norman: University of Oklahoma Press, 2005), esp. 172–75.

24. Davis, "Pioneer Days in Arizona," 140–41.

25. Davis and other military men believed the Mojaves, man-for-man, to be superior fighters, but the warriors had underestimated the soldiers' firepower and their ability to shoot their muskets with fixed bayonets. Ibid., 130–31, 137.

26. Iretaba, who stood well over six feet tall (Davis reported 6'8"), at first advocated resistance and may have been involved in the battle of 1859 but later became the first among the Mojave accommodation faction. Ibid., 130. Armistead established Fort Mojave in April 1859 and forced the tribe to negotiate a treaty in August that ended organized hostilities with the U.S. government. As a Confederate brigade commander, Armistead was killed in Picket's Charge at Gettysburg on July 3, 1863, soon after Fort Mojave was reestablished. Tuttle, "River Colorado," 58–60.

27. Davis, "Pioneer Days in Arizona," 61. For examples of policing Indians and whites, see ibid., 143; and *Daily Alta*, March 26, 1864, May 14, 1864.

28. McGinty, *Oatman Massacre*, 176–77, 192.

29. *Daily Alta*, June 12, 1864; Davis, "Pioneer Days in Arizona," 132–34. Throughout the 1860s, the government sponsored many such goodwill tours that included chiefs and headmen from some of the tribes most resistant to diplomatic and coercion efforts. Herman J. Viola, *Diplomats in Buckskins: A History of Indian Delegations in Washington City* (Norman: University of Oklahoma Press, 1995), 1–16.

30. Davis, "Pioneer Days in Arizona," 52; Tuttle, "River Colorado," 60–61.

31. General Orders (GO) No. 4, February 18, 1865, Department of New Mexico (DNM), *OR*, series 1, vol. 48, 909; Charles Atchisson to W. Forry, February 20, 1864, *OR*, series 1, vol. 50, pt. 2, 761–62; J. Ross Browne, *Adventures in the Apache Country* (New York: Harper, 1869), 29; *Daily Alta*, July 4, 1864, April 3, 1865; James Curtis to Atchisson, February 22, 1865, *OR*, series 1, vol. 50, pt. 2, 1152.

32. The Hualapai War, as it became known, continued after the departure of the California troops in April 1865. Davis, "Pioneer Days in Arizona," 64–65.

33. Carleton to Nathaniel Pishon, June 22, 1863, in Orton, *Records*, 72; GO No. 27, October 23, 1863, DNM, *OR*, series 1, vol. 50, pt. 2, 654; David Fergusson to James Whitlock, April 23, 1863, series 1, vol. 50, pt. 2, 413. See also Carleton's correspondence in U.S. Congress, *Condition of the Indian Tribes: Joint Special Committee Report: Appointed Under Joint Resolution of March 3, 1865. J. R. Doolittle* (Washington, D.C.: Government Printing Office, 1867), 98, 110, 115–16, 121, 135.

34. Davis, "Pioneer Days in Arizona," 53; *Daily Alta*, January 26, March 26, 1864, January 15, April 3, 1865; Mohave County Book of Claims, 1864–66, Office of the Mohave County Historian, Kingman, Arizona.

35. Davis wrote a chapter in J. Ross Browne's highly regarded book *Resources of the Pacific Slope*, first published in 1866. J. Ross Browne, *Resources of the Pacific Slope: A*

Statistical and Descriptive Summary of the Mines and Minerals, Climate, Topography, Agriculture, Commerce, Manufactures, and Miscellaneous Productions, of the States and Territories West of the Rocky Mountains (New York: D. Appleton, 1869), 443–81; Davis, "Pioneer Days in Arizona," 76–77.

36. Measles outbreaks in 1864–64 killed many in the Colorado River villages, and ineffective Mojave and Paiute doctors were in turn executed by the families of distraught victims. *Daily Alta*, March 26, 1864, December 24, 1864.

37. Davis, "Pioneer Days in Arizona," 61.

38. Comparative photographic analysis confirms that the tall orderly standing beside Atchisson is Davis. Though the purpose of d'Heureuse's photo excursion is not certain, it is likely that he was commissioned to document the region for Philadelphia mining investors. For more on d'Heureuse's journey, see Peter E. Palmquist and Thomas R. Kailbourn, "d'Heureuse, Rudolph," *Pioneer Photographers of the Far West: A Biographical Dictionary, 1840–1865* (Stanford University Press, 2001), 201–203.

39. Carleton ordered, "Each soldier will wear his [1858] uniform hat without trimmings, one blouse, one pair trousers, one pair stockings, one woolen shirt, one pair drawers, and may wear a cravat in lieu of the leather [neck] stock." The soldiers pictured retained the sky blue worsted wool hat cords with tassels even though the other "trimmings" were removed. GO No. 3, February 11, 1862, District of Southern California, *OR*, series 1, vol. 50, pt. 2, 858–59.

40. For examples of Davis's letters to the *Daily Alta*, see Masich, *Civil War in Arizona*, 263–327. Davis also wrote for the *Prescott Arizona Miner* over the pen name "A.E.D." See for example *Arizona Miner*, September 21, 1864.

41. *Daily Alta*, April 3, 1865.

42. Davis, "Pioneers Days in Arizona," 65–66; *Daily Alta*, July 19, 1864.

43. Davis, "Pioneers Days in Arizona," 60, 65.

44. Ibid., 62–64, 66–67.

45. Carleton to Lorenzo Thomas, September 13, 1863, in U.S. Congress, *Condition of the Indian Tribes*, 135–36; *Daily Alta*, July 4 and October 17, 1864.

46. Davis, "Pioneer Days in Arizona," 78–79, 81.

47. Ibid., 79–81.

48. Ibid., 82; Davis mustered out at Drum Barracks October 9, 1865. Orton, *Records*, 657.

49. *Daily Alta*, February 19, 1866.

50. Davis, "Pioneer Days in Arizona," 53, 93. California Volunteers provided the young territory with a corps of literate, formally educated, and energetic men to draw on for political leadership. During and immediately following the Civil War, Anglo-Americans began to dominate territorial politics, and a number of California soldiers, in addition to Davis, became civil officials: Capt. Converse Rowell, Fourth Infantry; Col. Charles Lewis, Seventh Infantry; and Lt. Edward Tuttle, Fourth Infantry, all served in the Arizona legislature. Rowell also served as U.S. district attorney for Arizona and later became district attorney for Yuma County. Charles Atchisson served as probate judge and postmaster in Mohave County. *Daily Alta*, June 12, July 19, and September 10, 1864.

See "Atchisson, Charles," "Davis, Alonzo Edward," "Lewis, Charles W.," "Rowell, Converse W. C." and "Tuttle, Edward" in Hayden Arizona Pioneer Biography Files, Arizona State University, Tempe; H. H. Bancroft, *History of Arizona and New Mexico* (San Francisco: History Company, 1889), 539, 634–36. See also Masich, *Civil War in Arizona*, 265, 269, 272.

51. Davis, "Pioneer Days in Arizona," 87–89, 101–104. The hotel he operated with his father-in-law nearly cost Davis his life as drunken soldiers of the Fourteenth U.S Infantry opened fire on him when he, under orders from their commander, refused to serve them liquor.

52. Ibid., 84–86, 107–108; Charles Atchisson to Drum, April 2, 1864, in Irene J. Brennan, ed., *Fort Mojave, 1859-1890: Letters of the Commanding Officers* (Manhattan: MA/AH Publishing, Kansas State University, 1980), 23–24; *Daily Alta*, April 3, 1865.

53. A respected lawyer and community leader, Davis died in Pasadena, California, on January 19, 1915, at the age of seventy-five. Alonzo E. Davis Pension File, application 794743, RG 15, NARA. His daughters, Louise and Jesse, typed the memoirs he had meticulously reconstructed from diaries he kept during the Civil War years. In an addendum, they wrote that their father fondly remembered his Arizona days, sang the songs of his youth, and often wore his old uniform, with buttons polished, for GAR meetings. They concluded that he "was always a power for good" and "always every inch a true soldier." *Los Angeles Times*, January 20, 1915; Davis, "Pioneer Days in Arizona," 171, 186–88.

6

Harry McConnell

Robert Wooster

On October 5, 1866, Harry Hall McConnell, a freight and ticket agent for the Catawissa Railroad Company, entered the U.S. Army recruiting office at Philadelphia, Pennsylvania. A native of the Pennsylvania coal country of Carbon County, McConnell, aged twenty-six, had grey eyes, brown hair, and a ruddy complexion; stood 5'6½" tall; and was the well-educated son of a physician. He volunteered for the cavalry, which entailed a five-year service obligation. The decision by a man born to the middle class to join the army was an unusual one, for most Americans of the period had little regard for the regulars, an attitude reinforced by the volunteer armies of the Civil War. In reminiscences published twenty-three years later, McConnell explained that he wanted "to see what I could of the lights and shadows of army life on the frontier," particularly the differences between volunteer and regular service. In a letter dated August 1, 1867, however, he maintained that "the best preparation" for a hoped-for appointment as a commissioned officer would come with "an actual experience as an enlisted man."[1]

Spending most of his time in the service in and around Fort Richardson, Texas, McConnell never became an officer, and was in 1871 discharged at the expiration of his first term of enlistment. He soon returned to Jacksboro, the civilian community adjacent to Fort Richardson and county seat of Jack County, settling down with his wife and two sons. There he lived a productive life, editing a newspaper, serving as the town's second mayor, and working as a druggist, postmaster, land agent, and commissioner for the Fifth Circuit Court. The region's first bank was built on land that he owned; his grandson later became that bank's president. He also wrote one of the most revealing accounts of life as an enlisted man in the post–Civil War regular army ever published.[2]

As both soldier and settler, McConnell assisted in the U.S. conquest of the Southwest borderlands. State and federal governments used organized violence to accelerate the process, and enlisted men like McConnell occasionally engaged independent Indians in combat. However, McConnell's story is illustrative in a sense that many soldiers stationed in the borderlands never saw any independent Indians and even fewer fought against them. During his five years in service, McConnell had just one violent engagement with a group of Indians (probably Kiowas). But by seizing and controlling strategic centers in environments with limited resources, the army reduced the capacities of Indians to resist the U.S. onslaught. Incoming civilian settlers, sometimes joined by former soldiers, completed the conquest. The civilians' presence increased the likelihood that the federal government would deploy its largest disposable resource—the U.S. Army—to advance the interests of the citizens.[3] Building homes, ranches, farms, and businesses, settlers soon monopolized the natural assets of the Southwest, ending any possibility that the earlier Indian inhabitants could challenge U.S. sovereignty. And, like McConnell, their quest for physical and economic security also eventually led the newcomers to control the violence that so often accompanied the wildest days of conquest.

UNCERTAIN MILITARY PAST

Harry Hall McConnell was born in 1837 at Mauch Chunk (now Jim Thorpe Township), Pennsylvania, the fourth child of Benjamin Rush and Mary Ann McConnell. Harry's father, a Philadelphia native and University of Pennsylvania graduate, had come to Carbon County as a physician for the Lehigh Coal and Navigation Company. The namesake of one of the nation's most celebrated physicians and scientists, Dr. McConnell published a short essay, "Notice of a Revolving Electro-Magnetic Instrument," in *The American Journal of Science and Arts* the same year as Harry's birth. In 1860, Harry was still living with his parents, who claimed an estate worth $3,000 (over $88,100 in 2014 dollars).[4]

With the Confederacy's firing on Fort Sumter, at least seventy young men from Mauch Chunk promptly volunteered for three months' service in the Sixth Pennsylvania Infantry. That summer they enrolled for three years in the reorganized Eleventh Pennsylvania Infantry Regiment. Following the community patterns that often characterized Civil War units, Mauch Chunk residents were especially prevalent in Company H. Others followed suit in the coming months, and the regiment fought at Second Bull Run, Antietam, Chancellorsville, Gettysburg, Petersburg, and Appomattox. In 1867 McConnell claimed to have served in the Sixth and Eleventh Pennsylvania, and to have earned a commission in the latter. In a special census of Union soldiers taken twenty-three years later, he attested to having been in Company H, Eleventh Pennsylvania, enlisting on April 21, 1861, and receiving his discharge in September 1864. While vague on details, he implied some type of volunteer Civil War service on four occasions in his published memoirs.[5]

Civil War records, particularly for individual soldiers, are often incomplete. For example, the regimental returns for the Eleventh Infantry in the Pennsylvania State Archives do not mention McConnell, but also fail to include companies H, I, or K, suggesting that the records from those organizations might have been lost or misplaced.[6] However, in 1867, and again in 1868, War Department clerks, following up on his application for a commission, could not locate any Civil War record for McConnell.[7] Nor does his name, or any reasonable variant, appear in published regimental rosters, the Civil War Soldiers and Sailors System (which includes names from muster rolls and compiled military service records), unit rosters on the Pennsylvania State Archives website, or the Eleventh Pennsylvania Infantry Descriptive Book and Order Book (both in the National Archives). Moreover, although he later filed for a disability payments based upon his regular army service, there is no indication that McConnell ever applied for a Civil War pension.

Other evidence regarding McConnell's Civil War whereabouts does exist. In September 1862, with the approach of Robert E. Lee's invading Confederate forces (which culminated in the Battle of Antietam), Pennsylvania assembled several emergency militia regiments. A man fitting McConnell's description enlisted in Company A, Nineteenth Infantry, for twelve days.[8] In addition, the Pennsylvania Septennial Census (1863) and city directories of 1864 and 1865 reveal one H. H. McConnell as a clerk living in Philadelphia, which is consistent with information found on the regular army's enlistment rosters and in papers included in his application for a commission.[9]

On December 24, 1863, McConnell married Jeannette Desire Connor in a ceremony held at Summitt Hill, just southwest of Mauch Chunk. The two had a child, Benjamin Rush, in 1865. When McConnell volunteered for the regular army, he left his wife and child behind at Mauch Chunk. Born in the 1830s, Jeannette was the daughter of the community's most prominent hotelier, Cornelius Connor. After an 1849 fire destroyed his hotel and much of the town's business district, Connor used the insurance settlement to build a larger brick structure, the New American House, which long served as the county seat's architectural showplace. But he died in 1858, and the estate was insufficient to allow his surviving family members (he had as many as fourteen children) to maintain their former lifestyle. Thus while her husband was away in the late 1860s, Jeannette rented out rooms to boarders (two civil engineers and a post office clerk) and claimed a modest estate of five hundred dollars in 1870.[10]

TO THE TEXAS BORDERLANDS

In contrast to most regular army enlistees, Harry McConnell, son of his hometown's first medical doctor, boasted a classical education and quickly became a favorite of officers seeking help filling out the army's myriad forms and paperwork. He was named an acting sergeant among the recruits, with whom he sailed from Baltimore to Indianola, Texas, en route to joining the Sixth Cavalry Regiment at Austin. In mid-January 1867, he arrived at Jacksboro, where two companies had established a camp. He fell in love with Texas, especially in spring: "After all these years, each recurring spring here is as delightful to me as ever; nowhere, in my knowledge, does nature so completely re-invigorate everything and fill everything with new life as it does each spring in Northwest Texas." To break the dull routine of army life, for a time McConnell and "the boys" produced a weekly manuscript paper, the *Little Joker*. The camp at Jacksboro was initially assumed to be temporary, so in late spring 1867 newly minted Sergeant McConnell was detached to Fort Belknap. With the abandonment of that post, he was sent to work for the quartermaster at the camp at Buffalo Springs, twenty-eight miles from Jacksboro.[11]

The army's reoccupation of the northern and western borderlands of Texas following the Civil War—in addition to Fort Richardson and the camp at Buffalo Springs, in 1867 it established Fort Griffin near the Clear Fork of the Brazos River to replace old Fort Belknap—had been uneven.

Maj. Gen. Philip H. Sheridan, commander of the military department (later district) of which Texas was a part, believed that unreconstructed white southerners, not independent Indians, posed the chief threat to order and security. As such, he had initially stationed most of the returning regulars in the interior of the state, so as to better preserve order between Unionists, freedmen, and former Confederates. White residents of north Texas, however, believed differently, their fears confirmed in spring 1866 when about thirty-five Comanches killed one woman and took three other captives during a raid into Jack and Wise Counties. In July, residents of Clay, Cooke, Jack, Montague, Wise, and Young Counties complained that Indians were attacking "with a boldness never known before, Committing Murders and Stealing horses and driving off cattle in large numbers and herds." Four persons were murdered about twelve miles from Jacksboro two months later, and in neighboring Wise County an Indian raid killed one woman and captured three others. In total, the state of Texas claimed that Indian attacks in Jack County from 1865 to 1867 killed seven white people and resulted in the loss of five thousand cattle and one hundred horses.[12]

For Harry McConnell, the threat of violence hit home on July 21, 1867, when word that Indian raiders (probably Satanta and a group of Kiowas) had attacked a work party of soldiers and civilians reached Buffalo Springs. Bvt. Maj. Benjamin Hutchins assembled all of the men with horses and full riding equipment—four noncommissioned officers and thirty-five men—in an exhausting pursuit. Lacking information about Indian whereabouts and unwilling to endure the privations demanded by a lengthy chase, Hutchins, whom McConnell later described as "very vain, and . . . imagined that he bore a striking resemblance to the first Napoleon," failed to catch any of the raiders. With desertions reaching 20 percent annually, suspicions that the Indian threat was overblown, and an army desperately seeking to save money whenever possible, both the inadequacy and unpreparedness of the strike force was common in the post–Civil War army.[13]

Remaining behind in camp were Lt. Theodore Majtheny, Sergeant McConnell, forty-four dismounted cavalrymen, and scores of civilian laborers and camp followers. Just before sunset on the 21st, nine panicky civilians hurried in, Indians hot on their heels. Lieutenant Majtheny, a native of Hungary who had seen limited field duty as a volunteer during the Civil War, shepherded the women and children into the forage house and directed McConnell to distribute the post's remaining arsenal—twenty-seven

Spencer carbines with about thirty-five rounds apiece—to some of the soldiers. The Indians, whom Majtheny estimated to number 200 (writing two decades later, McConnell increased the size of the attacking party to over 350), "came in a wild charge." The garrison's ragged volley broke up the assault, killing one Indian. The soldiers expected another assault the next day, "but it did not come," wrote Majtheny, "they knowing of our vigilance." The raiders having judged that potential costs of a full scale assault would outweigh any plunder they might garner, reinforcements broke up the short-lived siege at Buffalo Springs on the 23rd, with a rattled Majtheny reporting, "My men behaved cool, and performed their duty cheerfully."[14]

ARMY LIFE

A week after the assault, an emboldened McConnell petitioned for the chance to convince a board of officers to grant him a commission. As his commanding officer, Brevet Major Hutchins supported the claim, describing McConnell as "a gentleman and good soldier." Six other officers from the regiment also signed the application. But War Department officials denied McConnell's appeal, determining that he lacked the required two years of military service and was too old for an initial appointment. Undeterred by the setback, McConnell convinced his old boss Samuel V. Merrick, president of the Catawissa Railroad, to apply some political pressure to grease the squeaky wheels of the War Department bureaucracy. Merrick in turn secured a letter of support from Maj. Gen. Oliver O. Howard, who described McConnell as being "a young man of good family, intelligent, finely educated, a gentleman in manners and bearing" who enjoyed the backing of "gentleman of high standing and influence." But the adjutant general held firm: McConnell, now aged thirty, was too old to become an officer. Fourteen months after McConnell's initial letter, Secretary of War John M. Schofield finally closed the case, backing the adjutant general's conclusion that his age rendered him ineligible for a commission.[15]

Though unsuccessful, McConnell's efforts to become an officer seem entirely consistent with the class consciousness that characterized the army as well as Victorian society. The product of a middle-class family, his disdain for most of his fellow enlisted men, significant numbers of whom were immigrant laborers, was hardly unusual. He did acknowledge a few exceptions. "Now and then I came across a young man, well brought up and of good family," declared McConnell in *Five Years a Cavalryman*, "who had come into the army from a love of adventure and a desire to see frontier life, such as the army can alone afford, and who conducted himself with the same propriety as if under the best restrains and influences." Such comrades were, however, a distinct minority. "The majority" of his fellow recruits "were 'bounty jumpers,' blackguards and criminals of various degrees, or, at any rate, men who had sought the army as an asylum from the punishments that the law would have justly meted out to them had they remained in civil life."[16]

McConnell's contempt for many of his fellow soldiers was shared by most commissioned personnel, and reflected widely held ethnic stereotypes in the late nineteenth-century United States. Over 40 percent of white soldiers were born abroad, and second-generation immigrants comprised another fifth of the white regulars. The majority of immigrant soldiers were Irish or German, and McConnell's descriptions portray, to the twenty-first-century reader at least, an almost cartoonish quality. Germans, though "good army laborers," were too eager to endear themselves by doing a thousand menial and unmilitary tasks for their officers to be good soldiers. These "dog-robbers," he complained, hung around an officer's quarters, "fall heir to his cast-off clothing, drink his whiskey, run errands for his wife, build chicken-coops, draw rations, attend his horses, and, in short, gobble up all the 'crumbs' of whatever kind that 'fall from his table.'" The Irish, by contrast, made better soldiers, a quality McConnell attributed to their long struggle against English oppression. "Cheerful, apt to learn his duties, ready to adapt himself to every circumstance and condition, generally obedient to his superiors, and blessed with a robust frame," he wrote, "the Irishman is by far the best soldier in our army."[17]

The Irish were, however, merely the best of a very bad lot, for they, like their German- and American-born comrades, drank far too heavily for McConnell's liking. He joined virtually every contemporary observer in explaining that the arrival of a paymaster, chronically delayed by several months, sparked celebrations of bacchanalian proportions. His memoirs also included multiple tales of alcoholic old soldiers. Upon hearing that a fellow soldier had received ample quantities of whiskey following a snakebite, "Paddy Maloney" promptly waded barefoot among some weeds in hopes that he too might get bitten by a snake. An enlisted man named

Island Home, Fort Richardson, Texas. Although McConnell did not write about them in his memoirs, prostitutes (faintly visible in the background) accompanied soldiers throughout the West. Jacksboro, home to a garrison and a popular site for cattle drives, reputedly had several houses of prostitution. Courtesy Lawrence T. Jones III Texas Photography Collection, DeGolyer Library, Southern Methodist University.

Shields was "a constitutional drunkard"; a company clerk was "addicted to the flowing bowl"; John Quinn, though good at handling animals, was "capable of doing anything in order to get whiskey"; Sgt. Jim DeForrest had "the old soldier's fondness for whiskey."[18]

During his summer 1867 service at the camp at Buffalo Springs, McConnell contracted chronic diarrhea, which he believed stemmed from the post's poor water supply. He remained sick in his quarters for much of that fall. In March 1868, he returned to Jacksboro, home to newly minted Fort Richardson, before being summoned to San Antonio to testify at a court-martial. The following year, he secured access to a printing press at nearby Weatherford long enough to publish several editions of *The Flea*, described by its wisecracking editor as a "first-class journal devoted to Politics, Religion, Science, The Arts, Music and the Drama." In reality, most of *The Flea* was devoted to local advertisements and post gossip, but in a notable exception McConnell waxed eloquent in support of the new state constitution of 1869. Acknowledging that some items in the document "may be repugnant to the deeply rooted prejudices of many," he reminded readers that "fanatic leaders" had only eight years earlier led the state out of the Union. By restoring Texas to the Union, the document would inspire "a mighty wave" of new emigrants, "and before this generation has passed away, it will be justly called the Empire State of the Southwest."[19]

By late 1869, diarrhea and remittent fever had once again forced McConnell's absence from his regular military duties, and the following summer he remained behind in the Fort Richardson hospital while the Sixth Cavalry was transferred to Kansas. McConnell recovered enough to eventually make the trip, and five years to the day after his enlistment he was discharged from the regular army just outside Fort Hays, Kansas.

PROSPECTING

If near chronic illness coupled with class resentment and feelings of alienation had characterized much of McConnell's military experience, now he had to decide what to do with the rest of his life and where to do it. One thing seemed certain: Kansas had little appeal. Nearby Hays City had fewer "good people there" than there had been present "in Sodom when the angel of the Lord took the census of that place some years since," and the surrounding countryside "was barren and very uninteresting," McConnell penned. Texas, by contrast, seemed a better bet. The prairies and rivers surrounding Fort Richardson offered abundant supplies of game and fish and promised "vast mineral wealth." And Jacksboro, though still threatened by Indian attack and plagued by the ne'er-do-wells who inevitably made their way to frontier garrison towns, was nonetheless "the distributing point for about all the money current in Northwest Texas." McConnell thus made his way by train and stagecoach back to the Lone Star State.[20]

From McConnell's perspective, events soon vindicated his decision, for ethnic cleansing would replace the racial violence that had long ravaged northern Texas. During the 1860s, Kiowa and Comanche raids had reduced the non-Indian population of Jack County from about one thousand to less than seven hundred, and on May 18, 1871, a Kiowa raiding party had jumped a ten-wagon supply train and killed eight teamsters at Salt Creek Prairie, just eight miles from Fort Richardson. But this would be the last Indian military victory in the immediate region, for they had opted not to strike a preceding party of riders in hopes of securing the greater booty of the oncoming wagon train. Unbeknownst to the Kiowas, the earlier group had included William T. Sherman, commanding general of the U.S. Army, whose small escort they could easily have overwhelmed. The near miss transformed Sherman, long skeptical of Texas claims about the magnitude of Indian attacks, into a zealous advocate of stepped-up army activity throughout the region. Subsequent military operations, which culminated in the grinding campaigns of the Red River War (1874–75), eliminated Indian opposition and brought on a surge of white colonists. The army abandoned Fort Richardson in 1878, and by 1880 Jack County's population numbered 6,629, nearly ten times that of just a decade earlier. By 1890, the number of county residents approached ten thousand.[21]

A final grand adventure remained. McConnell was not alone in believing that the area west of Jacksboro held vast mineral wealth, and in 1871 a group of eastern investors formed the Texas Land and Copper Association to exploit those riches and to profit from the increased land values that white occupation would bring. The group's board of directors reputedly included Tom Scott (president of the Texas and Pacific Railway), R. Adm. David D. Porter (whose naval squadrons had helped to capture Vicksburg and Fort Fisher during the Civil War), and Jay Cooke (one of the age's most prominent financiers). Armed with a slick twenty-seven-page prospectus and the desire to beat a host of competitors—most notably the Wichita Colonization, Agricultural, Mining, and Manufacturing Company—the company's scientific team rendezvoused at Fort Richardson in late June 1872. Principles included "Colonel" W. C. McCarty, a former railroad agent and bookkeeper turned expedition leader; "Professor" Anton R. Roessler, the Hungarian-born cartographer and geologist who McConnell described as "the most thorough and ideal crank of any age"; Oscar Loew, "a droll looking little fellow" who would become a prominent agricultural chemist; and A. C. Troutman, the party's photographer. With the group's composition shifting almost daily, Harry McConnell was among those who signed on at Jacksboro.[22]

Some sixty strong, the expedition set out from Fort Richardson in mid-July, meandering west to Fort Griffin, where they hired some Tonkawa scouts and made their way to Kiowa Peak (present-day Stonewall County, Texas). Plagued by hot weather, poor water, and incompetent leadership ("a bigger fraud never was seen," wrote McConnell in describing McCarty), the party surveyed a few tracts and shot some buffalo but found little copper. Characterizing the group as largely "a mob of drunken & ½ drunken men," one diarist described McConnell as trustworthy and "sober." The demoralized expedition disbanded in mid-September.[23]

MIDDLE-CLASS MAN

His prospecting days having ended, Harry McConnell settled down at Jacksboro, determined to rejoin the middle class. In 1873, he brought his wife and son, Rush, out from Mauch Chunk, and the couple had another son, Harry Hall Jr. By mid-1875, former Sergeant McConnell was a city alderman and secretary of the Fort Richardson Masonic Lodge. With one partner, he also served as editor of the *Frontier Echo*, which debuted on June 30. The four-page weekly featured a range of local news and gossip, miscellaneous correspondence, short fiction, and advertisements. Undoubtedly trying to capture the sympathy of a local population that had voted 76–14 against secession and depended for its livelihood on the U.S. Army, its masthead featured quotations from Abraham Lincoln's Gettysburg Address: "Let us see to it, that a Government of the people, by the people, and for the people, shall not Perish from the Earth." Appealing to a growing populist sentiment, McConnell promised to deliver readers a "family paper," which would be "a true exponent of the principels [*sic*] of Good Government, opposing all rings and monopolies which in any way tend to fetter or oppress the laboring man." But with subscriptions meager and paper in short supply, in October McConnell handed over his interest in the newspaper to the new publisher-editor, George W. Robson, who expanded state and national reporting.[24]

Dabbling in dry goods, land, cattle raising, and the town drugstore, in March 1876 the former regular was selected mayor by the Jacksboro board of aldermen. With over two dozen saloons serving soldiers and cowboys amid the heyday of the Texas cattle drives, boomtown crime, rather than the older conflicts against the Indians, had become the chief threat. "Drunken men used to shoot up the town about every night," remembered one scout, "and sometimes during the day." No wonder that the *Echo* implored the new administration to focus on "maintaining peace and quiet." As the days of the freewheeling cattle drives came to a close, the violence subsided, and McConnell went on to become a trustee of the Jacksboro school community and secretary of the local literary society. By the late 1870s, McConnell's Drug Store, located on South Main Street, ran weekly advertisements in the *Echo*. In addition to serving as compounding pharmacist, druggist, and apothecary, the doctor's son stocked sewing machine needles and oil, paints, varnishes, dyes, stationery, tobacco and cigars, "fine wines and liquors for family and medicinal use . . . in fact a Full Line of Everything usually kept in a First Class Drug Store." Another advertisement promised "All kinds of blank books, croquet sets, playing cards, school books, lamps, pocket cutlery and a thousand and one other knick-knacks."[25]

Although the drugstore became the family's primary business, the McConnells dabbled in a variety of money-making enterprises. Though a sharp critic of the federal government's involvement in Reconstruction, McConnell saw no reason not to take advantage of Washington's largesse. Appointed the Jacksboro postmaster on September 11, 1877, he retained the office for much of the next decade. Local postmasters usually operated out of their own places of business in a part-time capacity; for McConnell, the position offered considerable financial security, with his $743 compensation in 1885 (roughly $18,900 in 2014 dollars) handsomely supplementing his work as a druggist.[26] In 1879 and again in 1881, he was also a U.S. commissioner for the Northern District, Fifth Circuit Court at Dallas. During the nineteenth century, such commissioners conducted preliminary investigations of those suspected of violating a federal law and assisted other law enforcement officers in issuing search and arrest warrants. Paid on a fee basis, they were allowed considerable discretion; these appointments reflected McConnell's considerable influence in Jack County.[27]

Jeannette McConnell was a full partner in the family's quest for economic security. The daughter of a hotelier, she managed several Jacksboro hotels. When she took over proprietorship of the Southern Hotel in early 1876, for instance, the *Echo* proclaimed, "We defy any town in the State to show a neater, better kept house than the Southern. Presided over as it is with grace and dignity by that estimable lady, Mrs. McConnell, we feel safe in saying the Southern is the best hotel of the north west." She also offered private lessons in piano, guitar, and voice. By 1878, the McConnells had shifted management to the Horton House, which promised its visitors "Good Rooms, a pleasant Dining Hall, fine Cistern water, a first-class Table, and attention to the comfort of guests." Patrons could also expect "a first-class Livery Stable in connection." Filing their city and county taxes under her name, in that year the family claimed a town lot, six cows, a hog, cash, and merchandise totaling $4,287 (roughly $105,000 in 2014 dollars).[28]

The McConnells had become one of the most respected families in Jacksboro. In 1877, Jeannette's sister Emma relocated there and married McConnell's sometime partner, J. W. Knox. Harry joined First Presbyterian Church, and he and his wife enjoyed the services of a live-in servant and gardener. Their son Benjamin Rush, a cattleman, played club baseball and was second violin in the community orchestra. In 1891, Harry served as one of the directors of the Jack County Educational Institution (later North Texas Baptist College), and was one of five speakers at that year's local reunion of the "Blue and Gray."[29]

Something of a local legend, in 1889 Harry H. McConnell published his reminiscences of his life in the regular army. Generally accurate, his sketches presented a decidedly mixed view of post–Civil War officers (unsurprising given his failure to secure a commission) and correctly identified the frequent quarrels between post commanders and surgeons as well as the daily routines of garrison life. They were also notable for his sharp criticisms of the failure by his fellow Texans to properly maintain the crumbling Alamo and for his censures of the Texas Rangers: McConnell charged that, although they might have been "tolerable Indian fighters," the legendary state forces spent most of their time "terrorizing the citizens and 'taking in the town.'"[30]

For the most part, however, the narrative reflected the values and beliefs of the respectable, middle-class white Texas society to which the ex-soldier now belonged. Roundly critical of the Freedmen's Bureau, Reconstruction, and the federal government's often-vacillating Indian policy, it praised the qualities of white settlers and even some army officers like Col. Ranald Mackenzie, whose ruthless campaigns had pushed aside many of the earlier

Indian residents across Texas. Acknowledging that Indians were the victims of white expansion, McConnell nonetheless expressed little guilt about this conquest, proclaiming that peaceful efforts to transform such "savages" had about as much chance as "civilizing a coyote or rattlesnake." Adopting the racist language of the period, McConnell frequently referred to Hispanics as "greasers," dubbed one African American a "darkey" and described black regular cavalrymen as "unsoldierlike and slovenly."[31]

His past brushes with violence were now replaced by a growing struggle to preserve his health and his fortune, for despite his efforts to conceal it, the old soldier's health had become increasingly fragile. "He was never entirely rid of the diarrhea while I knew him," remembered his sister-in-law, and a doctor testified to his chronic bowel movements, nervousness, and occasional numbness in his legs. "He was never a strong man," added a business associate. McConnell sold his share of the drugstore in 1891; reconciling with his oldest son, the two organized McConnell & McConnell, General Agents, with Harry acting as a notary public and Benjamin specializing in abstracts, lands, and loans. In May 1892, the elder McConnell began receiving partial invalid pension of six dollars a month ($161 in 2014 dollars), having successfully tied his chronic diarrhea and dysentery to the water supply at Buffalo Springs while he was a soldier. He died on July 31, 1895.[32]

Defending her interests to the end, his widow wrangled an appointment as Jacksboro postmaster and managed to secure her claim to her husband's disability payments; the exasperated government investigator on the case described her as "an everlasting talker." Following a long illness, Jeannette McConnell died on February 13, 1917, survived by her eldest son and two sisters. Her story, as well as that of her soldier-husband, suggests that even among the violence of the wars against the Indians, Reconstruction, and a turbulent borderlands, many—probably most—Americans devoted the majority of their lives to the quest for order and the promise of a settled, comfortable life.[33]

NOTES

1. Register of Enlistments in the U.S. Army, 1798–1914, M233, roll 31, p. 297, Record Group (RG) 94, National Archives and Records Administration, Washington, D.C. (NARA); H. H. McConnell, *Five Years a Cavalryman; or, Sketches of Regular Army Life on the Texas Frontier, 1866–1871* (1889; repr., Norman: University of Oklahoma Press,

1996), 26 [first quotation]; Harry McConnell to Adjutant General (AG), August 1, 1867, M1070/1867, Letters Received (LR), Commission Branch (CB), 1863–1870, M1064, roll 355, RG 94, NARA [second and third quotations].

2. For the McConnell connection with the First National Bank of Jacksboro, see "Our History," *First National Bank of Jacksboro*, http://www.fnbjacksboro.com/home/about (accessed August 15, 2014).

3. See especially Andrew Cayton, "'Separate Interests' and the Nation-State: The Washington Administration and the Origins of Regionalism in the Trans-Appalachian West," *Journal of American History* 79 (June 1992): 39–67; Janne Lahti, *Cultural Construction of Empire: The U.S. Army in Arizona and New Mexico* (Lincoln: University of Nebraska Press, 2012).

4. Alfred Mathews and Austin N. Hungerford, *History of the Counties of Lehigh and Carbon, in the Commonwealth of Pennsylvania* (Philadelphia: Everts and Richards, 1884), 623; Sixth Census of the United States (1840), Mauch Chunk, Northampton County, Pennsylvania, M704, roll 479, NARA; Benjamin Rush McConnell, "Notice of a Revolving Electro-Magnetic Instrument," *American Journal of Science and Arts* 32 (July 1837): 188–90; Seventh Census of the United States (1850), Mauch Chunk Township, Carbon County, Pennsylvania, M432, roll 762, NARA; Eighth Census of the United States (1860), Mauch Chunk Township, Carbon County, Pennsylvania, M653, roll 1089, NARA. For estimates of the modern value of nineteenth-century dollars, see "Purchasing Power of Money in the United States from 1774 to Present," https://www.measuringworth.com/ppowerus/ (accessed June 23, 2016).

5. William Henry Locke, *The Story of the Regiment* (Philadelphia: J. B. Lippincott, 1868); McConnell to AG, August 1, 1867, M1070/1867, LR, CB, M1064, roll 355, RG 94, NARA; Special Schedules of the Eleventh Census (1890), Enumerating Union Veterans and Widows of Union Veterans of the Civil War, M123, roll 102, RG 15, NARA; McConnell, *Five Years a Cavalryman*, 42, 53, 83, 212. For Sixth Pennsylvania rosters, see "Registers of Pennsylvania Volunteers, 1861–1865," vol. 1, RG 19, Records of the Department of Military and Veterans' Affairs, Pennsylvania Historical and Museum Commission, Bureau of Archives and History, Pennsylvania State Archives, Harrisburg, http://www.phmc.state.pa.us/bah/dam/Rg/di/r19-65RegisterPaVolunteers/r19-65MainInterface.htm (accessed June 23, 2016). Of the 183 enlisted men who served in Company H, 29 died during the war. Descriptive Book, Eleventh Pennsylvania Infantry, vol. 3, Records of Volunteer Union Organizations, RG 94, NARA. McConnell seems to have had no connection with any of the other ten surviving Union veterans in Jack County.

6. "Registers of Pennsylvania Volunteers, 1861–1865," vol. 2, RG 19, Records of the Department of Military and Veterans' Affairs, http://www.phmc.state.pa.us/bah/dam/rg/di/r19-65RegisterPaVolunteers/r19-65%20Reg23-39Interface.htm (accessed June 23, 2016). Rosters may also be found in Samuel P. Bates, *History of Pennsylvania Volunteers, 1861–65*, 5 vols. (Harrisburg, Pa.: B. Singerly, 1869–71), and Janet Hewitt, *History of Pennsylvania Volunteers, 1861–65*, 4 vols. (Wilmington, N.C.: Broadfoot, 1993–94).

7. Endorsements to Harry H. McConnell files, M1070/1867 and M429/1868, LR, CB, M1064, rolls 355, 407, NARA.

8. Pennsylvania Civil War Veterans' Card File, 1861–66, Indexes, Pennsylvania State Archives, http://www.digitalarchives.state.pa.us/archive.asp?view=ArchiveItems&ArchiveID=17&FID=1301633&LID=1301682&FL=M&Page=3 (accessed November 15, 2014). The typed card reads "Henry H." rather than "Harry H." McConnell, but that seems a transcription error, as he was listed as age twenty-five and a resident of Mauch Chunk, both characteristics which were consistent with his known identity.

9. Jeannette McConnell, Widow's Claim, April 1, 1896, Harry H. McConnell and Jeannette D. McConnell Pension File (McConnell Pension File), Applications 1110293 and 632006, Certificates 850603 and 5114456, RG 15, NARA. *Pennsylvania, Septennial Census, 1779–1863*, www.Ancestry.com (accessed August 16, 2014), lists McConnell's birthdate as about 1839. *McElroy's Philadelphia City Directory for 1864* (Philadelphia: E. C. and J. Biddle, 1864), 426, and *McElroy's Philadelphia City Directory for 1865* (Philadelphia: A. McElroy, 1865), 452, both identify his employer as the Catawissa Railroad Company.

10. Archibald McElroy, "Cornelius Connor and the Mauch Chunk Inferno," *Carbon County Magazine* http://www.carboncountymagazine.com/CarbonCountyMagazine/2014/2014-07/Articles/Article07.html (accessed December 23, 2014); Ninth Census of the United States (1870), Mauch Chunk Township, Carbon County, Pennsylvania, M593, roll 1320, NARA. Jeannette's exact birthdate remains a mystery. An obituary and her tombstone both list her year of birth as 1835. Census records, however, variously suggest 1833, 1837, 1840, or even 1845. "Personals; Jeannette McConnell Dies," *Jacksboro (Tex.) Gazette*, February 15, 1917, http://www.newspaperabstracts.com/print.php?id=28085 (accessed August 16, 2014); http://www.jackcountytexas.info/Cemeteries/images/Oakwood-2/Oakwood-1330.jpg (accessed December 22, 2014); Sixth Census of the United States (1840), Mauch Chunk, Northampton County, Pennsylvania, M704, roll 479, NARA; Seventh Census of the United States (1850), Mauch Chunk Township, Carbon County, Pennsylvania, M432, roll 762, NARA; Tenth Census of the United States (1880), Precinct 1, Jack County, Texas, T9, roll 1313, NARA; Twelfth Census of the United States (1900), Jacksboro, Jack County, Texas, T623, roll 1648, NARA.

11. McConnell, *Five Years a Cavalryman*, 19, 48, 56, 62–63 [first quotation], 60 [second quotation], 84–86; Fort Belknap, May 1867, Returns from U.S. Military Posts, 1800–1916, M617, roll 95; and Fort Richardson, April 1867, roll 1008, both in NARA.

12. Phil Sheridan to John Rawlins, November 8, 1866, roll 24, Ulysses S. Grant Papers, Library of Congress, Washington, D.C.; "Report of Gen. Phil Sheridan," November 14, 1868, in U.S. War Department, *Annual Report of the Secretary of War*, House Ex. Doc., No. 1, 40th Cong., 3d Sess., Serial 1367, 48; Gary Clayton Anderson, *The Conquest of Texas: Ethnic Cleansing in the Promised Land, 1820–1875* (Norman: University of Oklahoma Press, 2005), 348–49; Dorman H. Winfrey and James M. Day, eds., *Texas Indian Papers* (Austin: Texas State Library, 1961), 4, 97 [quotation], 232–36; Allen Lee Hamilton, *Sentinel of the Southern Plains: Fort Richardson and the Northwest Texas Frontier, 1866–1878* (Fort Worth: Texas Christian University Press, 1988), 18, 184n10.

13. McConnell, *Five Years a Cavalryman*, 48 [quotation], 52, 93–95; Benjamin Hutchins to Assistant Adjutant General (AAG), July 23, 1867, Entry 1, Letters Sent (LS),

vol. 66, pt. 5: Military Installations, RG 393, NARA. The Fort Richardson post returns for May 1868, for example, admit that two separate expeditions "against depredating Indian . . . accomplished nothing." Fort Richardson, May 1868, Returns from U.S. Military Posts, M617, roll 1008, NARA. For the identification of Satanta and the Kiowas, see Hamilton, *Sentinel of the Southern Plains*, 185n34.

14. Theodore Majtheny to AAG, July 24, 1867, Entry 1, LS, vol. 66, pt. 5: Military Installations, RG 393, NARA [quotations]; McConnell, *Five Years a Cavalryman*, 95–100. McConnell remembered distributing only twenty-one rounds to each soldier.

15. McConnell's quest for a commission encompasses four different files: M1070/1867 [first quotation], M1190/1867, M1388/1867 [second and third quotations from Oliver Howard's letter of September 13, 1867], and M429/1868, all in LR, CB, M1064, rolls 355, 356, 407, NARA.

In 1866 and 1867, 1,530 officers were appointed to the army. Of these, 88 percent came from civil life and boasted of at least two years of "distinguished" service during the Civil War. Just under 7 percent came from West Point, and about 5 percent were from the regular ranks. Edward M. Coffman, *The Old Army: A Portrait of the American Army in Peacetime, 1784–1898* (New York: Oxford University Press, 1986), 219.

16. McConnell, *Five Years a Cavalryman*, 17 [first quotation], 13 [second quotation]. For a splendid assessment of the importance of class and race in the post–Civil War army, see Kevin Adams, *Class and Race in the Frontier Army: Military Life in the West, 1870–1890* (Norman: University of Oklahoma Press, 2009).

17. Adams, *Class and Race*, 23–25; McConnell, *Five Years a Cavalryman*, 106, 107 [quotations]. Adams, who describes McConnell's writing as "proto-racism," argues that class tensions in American society during the late 1870s and 1880s explained a growing sense of nativism among military leaders, which culminated in an 1894 law which required that first-time enlistees know English and either be citizens or have announced their intention to become citizens. Adams, *Class and Race*, 187–91; Coffman, *Old Army*, 330–31. First published in 1889, McConnell's memoirs probably reflected that trend.

18. McConnell, *Five Years a Cavalryman*, 54, 156–58, 110–11 [first quotation], 89 [second quotation], 88 [third quotation], 205 [fourth quotation], 31 [fifth quotation].

19. Ibid., 120, 173, 177; Declaration for Original Invalid Pension, April 11, 1892; John Cameron, Neighbor's Affidavit, April 16, 1892; William H. Appleby, Neighbor's Affidavit, April 16, 1892, all in McConnell Pension File, RG 15, NARA; *The Jacksboro (Tex.) Flea*, April 15, 1869 [quotations]. In his memoirs, McConnell mistakenly recalls the trip to San Antonio as having been in 1869, but military records set it during the previous year. McConnell, *Five Years a Cavalryman*, 177; Special Order No. 107, July 7, 1868, Entry 9, General Orders, Special Orders, and Circulars, vol. 9, pt. 5: Military Installations, RG 393. NARA.

20. Regimental Returns, Sixth Cavalry, November 1870 and October 1871, Returns from Regular Army Cavalry Regiments, M744, roll 62, NARA; William H. Appleby, Neighbor's Affidavit, April 16, 1892, McConnell Pension File, RG 15, NARA; Register of Enlistments in the U.S. Army, M233, roll 31, 297, NARA; McConnell, *Five Years a Cavalryman*, 269–70 [first, second, and third quotations], 71 [fourth quotation], 81 [fifth

quotation]. The 1871–72 city directory of Fort Leavenworth, Kansas, listed one Harry McConnell as a clerk, although the veteran's reminiscences assert that after spending "a day or two" with Captain John A. Irwin, he immediately set forth for Texas. *Callis, Lynch & Edge's Leavenworth City Directory and Business Mirror, for the Years 1871–72* (Leavenworth, Kans.: Daily Commercial Print, 1871).

21. Anderson, *Conquest of Texas*; Robert Wayne McDaniel, "Jack County," *Handbook of Texas Online*, http://www.tshaonline.org/handbook/online/articles/hcj01 (accessed December 17, 2014); Robert M. Utley, *Frontier Regulars: The United States Army and the Indian, 1866–1891* (1973; repr., Lincoln: University of Nebraska Press, 1984), 207–14.

22. Llerena Friend, introduction to *M. K. Kellogg's Texas Journal 1872* (Austin: University of Texas Press, 1967). Quotations are from McConnell, *Five Years a Cavalryman*, 294–95. See also "Scientific Exploration: The Mineral Resources of Texas to be Developed," *Dallas Herald*, June 1, 1872; A. R. Roessler, "Texas Minerals," *Dallas Herald*, June 8, 1872. Many of Troutman's photographs are available as part of "Lawrence T. Jones III Texas Photographs," DeGolyer Library, SMU Central University Libraries Digital Collections, Dallas. See http://digitalcollections.smu.edu/all/cul/jtx/.

J. W. Forney, publicist for the Texas and Pacific Railroad, proclaimed, "God, in his generosity, seems to have given a share of all his best gifts to Texas. . . . The copper of Texas depends on no hypothesis, but is a fact." John W. Forney, *What I Saw in Texas* (Philadelphia: Ringwalt and Brown [1872]), 27.

23. McConnell, *Five Years a Cavalryman*, 295 [first quotation]; *M. K. Kellogg's Texas Journal 1872*, 148 [second and third quotations].

24. Benjamin R. McConnell, Deposition B, March 5, 1901, McConnell Pension File, RG 15, NARA; Ninth Census of the United States (1870), Mauch Chunk Township, Carbon County, Pennsylvania, M593, roll 1320, NARA; Tenth Census of the United States (1880), Precinct 1, Jack County, Texas, T9, roll 1313, NARA; McDaniel, "Jack County"; *Jacksboro (Tex.) Frontier Echo*, July 21, 1875 [quotations]. The memorial stone for the younger son at Jacksboro's Oakwood Cemetery provides his birth date. Following the westward push of the cattle industry, Robson later moved operations to Fort Griffin. "Frontier Echo," *Handbook of Texas Online*, http://www.tshaonline.org/handbook/online/articles/eef06 (accessed December 17, 2014).

25. Benjamin R. McConnell, March 5, 1901, Deposition B, McConnell Pension File, RG 15, NARA; Robert K. DeArment, *Alias Frank Canton* (Norman: University of Oklahoma Press, 1996), 21 [first quotation]; Ida Lasater Huckabay, *Ninety-four Years in Jack County, 1854–1948* (n.p., 1949), 109, 119–26, 268; *Frontier Echo*, March 17, 1876 [second quotation], September 14, 1877, November 23, 1877, October 5, 1877 [third quotation], October 25, 1878 [fourth quotation].

26. Appointment Date September 11, 1877 (vol. 35); Appointment Date May 27, 1881, (vol. 55); Appointment Date August 14, 1882, (vol. 55), all in Record of Appointment of Postmasters, 1832–1971, M841, roll 124, NARA; U.S. Department of the Interior, *Official Register of the United States, Containing a List of the Officers and Employees in the Civil, Military, and Naval Service on the First of July, 1881*, vol. 2, *The Post-Office Department*

and the Postal Service (Washington, D.C.: Government Printing Office, 1881), 575; U.S. Department of the Interior, *Official Register of the United States, Containing a List of the Officers and Employees in the Civil, Military, and Naval Service on the First of July, 1885*, vol. 2, *The Post-Office Department and the Postal Service* (Washington, D.C.: Government Printing Office, 1885), 650.

27. U.S. Department of the Interior, *Official Register of the United States, Containing a List of the Officers and Employees in the Civil, Military, and Naval Service on the Thirtieth of June, 1879*, vol. 1, *Legislative, Executive, Judicial* (Washington, D.C.: Government Printing Office, 1879), 439; U.S. Department of the Interior, *Official Register of the United States, 1881*, 1:731–32; Charles A. Lindquist, "The Origin and Development of the United States Commissioner System," *American Journal of Legal History* 14 (January 1970): 1–2, 9.

28. Huckabay, *Ninety-four Years in Jack County*, 143; *Frontier Echo*, February 11, 1876, March 17, 1876 [first quotation], October 9, 1875, September 13, 1878, September 20, 1878 [second and third quotations]; Jack County Tax Rolls, 1877, 1878, Jack County Courthouse, Jacksboro, Texas. By February 1879, McConnell proclaimed the Horton House as "thoroughly renovated and rebuilt." *Fort Griffin (Tex.) Echo*, February 8, 1879.

29. Emma L. Knox, March 7, 1901, Deposition F; Record Proof of Death of Soldier, Affiant Henry A. Howard, both in McConnell Pension File, RG 15, NARA; Tenth Census of the United States, Precinct 1, Jack County, Texas, T9, roll 1313, NARA; Huckabay, *Ninety-four Years in Jack County*, 244, 289, 291, 426,

30. McConnell, *Five Years a Cavalryman*, 196 [quotations]. For his descriptions of the Alamo in the 1870s, see pp. 36, 190.

31. Ibid., 59 [first quotation], 239 [second quotation], 34, 190 [third quotation], 181 [fourth quotation], 237 [fifth quotation].

32. Benjamin R. McConnell, March 5, 1901, Deposition B, Case of Jeannette D. McConnell; Emma L. Knox, March 7, 1901, Deposition F [first quotation]; R. L. McClure, October 5, 1892, Surgeon's Certificate; Henry A. Wills, March 5, 1901, Deposition C [second quotation]; McConnell, Declaration for Original Invalid Pension, April 11, 1892; and Record Proof of Death of Soldier, Affiant Henry A. Howard, all in McConnell Pension File, RG 15, NARA. McConnell to Commissioner of Pensions, February 5, 1894, McConnell Pension File, RG 15, NARA, is written on letterhead paper from the new business. In 1893 and 1894, the War Department denied McConnell's appeal for an increase.

33. U.S. Congress, *Journal of the Executive Proceedings of the Senate of the United States, Fifty-Sixth Congress*, vol. 32 (Washington, D.C.: Government Printing Office, 1909), 341; "Personals," *Jacksboro Gazette*, February 15, 1917; E. E. Hoge to H. Clay Evans, March 18, 1901 [quotation]; and J. W. Gaskin to Bureau of Pensions, May 13, 1917, both in McConnell Pension File, RG 15, NARA. Her tombstone incorrectly gives her death as 1914.

7
George Goldsby

James N. Leiker

Ellen Lynch had been denied a pension claim before. Her husband, William, had been a private in the Ninth U.S. Cavalry, serving against the Sioux Indians of South Dakota in 1890 and 1891. The irony of an African American soldier—certainly no stranger to racial oppression—fighting Native Americans during that brutal winter of Wounded Knee would not have been lost on the couple. After all, Ellen herself was a mixed-blood Afro-Cherokee. But irony was likely not on her mind in summer 1922. William Lynch had died six years earlier at their home in Fort Gibson, Oklahoma. Then, in her late fifties, with limited means of support, she had filed for a pension as his widow and had been denied on the grounds that she had never properly divorced her first husband, one William Scott, alias George Gooseby, alias George Goldsby. After Scott passed away, Ellen had another opportunity; if the Veterans Bureau would not acknowledge her marriage to the soldier with whom she had lived for twenty-seven years (Lynch), then perhaps it would acknowledge her marriage to a man she had seen but once in nearly half a century (Scott). Ellen quickly filed her claim but ran into a snag. Effie Scott, who shared William's home and bed at the end of his life, likewise claimed a widow's pension based on documents asserting their marriage in a ceremony performed by a black minister in Eureka Springs, Arkansas, in 1880. Complicating matters was the fact that Effie Scott was white, meaning any marriage to a "quadroon" (how the pension file classifies William Scott aka George Goldsby) carried no legal weight under Arkansas's anti-miscegenation laws, which federal agencies were bound to respect. Effie, however, produced records certifying that in 1886 she had remarried Scott in Kansas, a state with no such legal barrier.[1]

The contesting claims of Ellen Lynch and Effie Scott put the Veterans Bureau in quite a pickle, for in being asked to rule for one woman over the other, it had to consider complicated questions about marriage, race, and identity. In determining who exactly was William Scott's spouse at the time of his death, the bureau had to decide which of his three known marriage ceremonies—one to Ellen, two to Effie—was legally binding. If Scott was black, his 1880 ceremony with Effie in Arkansas would certainly have been nullified, thus strengthening Ellen's case. Evidence suggests that he was black, having served for twelve years in the African American Tenth U.S. Cavalry, the recruiter for which in 1867 described Scott, aka Goldsby, as "light." Still, illustrating the subjective nature of racial perception, Scott/Goldsby evidently had been light enough to enlist in a white volunteer regiment during the Civil War three years before. In that regiment of the Union Army, the "black" Goldsby served honorably as a "white" soldier against the Confederacy for ten months. Which war then defined him best, the one against slavery or the one against Indians? Was he black or white? Most crucially for the bureau's decision, was he George Goldsby or William Scott or someone else? Through eight decades of life, he transitioned from slavery to freedom, from soldier to civilian, from southerner to westerner, and through multiple names and racial categories to a degree that renders a search for any essential identity almost pointless.

Frustrating though the case may have been for the Veterans Bureau, the life of Sgt. George Goldsby—and secondarily, who was his true widow—should pique the curiosity of the social historian. From a certain perspective, Goldsby was a conqueror, but he was other things too: possibly a runaway slave; a mixed-race father of mixed-race children; a soldier who confronted racial violence; a military deserter; possibly a bigamist; an inspiration for black pride in the post–civil rights era; and, in his own lifetime, a mythic figure whose deeds became entwined with popular southwestern legend. Most significantly, Goldsby or Scott or whoever he was lived a borderless life that defied nineteenth-century understandings of race and identity. Like the typical enlisted man, he did not leave scholars much to go on—descendants' recollections, meager military records, scattered references on genealogical websites, and a great deal of literary conjecture—but he left enough to reconstruct a life that was shaped by the racial constructs of its day while simultaneously exposing those constructs' fractures.

The man whom both Effie Scott and Ellen Lynch claimed as their husband once testified that he was born in Perry County, Alabama, on February 22, 1843. This is remarkably specific considering that slaves often did not know their birthdates or, as in cases when the father was white, did not even know their precise parentage. But given that he used the name "Goldsby" during his military service, we might assume that George at least identified with the paternal side of his family and therefore knew more specifics than usual. In a 1912 deposition, he claimed his parents to be a "mulatta" woman named Hester King and a plantation owner named Thornton Boykin Goldsby. Thornton Goldsby was known in the area of Selma as a prosperous planter and horse breeder. Born in Georgia on September 14, 1796, he likely was part of the generation of white southerners who crowded into Alabama following the War of 1812 and removal of Muskogean (Creek) peoples to Indian Territory, where George would later devote much of his life. Thornton settled on a plantation named Meed Hall near Marion and gradually acquired property in Selma. One of his "white" children, also named George, was born in 1825, became a lawyer, and served in the Alabama legislature. About Sergeant Goldsby's mother, Hester, nothing is known outside of his claim that she lived between Selma and Marion and that she had six other children—Crawford, Abner, Joseph, Blevens, Mary, and Susie—with Thornton. This indicates some kind of long-term relationship between Goldsby's parents that historians of slavery would be very reluctant to classify as romantic. Actually, Goldsby seems not to have mentioned his mother having been a slave, neither Thornton's nor anyone else's, raising the possibility that he and his siblings were raised as free black people, perhaps even acknowledged by their biological father. Such would have been an oddity in antebellum Alabama, but it might explain his later ability to blend easily with whites. Whether as master or as father, Thornton Goldsby was gone early from his life, having relocated to Summerfield in Dallas County and dying on September 4, 1858, before George's sixteenth birthday.[2]

AMERICAN SOLDIER

In the racial typology of the time, Goldsby was a quadroon, meaning one-quarter black and three-quarters white. No known picture of him survives, but several sources claim him as light-complexioned, a trait that permitted him to pass among Euro-Americans and claim some benefits of white privilege. It also provided an introduction to military service. While employed as a hired servant with Lee's Army of Northern Virginia at Gettysburg in 1863, he escaped to Harrisburg, Pennsylvania, and worked for a year as a teamster in a Union quartermaster's unit. On August 4, 1864, he enlisted as a white man (albeit described as "dark" by the recruiting officer) under the name "George Gooseby" in the Twenty-First Pennsylvania Cavalry. The Twenty-First fought a number of engagements in central and eastern Virginia during Grant's final Richmond campaign. Other than his rank of private, no specifics are known of Gooseby's war record. He was honorably discharged on June 16, 1865, three weeks before the entire Twenty-First mustered out at Lynchburg, Virginia. Uncorroborated sources say that he returned briefly to Selma after the war, then departed upon hearing that he was to be lynched for his service to the Union Army. His next appearance in military documents comes on September 12, 1867, when he enlisted under the name "George Goldsby" with the Tenth U.S. Cavalry at Fort Gibson, Indian Territory.[3]

The late 1800s saw thousands of newcomers like Goldsby settle in eastern Indian Territory, where they exacerbated an already complicated situation. As in white communities, slavery and war had divided the Cherokee Nation. Since removal from the South a generation earlier, the tense relationship between Cherokees and blacks had wavered between affection and coolness. Following passage of the Thirteenth Amendment and ratification of a post-emancipation treaty in 1866, the Cherokee Nation's power to maintain its land base and determine its own citizenry dwindled considerably. Non-Indians, black as well as white, claimed the recently opened lands and pressured lawmakers to clear a legal path to full title by abolishing Native ownership. As distinctions between Cherokees, Afro-Cherokees, and newly arrived blacks began to blur, Indian leaders tried to evict all people of African descent from their tribal polities. Some even developed a certain parity with southern whites by adopting their prejudices against freedmen. Blacks for their part grew frustrated with whites' continual invitation—insistence even—that Indians assimilate. African Americans established dozens of towns and businesses in Indian Territory, illustrating what Booker T. Washington would label "self-help." Individual black men worked as soldiers, cowboys, even deputy marshals. Despite examples of entrepreneurial spirit, as one scholar claims, "White officials discouraged in African Americans the very ideals and values they so fervently sought to inculcate in Native Americans." The later Dawes regulations, besides undermining Cherokees' own efforts at self-definition, classified Afro-Cherokees as freedmen and thereby excluded them from tribal membership, laying the foundation for an expansion of segregation following statehood in 1907. Leaving Alabama for the West may have been Goldsby's attempt at a fresh start. But his arrival and subsequent marriage to an Afro-Cherokee coincided with Indian Territory's evolution from a fragmented racial atmosphere of multiple, overlapping identities toward a fixed, triangular hierarchy of blacks as subordinate to whites and Natives.[4]

In such an environment, a young man with military training and few options would have sought refuge in the U.S. Army. One year after Appomattox, Congress approved a reorganization act that authorized establishment of several new regiments comprised exclusively of blacks. By 1869, African Americans constituted nearly 10 percent of an enlarged U.S. Army through enlistment in the Twenty-Fourth and Twenty-Fifth Infantries and Ninth and Tenth Cavalries. Blacks' distinguished record in the Civil War, combined with Radical Republicans' intent to humiliate the South through recruitment of freedmen, prepared lawmakers to see the army as a tool for transforming former slaves into productive citizens. White officers, who often clashed with civilian politicians, saw it differently. As Gen. William T. Sherman wrote in 1877, "The experiment of converting them [blacks] into soldiers has been honorably and in good faith tried . . . but the army is not and should not be construed a charitable institution." The term "buffalo soldier," which probably originated with Plains Indians to describe the black cavalry, has been applied colloquially to all African American enlisted men. Yet as one study has shown, the term's popular usage began in the early twentieth century and was not used by contemporaries like Goldsby. Black soldiers were not the systematic victims of racism, singled out for institutional discrimination, that they have often been depicted as. Charged with occupying a vast western region with skimpy resources and manpower, the army could ill afford to discriminate even if it wanted to. Still, regiments were segregated by race, and commanders did sometimes consider local civilian prejudice when issuing assignments.[5] In signing on with a black regiment, Goldsby naturally made no mention of his previous Union Army experience, which would have put his racial identity and his eligibility to join the Tenth into question.

Fortunately, he joined the command of an officer with relatively enlightened views. A former music teacher, Benjamin Grierson achieved a distinguished Civil War record, which inspired his commission as colonel in July 1866. Recruitment of men and officers for the Tenth proceeded slowly at first because of Grierson's high standards. Through early 1867, recruiters' focus on the Upper South produced a pittance of only eighty enlisted men. After Grierson shifted these efforts to northern cities, the Tenth's numbers began to increase. By the time Goldsby enlisted in late summer, Grierson and his staff had organized eight companies with roughly a hundred men each. This marked the beginning of a decade of near-constant service against the Southern Plains tribes. As of 1867, Southern Cheyennes and Arapahos still hunted in western Kansas while Kiowas and Comanches launched raids against both whites and agricultural Indians in the extended borderlands stretching from Indian Territory and Texas to Coahuila and Chihuahua in northern Mexico.[6]

Assigned to Company D, Goldsby participated in no military campaigns but encountered plenty of danger and hard work during his first few years with the Tenth. He also witnessed more than his share of violence. Through 1868, soldiers delivered mail and payroll shipments from Fort Gibson to isolated points farther west, traversing areas controlled by white outlaws and nomadic raiders. Troops performing such duties were sometimes robbed and murdered, their remains discovered months later. By the end of the year, Companies D, L, and M had been relocated to Fort Cobb in west-central Indian Territory, where they guarded Indians detained during Lt. Col. George A. Custer's winter campaign against the Cheyennes along the Washita. In January 1869, Fort Cobb's role as agency headquarters for the Kiowas and Comanches was replaced by a new base, Fort Sill, near the Wichita Mountains. Fort Sill became the army's main center of control over Southern Plains tribes, and, like other black recruits, Goldsby cut and transported limestone from local quarries for its construction.

In 1872, most troopers' five-year enlistments expired. Fort Sill alone averaged dozens of discharges per month in that year, dropping its total garrison from 650 to 452 between March and October. Happening simultaneously with the Tenth taking responsibility for the western half of modern Oklahoma, Grierson authorized employment of discharged soldiers as civilian blacksmiths and teamsters. Goldsby was in the minority—about 15 percent—of troopers who quickly reenlisted and received a dollar-a-day increase for continuous service. By then, he also had been promoted to First Sergeant of D Company.[7]

Goldsby's 1872 reenlistment registry provides some detail about his physical appearance: age twenty-nine, black hair, fair complexion, hazel eyes, and six feet tall. Despite being stationed at Fort Sill, he maintained social connections to eastern Indian Territory, evident both in his reenlistment at Fort Gibson and his marriage two years later to a local freedwoman. Ellen Beck was born February 16, 1859, in the Delaware district, daughter of Luge and Tempy Beck, who had been enslaved to Jeffrey Beck, a Cherokee Indian. Family accounts describe Luge as having both Cherokee and black ancestry. Presumably, Ellen's parents—and Ellen herself at age six—were emancipated at the end of the war and joined the swelling numbers of freedmen and others of African descent. In 1874, when Ellen was only fifteen years old, her marriage ceremony to George on July 4 was officiated by an army chaplain at Fort Sill. Generally, the army refused to recruit married men, but experienced soldiers could marry with their commanders' permission. In many western forts, black women supplemented their husbands' income through jobs as cooks and officers' servants. In Ellen's case, she secured employment at Fort Sill as one of four laundresses assigned to each company, earning rations for washing men's clothes. An observer smugly claimed that the laundresses provided "care and service particularly necessary for the colored troops," implying prostitution. George and Ellen resided at Fort Sill less than a year, and in time had four children: a daughter named Georgia, and three sons, Crawford, Clarence, and Luther.[8]

Like everyone at Fort Sill, the newlyweds endured a tense social atmosphere. White infantry troops objected to being quartered outdoors while black cavalrymen, most of whom had been in the field since 1867, occupied the barracks. Officers with moral objections to the laundresses' presence—another hint at prostitution—earned black troops' scorn by trying to evict the women from the base. Grierson himself contributed to some of the problem. An advocate of President U.S. Grant's Peace Policy, he struggled to contain young Kiowas and Comanches who used their reservations to launch raids into Texas and beyond. Local civilians, journalists, and even Bureau of Indian Affairs agents directed a steady stream of abuse at Grierson's perceived lack of aggression. Following a scandal in 1872 in which he dispatched black troops to remove illegal settlers (boomers) and intervene in a dispute between factions of the Creek people, Grierson accepted a position with the General Mounted Recruiting Service in Saint Louis. His replacement had no success at improving the climate, soon embroiling the community in a host of accusations ranging from insubordination to marital infidelity among the officer class. By November 1874, Gen. Philip Sheridan personally promised to "break up the nest at Fort Sill" by transferring the Tenth's headquarters to Fort Concho, Texas, and scattering its companies. Historian Bruce Dinges maintains that Sheridan's decision to exile the black regiment and its squabbling officers to West Texas "was based more on social, than purely military, necessity."[9]

Even so, the Texas borderlands provided ample opportunity for military action. Resuming command of the Tenth in April 1875, Grierson assembled the largest military force ever to invade the Staked Plains. Led by Lt. Col. William Shafter, this combined army of cavalry and infantry—650 black soldiers in all—headed west from Fort Concho—where Goldsby was stationed—in July, and through November destroyed numerous Comanche encampments and drove hundreds of Native men and women onto reservations in the Indian Territory. The following year, Goldsby's D Company joined two other units in scouting more than a thousand miles in search of Indian and Mexican raiders who crossed the international line. Goldsby and his fellow troopers did not earn a rest until winter when Grierson treated the entire garrison to a Christmas feast. Through spring 1877, black cavalrymen worked with Seminole scouts at Fort Clark, Texas, in a border-crossing campaign against Kickapoos and Lipan Apaches in Mexico.[10] Records are vague about Sergeant Goldsby's personal involvement in these excursions, but clearly he was part of a massive, successful mission to drive independent Indians from the region and ready it for Anglo development.

THE SANTA ANGELA INCIDENT

Fort Concho and its neighboring civilian community of Santa Angela (renamed San Angelo in 1883) provided the setting for a turning point in Goldsby's life that reshaped his family's future and directed his borderless life into the realm of myth and memory. Colonel Grierson once wrote his wife that all the men in his command were more or less disgusted with the surrounding country; saloon-ridden Santa Angela attracted dangerous, degenerate characters, many of whom despised the army's presence. In 1870 alone, the town, then numbering no more than a hundred residents, saw at least seven murders. A surgeon wrote in the late 1870s that, while officers never left the garrison after dark, enlisted men squandered their pay among "human sharks who follow . . . the army like parasites."[11]

Gamblers, prostitutes, pimps, gunfighters, Mexican revolutionaries, and unrepentant Confederates created an unsavory, violent atmosphere that permeated the base itself. As at Fort Sill, officers requested removal of some laundresses because of "utter worthlessness, drunk[en]ness, and lewdness" and for stirring sexual jealousy among the men. Ellen Goldsby, a laundress in Company D, was not named specifically, but she and George would certainly have been immersed in the social and racial intrigues of fort and town. In fall 1877, a group of Texas Rangers, always resentful of federal soldiers, disrupted a dance in Nasworthy's saloon, where black cavalrymen waltzed with local Hispanics. After rangers under Capt. John Sparks pistol-whipped the soldiers, an angry group of armed blacks returned to Nasworthy's and opened fire, killing a bystander. Grierson demanded an apology from Sparks for brutalizing his men. Obtaining none, he reported the incident to the state adjutant general and got Sparks dismissed from ranger service.[12]

The Sparks affair was a mere prelude to the event that defined Goldsby's legacy. In February 1878, a gang of cowboys and buffalo hunters assaulted him in Morris's tavern, slicing the chevrons from his uniform and forcing him to leave. Goldsby returned to the post and rallied a group of followers, leading them to the company arms rack to which he had access as first sergeant. Seizing carbine rifles, they returned to the saloon and engaged the cowboys in a gunfight. A white hunter and two other civilians, as well as a soldier, Pvt. John L. Brown, were killed in the melee. G. W. Arrington, who succeeded Sparks as Texas Ranger captain, later confronted Grierson by marching across Fort Concho's parade ground, storming into the post commander's office, and demanding Goldsby's arrest and prosecution. An angry exchange followed during which Grierson challenged Arrington's authority on a federal military base and ordered him to get out. In time, a civil court indicted for murder nine black troopers, all from Company D. George Goldsby was not among them because on May 23, 1879, fifteen months after the shooting, he jumped bond and went AWOL from the U.S. Army, effectually becoming a military deserter.[13]

Desertions happened frequently in the army, and for a variety of reasons: exhausting physical labor, boredom, fear, frustration with officers—more than 30 percent of the army's total strength deserted in 1871 following a reduction in pay. Goldsby's desertion, however, seemed motivated principally by a desire to escape civil prosecution, or worse, lynching at the hands of white Texans eager to punish a black soldier who met violence with violence. Hostility at Fort Concho and Santa Angela continued well after Goldsby's departure. Two years later, soldiers retaliated against the killing of a white infantryman and a black private by kidnapping the local sheriff and riddling the Nimitz Hotel with bullets. After his troops published a manifesto promising death to any civilian who harassed them, Grierson began arrangements to relocate headquarters to Fort Davis, 250 miles southwest.[14] By then, George Goldsby—son of an Alabama horse breeder, dark-complexioned veteran of a white Union regiment, and light-skinned buffalo soldier—had disappeared for the second time in his life, assuming a new name and even a new racial identity.

Perhaps more significant than his abandonment of the army was his abandonment of Ellen. In her 1922 petition for a widow's claim, Ellen stated that she met Goldsby briefly at Fort Gibson a year after his desertion but never saw him again until decades later. Had their marriage been solid, the two could have braved a new life together as runaways; instead, Ellen returned to her laundress job with the Tenth Cavalry, relocating to Fort Davis and later Fort Grant, Arizona. Her four children with George were scattered among relatives in Indian Territory, with the oldest son, Crawford, placed in the care of a woman called "Aunty" Foster, who sent him to Indian boarding schools in Kansas and Pennsylvania. No evidence points to George having any kind of regular contact with his children or their mother, suggesting marital strife as one possible motive for his departure. On June 27, 1889, Ellen married Pvt. William Lynch, Ninth Cavalry, Company K, in Kansas City, Missouri. A native of Ohio, Lynch served previously with the Tenth Cavalry, so it is possible that he and George knew one another. After a military career that included a stint in the South Dakota Sioux campaign, Lynch opened a barbershop and settled with Ellen in her home area around Fort Gibson.[15]

BORDERLESS MYTH

In a very real sense, the life of George Goldsby—soldier, husband, father—ended with his desertion. But his central role in the Fort Concho shooting lent a luster that elevated his name to the level of frontier myth, with all accompanying exaggerations and distortions.

Part of that mythic status entwined with the lives and reputations of his children. Crawford Goldsby returned to Indian Territory in the late 1880s and reportedly developed a hostile relationship with Lynch, his stepfather, and with Mose Brown, who had married Crawford's sister Georgia and occupied a freedman's claim near Nowata. In spring 1894, eighteen-year-old Crawford shot a black man named Jake Lewis during a quarrel in a Fort Gibson dance hall. When Cherokee authorities tried to arrest him, he entered Creek and Seminole jurisdictions as part of an outlaw gang, the Cook brothers. Under the sobriquet "Cherokee Bill," he murdered more than a dozen men—most notoriously Brown, his own brother-in-law—and robbed and wounded many others. Popular western writers have found the exoticized image of a black Indian outlaw impossible to resist, emphasizing Crawford's combined Native and African American ancestry. In the words of Art Burton: "Only the color of his skin revealed his Indian blood; his features were distinctly Negroid, including thick lips and kinky black hair." William Loren Katz, author of numerous books on black western history for juvenile readers, claimed that Crawford "could travel through Oklahoma's Indian lands without fear of attack and this gave him a decided advantage over his pursuers."[16]

Crawford's violent activities coincided with vast confiscation of Indian holdings, part of the many land rushes in Oklahoma during the mid-1890s. Administrators pressured Cherokees with land claims to sell them for a onetime payment of $265.70. Crawford evidently must have owned such a claim because, while trying to collect his payment, he was arrested by a deputy marshal named Ike Rogers, tried, convicted, and finally executed in March 1896 at Fort Smith, Arkansas. One newspaper described Ellen's stoic reaction to her son's hanging: "Her parting was an affectionate one but she strove as much as lay in her power to restrain her emotion. Bill [Crawford] was affected by it, but following the example of his mother, gave little or no indication that he was other than perfectly composed." A year later, Clarence Goldsby, Crawford's younger brother, shot and killed Ike Rogers, eluded capture, and, according to family lore, enlisted in the army (likely using an assumed name) and worked as a Pullman porter until his death. In 1938, the Oklahoma Historical Society interviewed Maud Brown Surrell, daughter of Mose and Georgia Goldsby Brown, and granddaughter of

George and Ellen Goldsby. Maud harbored no resentment against "Uncle Crawford" for killing her father, claiming that Mose had mistreated him. Though her uncles' criminal careers were well-known in eastern Oklahoma, Maud believed, "If they could have had an opportunity, different environment and proper training during their younger life, they would have been different men."[17]

If local memory recalled George Goldsby as the absentee father of mixed-breed outlaws, national memory found a more honorable place for him. Artist and sculptor Frederic Remington, whose work supplemented that of his friends Owen Wister and Theodore Roosevelt in shaping and solidifying iconic perceptions of the American West, produced more than one hundred articles and stories for magazines at the turn of the century. One of these, a brief yarn titled "How the Worm Turned," appeared in a May 1901 issue of *Collier's*. Set in Cuba just before the outbreak of war with Spain, the narrator (presumably Remington himself) strikes conversation with "a big yellow infantryman," who declares his dislike of the heat:

> "A man of your color ought not to mind this hot country."
>
> "No, sah," he protested. "Ah don't belong heah. Ma father was a Mexikin white man and ma mother was colored."

After the soldier describes previous fights with "Injuns," Mexicans, and white men, Remington's narrator inquires how and where he might have fought whites. "Out in Texas" came the reply:

> "Them punchers and buffalo hunters and whiskey men didn't think no mo' of shootin' a po' nigger man than yu would of lightin' a cigarette. . . . What du yu think 'bout that—shootin' a poor soldiers, what was only 'beying orders, jus' fer fun?"
>
> "Outrageous—perfectly outrageous."
>
> "Well, that was what Sergeant Gadsby of F Troop said—'perfectly outrageous,' said he. We held a meetin' in the quarters, and the Sergeant he made a speech, and the soldiers was wild. He ended up by sayin', 'If we was men, to come on.'"

Once trust has been established with the narrator, the infantryman relates in detail the shootout in a Santa Angela saloon. "Gadsby" leads twenty-one black soldiers in single-file formation into a room filled with almost forty

Frederic Remington, *How the Worm Turned*, 1901. This painting is also known by the title *Say Boss, Ah Wasn't Thar—Ah Only Heerd 'Bout It from Men What Was.* Courtesy Richard F. Brush Art Gallery at St. Lawrence University, Canton, New York.

"Texicans." Pouring themselves whiskey, they face the bar and drain their glasses before Gadsby yells, "Bout face—give 'em hell!"

> "and every nigger turned his guns loose. Ah don't know just how it all was. Yu couldn't hear your own gun go off, and yu couldn't see nothin'. Pretty soon, Ah got to the do' by slidin' 'long the bar and thar was Sergeant Gadsby, who had it open. By this time they was only a shot now and then in the room back of the smoke, but the gro'nin and cussn' on the flo' was awful. One white man come a crawlin' tro' the smoke toward the do', and the Sergeant shot him as he lay."

Although the soldier carefully insists he was not present at the gunfight, the details he shares with Remington's narrator imply otherwise. The ending even hints that the soldier is Gadsby himself: "We knew the Texicans had the law all right, so after stables, we got on our horses with our arms, and we got whar ther' wa'nt no Law."[18]

How a writer of Remington's stature would have even known of Goldsby, and why he chose to portray him in a semi-fictional story, requires some speculation. Remington began his literary career of visiting western locales and collecting anecdotes almost a decade after the events at Fort Concho. That he would have heard about them at all suggests a certain oral tradition, with Sergeant Goldsby as protagonist. Not coincidentally, Remington's description of the soldier as black and Mexican squares with local and familial accounts from Indian Territory that (inaccurately) place Goldsby's paternity in Mexico. The 1890s and early 1900s marked the nadir for Euro-American/African American relations, with a horrific rise in lynching and racial segregation given sanction by the U.S. Supreme Court's *Plessy v. Ferguson* decision. Certainly, it is easy to dismiss Remington's story, especially its use of dialect, as bigoted stereotyping. But any account of African American men retaliating against racist violence with gunfire provides reason to rethink that characterization. During and after the Spanish-American War, newspapers and government officials openly debated the role of blacks in a post-frontier, modern army. Even Roosevelt, Remington's longtime friend, described blacks' participation in the Cuban conflict as cowardly. Remington's article presents an alternate view: black men refusing to riot or retreat but attacking calmly and deliberately, in disciplined military style. He closes with the line, "When the great epic of the West is written, this is one of the wild notes that must sound it."[19] If not a call for racial egalitarianism, Remington's aptly titled piece at least asserts that men like "Sergeant Gadsby" earned their place in military ranks, and that disrespecting them carried awful risks.

The paucity of information about Goldsby's life, especially his unknown whereabouts, fueled tall tales and conspiracy theories. The most bizarre of these linked him to Francisco "Pancho" Villa, the Mexican revolutionary. In 1910, Mexico erupted into a decade of factionalism and civil war that bled across the border into U.S. communities. Most Americans only heard of Villa after his 1916 attack on Columbus, New Mexico, which motivated the ill-fated Punitive Expedition into the Chihuahua Desert. By then, Villa's military successes had attracted attention in border areas, and oddly in black newspapers. The *Indianapolis Freeman* found curious the prolific rumors that Villa had African ancestry, while another periodical, the *Washington (D.C.) Eagle*, claimed Villa to be in actuality Henry Flipper, the first black graduate of West Point.[20]

In February 1914, the *San Francisco Chronicle* ran a story—reprinted nationwide—that identified Villa as a U.S. citizen, a native of Maryland.

In the story, W. A. Haynes, a quartermaster employee and former soldier in Company D, Tenth Cavalry, claimed to recognize Villa from his picture as George Goldsby. Another source claimed that he had crossed the border recently, met with Goldsby/Villa, and reminisced about their time together in the Tenth. Said Haynes: "He was a good soldier, although he was rather wild. When he left the Service at Fort Davis, Texas, he got into some scrape and went across the line into Mexico," became an outlaw and then a major in the Mexican army. Haynes observed, "He probably was the best professional bandit Mexico ever saw. The generalship he now displays comes, in my opinion, from his military training in the United States Army."[21] Haynes's account found its way to Indian Territory (by then Oklahoma) and prompted comment by people who remembered Cherokee Bill and his parents. Jane Thomas, an African American living in Vinita, recalled the senior Goldsby from the 1870s when her husband was stationed at Fort Sill: "It was generally talked many years ago that when Goldsby left the army he went to Mexico as an outlaw." According to Thomas, George was "a viciously bad man" who supposedly robbed and murdered a government mail agent named Jim Dooty, as well as another man with whom he had partnered in a wood contracting business.[22]

The motif of the badman who avoids punishment south of the border became a familiar trope in twentieth-century western mythology. Yarns circulated about white outlaws like Butch Cassidy and Billy the Kid, which claimed that they avoided punishment by escaping into Latin America and later died in obscurity. Significantly, that mythology provided some small accommodation for the vanished black soldier George Goldsby, who, after "jumping the border," gained fame and respect in his new identity as a Mexican bandit and general.

As frontier conquest receded into memory, these stories became embedded in popular culture, toward which Americans increasingly turned for understanding nineteenth-century expansion. Films, television programs, and Old West magazines and novels all reinforced earlier ideas about Manifest Destiny, while providing scintillating entertainment. Initially, African Americans received little attention in that narrative. For instance, in a 1955 episode of the TV series *Stories of the Century*, a white actor named Pat Hogan portrayed Cherokee Bill, with no reference to the actual ancestry of Crawford Goldsby.[23] However, starting in the 1960s, perhaps empowered by the civil rights movement, black characters began appearing more frequently in western genres. Books like Katz's *The Black West* and scholarly studies like William Leckie's *The Buffalo Soldiers* exposed a frontier past considerably more complex than a duality of white cowboys and red Indians. Novelists working in this new milieu included West Texas fiction writer Elmer Kelton, whose 1980 novel *The Wolf and the Buffalo* depicts a character with strong resemblance to George Goldsby. Set at Fort Concho in the 1870s, the story centers on a former slave named Gideon Ledbetter who heads west, joins the Tenth Cavalry, and finds himself in the hostile racial terrain of Santa Angela:

> Small as it was, that town frightened him more than the half-explored Indian lands that stretched almost to infinity beyond it. . . . Out there he seemed free from the constraints of his blackness. The land made equal demands upon all men and neither gave credit nor demanded extra for their color. In Santa Angela he was aware every minute of being black, tolerated only for the money in his pockets. Even when mouths smiled, the eyes showed hate.

Besides representing the inner fear and rage that Goldsby must have known before the famous gunfight, Kelton speculates on his relationship with Ellen. Ledbetter falls in love with and intends to marry a black laundress named Hannah, but his romantic plan goes awry upon discovering that she has been prostituted by her mother into servicing white officers and fellow enlisted men.[24]

Goldsby's mythic life continues in the twenty-first century as stories about buffalo soldiers satisfy the needs of a post–civil rights era for strong, assertive black men. In the process, storytellers have enveloped that life in a fog of rumor and fable, just as earlier storytellers did with white icons like Custer and Hickok. Fred Staff's recent self-published novel *Sergeant Goldsby and the 10th Cavalry* takes considerable liberties with Goldsby's documented past. The novel begins on an Alabama plantation where "Master Winthrop" uses George, a handsome, light-colored slave, as a breeder to produce beautiful girls who are sold for sex trafficking. After impregnating several of Winthrop's female slaves, as well as his daughter, George accompanies his master to Vicksburg and Chancellorsville. When Winthrop is wounded, George stands above him on the battlefield, gun in hand, ready to fulfill the reader's revenge fantasy:

"Now before you go, I want you to know that you are goin' a be a grandpa. That's right, your sweet little Miss Daisy is goin' to have a little nigger baby. And I be the daddy." . . .

Winthrop's eyes widened. . . . As he struggled to get to his feet he yelled, "You nigger son-of-a-bitch. I'll kill you with my bare hands. There is no nigger going to live and talk to me like that. You lying bastard, my Daisy wouldn't have a damn thing to do with your black ass."

"Well, sir, you may think that, but if you were home you could see her risin' belly, and I want you to know that I put it there, and she enjoyed it greatly."

George cocked the pistol and pushed it hard against the master's head and pulled the trigger. He didn't hesitate and he didn't give it a second's thought.

From there, Staff follows the general outline of Goldsby's known history: his brief return to Alabama, his absconding to Indian Territory, his marriage to Ellen Beck, and particularly, his service in the Tenth. After numerous adventures against outlaws and Indians, George, Ellen, and their daughter Georgia arrive at Fort Concho, where racist discrimination against black soldiers provokes the fateful shootout. In Staff's rendition, however, George remains a devoted family man to the end, saying a tearful good-bye to Ellen before deserting the army, promising he will see her again at her father's farm near Fort Smith.[25]

KANSAS FARMER

Many African American soldiers of the post–Civil War regular army fought back against civilian racism. Most have been forgotten while Goldsby's name endures. This may be partly because of his marriage to a Native American and his paternity of a famous black Indian criminal. Indeed, the interconnected lives of George, Ellen, and Crawford provide a literary vehicle for understanding intricate relations between multiple ethnic groups through the lens of one family's drama. It seems reasonable to conclude that in a world where racial and national borders separating people and groups are growing increasingly ill-defined, Goldsby's borderless life will continue to attract artists and fiction writers eager to project African American militancy or mixed-race consciousness onto the century of Manifest Destiny. There is nothing inherently wrong with such an endeavor; each generation creates a mythic past to serve present circumstances. But by immortalizing Goldsby's *mythic* life, do we lose track of his *human* one? Before the proliferation of stories lived a flesh-and-blood person who vanished from West Texas in May 1879. Did he live to mourn the execution of his oldest son, or read Remington's article, or hear his name associated with Pancho Villa? What became of that person?

We would likely never know if not for his ex-wife. In her 1922 widow's pension application, Ellen Lynch identified one William Scott of Cherryvale, Kansas, as the man previously known as George Goldsby. Cherryvale, in Montgomery County, lay less than thirty miles from Oklahoma's northern border and less than 150 miles from Fort Gibson, where Ellen lived most of her life; the father of her children had not gone far. Scott's marriage in November 1880 to a white woman, Effie Henshaw, carried legal complications. Eureka Springs, Arkansas, where the ceremony occurred, lay just across the border from Indian Territory in a state that did not recognize mixed-race marriages. Evidently, Scott sufficiently passed as white, a designation he carried the rest of his life although some sources suggest he claimed Mexican and Sioux ancestry as well. Census records through 1920 show the Scotts moving repeatedly along the Oklahoma-Kansas border, living mostly as farmers on rented or mortgaged property. The couple had six children, Florence, Peter, Frankie Emeline, Paul Thornton (the name of George Goldsby's father), Byron, and Horace. Information about his later life is vague, but Scott did attempt unsuccessfully to collect a pension in 1912, which would have necessitated revealing his previous name. In her own claim a decade later, Ellen revealed that Goldsby/Scott visited her after thirty-two years to obtain a legal divorce, which the couple never formalized. Scott must have had concerns about the legality of his union since he had remarried Effie in Cherryvale on April 15, 1886. By the time of his death on May 9, 1922, at age seventy-nine, the former soldier had spent almost half of his life as William Scott, Kansas farmer.[26]

However admirable his uncanny ability to reinvent himself, the bureau could recognize only one soldier with one surviving widow. A search in numerous jurisdictions turned up no legal proof of divorce between George and Ellen, abrogating both his marriage to Effie and hers to William Lynch.

Ellen's claim, the second one she had filed with the bureau, was successful; she was the legal widow of George Gooseby, veteran of the Twenty-First Pennsylvania Cavalry. That victory might have provided comfort during her remaining years when her health declined. Growing feeble, she moved in with her granddaughter, Maud Surrell, in Muskogee, Oklahoma, and died there on November 17, 1932. In validating Ellen's claim, the government upheld George's Civil War record, not his deserter status from the Tenth Cavalry, and likewise confirmed his participation in a white regiment and by extension his racial designation as white.[27] Strangely, the defining moment of Goldsby's mythic image—a proud black man who led other black soldiers in confronting racist violence—conflicts with the army's official record of his legal identity and of the preponderant weight of his own life as William Scott.

Of course, legality comprises only a fraction of the sum. We know that a biological person with multiple names lived from 1843 to 1922; beyond that, we know very little. Sergeant Goldsby's borderless life illustrates better than most than the salience of situational identity, the human capacity to shift modes of thought, relations with others, and even self-identification depending on circumstance. In an existence filled with border crossings of one kind or another, violence remained his only true constant. The violence of sectional war between North and South abolished slavery and provided his first opportunity to escape oppression; violence against Native Americans, and of Natives against each other, resulted in the confiscation of indigenous lands on which he spent his adulthood; his skilled use of violence made him an asset to both the Union and regular U.S. Armies; racist violence and his own reaction to it prompted his desertion and decades-long disappearance; and, finally, violence defined the image which brought fame to his most enduring alias. Whether he was Goldsby, or Gooseby, or Gadsby, or Scott, or Pancho Villa, white, black, Native American, or Mexican, the question of who he truly was remains a difficult existential one over which the historian has no special expertise.

NOTES

1. Ellen Lynch, Widow's Claim, George Goldsby Pension File, application 946600, Record Group (RG) 15, National Archives and Records Administration, Washington,

D.C. (NARA); Ellen Lynch, Widow Claim, January 21, 1924, "Decisions relating to Pensions and Annuities," Ancestry.com, http://freepages.genealogy.rootsweb.ancestry.com/~hinshaw/h15517b.jpg (accessed March 12, 2015), 438–41.

2. "Perry County, Alabama," U.S. Gen Web Project, http://www.algw.org/perry/biog4.html (accessed March 9, 2015).

3. George Goosby Compiled Military Service Record (CMSR), (Twenty-First Pennsylvania Cavalry), Adjutant General's Office (AGO), RG 94, NARA; George Goldsby File, Enlistment Documents, September 12, 1867, AGO, RG 94, NARA.

4. Murray R. Wickett, *Contested Territory: Whites, Native Americans and African Americans in Oklahoma, 1865–1907* (Baton Rouge: Louisiana State University Press, 2000), 205–10 [quotation on 209]. See also Tiya Miles, *Ties That Bind: The Story of an Afro-Cherokee Family in Slavery and Freedom* (Berkeley: University of California Press, 2005), 192–95.

5. James N. Leiker, *Racial Borders: Black Soldiers along the Rio Grande* (College Station: Texas A&M University Press, 2002), 29–30 [quotation on 30]; William A. Dobak and Thomas D. Phillips, *The Black Regulars, 1866–1898* (Norman: University of Oklahoma Press, 2001), xvi–xvii.

6. William H. Leckie and Shirley A. Leckie, *The Buffalo Soldiers: A Narrative of the Black Cavalry in the West*, rev. ed. (Norman: University of Oklahoma Press, 2003), 13–22; Bruce J. Dinges, "Benjamin Grierson," in *Soldiers West: Biographies from the Military Frontier*, ed. Paul Andrew Hutton and Durwood Ball, 2nd ed. (Norman: University of Oklahoma Press, 2009), 295–303.

7. Leckie and Leckie, *Buffalo Soldiers*, 28–29; Robert W. Frazer, *Forts of the West: Military Forts and Presidios, and Posts Commonly Called Forts, West of the Mississippi River to 1898* (Norman: University of Oklahoma Press, 1965), 120–21; Dobak and Phillips, *Black Regulars*, 268–70.

8. Goosby CMSR; "Decisions relating to Pensions and Annuities," 438; Leiker, *Racial Borders*, 85; Dobak and Phillips, *Black Regulars*, 173; Wickett, *Contested Territory*, 133–38 [quotation on 135]. Family information on Ellen Beck Goldsby Lynch can be found also at http://www.findagrave.com/cgi-bin/fg.cgi?page=gr&GRid=8814944.

9. Wickett, *Contested Territory*, 133–38; Dinges, "Benjamin Grierson;" Bruce J. Dinges, "Scandal in the Tenth Cavalry: A Fort Sill Case History, 1874," *Arizona and the West* 28 (Summer 1986): 125–40 [quotation on 140].

10. Leckie and Leckie, *Buffalo Soldiers*, 142–55; Leiker, *Racial Borders*, 49.

11. Samuel Smith, November 20, 1878, in John Neilson, ed., "I Long to Return to Fort Concho: Acting Assistant Surgeon Samuel Smith's Letters from the Texas Military Frontier, 1878–1879," *Military History of the West* 24 (Fall 1994): 145–46; Dinges, "Benjamin Grierson," 303–14.

12. Leckie and Leckie, *Buffalo Soldiers*, 164–65; Leiker, *Racial Borders*, 73; J. Evetts Haley, *Fort Concho and the Texas Frontier* (San Angelo, Tex.: *San Angelo Standard Times*, 1952), 271–73; Dobak and Phillips, *Black Regulars*, 174 [quotation].

13. The Morris saloon shootout is described in *Galveston (Tex.) Daily News*, March 1, 1878. Goldsby's date of desertion is identified in "Decisions relating to Pensions and

Annuities," 438. See also Leiker, *Racial Borders*, 88–91; Haley, *Fort Concho and the Texas Frontier*; and Leckie and Leckie, *Buffalo Soldiers*, 165.

14. Leiker, *Racial Borders*, 82–83, 90–91.

15. "Decisions relating to Pensions and Annuities," 438.

16. Arthur T. Burton, *Black, Red and Deadly: Black and Indian Gunfighters of the Indian Territory, 1870–1907* (Austin, Tex.: Eakin Press, 1991), 41–44 [quotation on 44]; William Loren Katz, *The Black West* (1971; repr., Seattle: Open Hand Publishing, 1987), 152–55 [quotation on 155]; William Loren Katz, *Black Indians: A Hidden Heritage* (New York: Atheneum, 1986), 158–65.

17. Burton, *Black, Red and Deadly*, 77–82; Maud Brown Surrell interview, Indian Pioneer Papers, Oklahoma Historical Society, Oklahoma City, http://digital.libraries.ou.edu (accessed March 10, 2015).

18. Remington's *Collier's* article "How the Worm Turned," from May 4, 1901, is reprinted in *The Collected Writings of Frederic Remington*, ed. Peggy and Harold Samuels (Garden City, N.Y.: Doubleday, 1979), 432–35. See also editors' commentary on pp. xv–xx.

19. Ibid., 435. See also Frank N. Schubert, *Voices of the Buffalo Soldier: Records, Reports and Recollections of Military Life and Service in the West* (Albuquerque: University of New Mexico Press, 2003), 114–17. On Roosevelt's description of black soldiers in Cuba and general sentiments about blacks in the military, see Leiker, *Racial Borders*, 98–107. Significantly, Remington also produced a painting titled *Done in the Open* (1902), depicting the famous San Angelo shootout.

20. Leiker, *Racial Borders*, 153–54.

21. The *Chronicle* article was reprinted in *Army and Navy Journal*, February 28, 1914.

22. *Vinita (Okla.) Weekly Journal*, February 27, 1914.

23. "Stories of the Century: Episode List," IMDB, http://www.imdb.com/title/tt0046647/episodes?year=1955&ref_=tt_eps_yr_1955 (accessed July 1, 2015)

24. Elmer Kelton, *The Wolf and the Buffalo* (Fort Worth: Texas Christian University Press, 1980), 145.

25. Fred Staff, *Sergeant Goldsby and the 10th Cavalry* (N.p.: self-published, 2014), 49.

26. "Decisions relating to Pensions and Annuities," 438; "Effie A. Henshaw," Hinshaw Family Association, http://www.rawbw.com/~hinshaw/cgi-bin/id?15517 (accessed July 28, 2016).

27. "Decisions relating to Pensions and Annuities," 438. The date and location of Ellen's death is recorded in the Maud Brown Surrell interview, Indian Pioneer Papers.

8
Emil Bode

Thomas T. Smith

A borderlands U.S. Army barracks in the latter half of the nineteenth century generally was a place of working-class immigrants from all over Europe, often near illiterate. Cpl. Emil A. Bode stood out in many ways. He was not only highly literate but was raised in very comfortable middle-class circumstances. That Bode also penned memoirs of serving in the post–Civil War army only made him stand out even more. While the bulk of frontier military personal accounts were penned by officers or their wives, Bode was an infantryman, a common foot soldier. Most of these officers and enlisted authors, diarists, and journal keepers were native-born, English-speaking Americans, while Bode was a German-born immigrant with English as a second language.

Emil Georg Adolph Bode was born in Schoenhagen, Hanover, on January 8, 1856, the son and grandson of schoolmasters. His father, Georg Heinrich Theodore Bode, died in 1868. The daughter of a master mirror maker, his mother, Charlotte Friederike Emile Forster, died a year later in 1869, leaving the fourteen-year-old Emil Bode and his three brothers orphans.[1]

The Bode boys had several uncles already living in the United States, Kaufmann Adolph Forster in Philadelphia, and George Heinrich Forster and his American-born wife, Rose, in Baltimore. In November 1869, Emil's seventeen-year-old brother Gustav took the German steamship *Leipzig* to join his uncle in Baltimore. Two years later the almost sixteen-year-old Emil departed Bremen on the same *Leipzig*, docking in Baltimore November 18, 1871. Rather than travel below decks cramped in steerage, both brothers had cabins and are noted on the manifest as merchants.[2]

ARMY LIFE

In 1877, in the aftermath of the depression and with unemployment still lingering from the Panic of 1873, Bode, at age twenty-one, briefly lived in Cincinnati and then found himself in New Orleans, apparently broke and jobless or, as he put it, "Finding myself under somewhat peculiar circumstances and my vital powers gradually decreasing without hope of a speedy relief in civil life, I concluded to go under the protecting shield of Mars and join the United States Army, with its well-fed, well-dressed, and citizen-honored sons."[3] On March 1, 1877, Bode enlisted for the required five years in Company D, Sixteenth Infantry, at the time on Reconstruction duty in New Orleans. He listed his occupation as laborer, and is described on his register of enlistment as five foot ten inches tall with blue eyes and sandy hair.[4]

The U.S. Army that Bode joined in 1877 was still very much a borderlands force enmeshed in what Secretary of War William W. Belknap called "the Indian problem," as well as an army scattered in the South and West as nation builders—protecting freedmen, enforcing the end phases of Reconstruction, running national cemeteries, improving rivers and harbors, conducting geological and mapping surveys, escorting mail and cattle drives, and building forts, telegraph lines, and roads. Reduced to 27,000 men in 1874, the army had forty regiments, ten of cavalry, five of artillery, and twenty-five infantry, the latter of which the bulk of nation building fell to. Bode recorded that he and his fellow infantrymen became "as well acquainted with handling a crowbar as . . . the manual of arms or any other military exercises." He also observed, "There is more laboring than soldiering in the U.S. Infantry."[5]

Bode's initiation in the army came at Jackson Barracks, three miles south of New Orleans, where he received a medical exam, oath of enlistment, uniforms, a first taste of rations, and introduction to discipline and fellow soldiers. Army rations he found plentiful and hardy, although apparently the coffee disappointed as it was "made by boiling the shadow of a coffee bean suspended above the pot." As for fellow recruits, with his trademark dry sense of humor, Bode noted, "Oh what a variety of humanity, from a very intelligent society man, to Darwin's missing link . . . with brains to match a monkey." A poignant observer armed with a sharp tongue, Bode saved few punches in his memoirs. He did not see much to recommend in the military training the army provided. After just a few weeks of effort, he mused, "I was considered an accomplished warrior after receiving thorough instruction in drill and the manual of arms." Bode was now qualified for guard duty, which, he lamented, "in a recruit's eyes is the highest accomplishment, a knight's last stakes to a soldier." Placed to guarding prisoners, Bode quickly lost count of those coming and going from the guardhouse, so the sergeant, "for his own good and mine," posted "me in a quiet corner to watch the woodpile." If he had any high hopes of the chivalry of a soldier's life, they all quickly vanished. On his future in the service, he noted, "I confess after seeing a little deeper under the shining exterior, was not a very brilliant one." Nevertheless, he stuck it out. "Men came, enlisted and deserted, and still I was there," Bode commented.[6]

Three months after Bode enlisted, his company was transferred to Fort Sill in the Indian Territory, and the remaining companies of the regiment were scattered to small posts across Kansas and the Indian Territory. The train journey to Caddo, in southeastern Indian Territory, took two weeks, followed by an overland westward march of 150 miles to Fort Sill. The march offered Bode his first glimpse into reservation Indian life and Native American culture. He observed the Choctaw Reservation and people, who, Bode reflected, "were further advanced than a great many whites and farmers in the states, not to mention the negroes." He also noted how the Choctaw country was overrun with lawless whites, who "impressed the Indians with a very low standard of our civilization."[7]

This march became Bode's initiation into soldiering as he discovered the dangers of river crossings, the destructive power of Great Plains thunderstorms, and the beauty of the prairie. He also first revealed his attitude concerning beauty of another sort: "Indian maidens, the most bewitching beings I ever beheld, made their appearance, mounted their ponies and were off before I knew that I was head over heels in love with one of them. . . . Cupid had sent an arrow clear through the old rusty armor of my bachelorhood."[8] Scholars such as Sherry L. Smith, who have studied army perceptions of Indians, find that soldiers' descriptions of Indian women generally fall into two stereotypes, the "Indian princess," or the "dirty squaw." Bode's perceptions, throughout his memoir, more often than not, fall into the "Indian princess" category. Typical of his passages was his observation of a young Wichita woman riding by: "Her attitude was commanding and we bowed in homage and admiration as she passed us as proud as a queen. My

Panoramic view of Fort Sill, Indian Territory, 1873, view to north from guardhouse. In the center foreground is Pvt. Emil Bode's infantry barracks, the only one built of wood, which he described as "very neglected." #P1406, Courtesy Fort Sill National Historical Landmark and Museum.

heart was rolled at this occasion." Bode's apparent lack of bigotry may be explained by the simple fact that he was an intelligent twenty-one-year-old romantic who found it difficult to develop prejudice against a pretty girl of any race.[9]

Private Bode and his Company D, Sixteenth Infantry, with all three officers and thirty-three of thirty-seven authorized enlisted men, along with Company B, arrived into Fort Sill on June 29, 1877. Fort Sill, established in 1869 to supervise the Kiowa-Comanche Reservation, was commanded by Col. Ranald Mackenzie, the regimental commander of the Fourth Cavalry, who boasted a reputation for fierce effectiveness in the field. Bode and his infantrymen would share the garrison with six troops of cavalry.[10]

In 1877, the post surgeon reported that the most common illness at Fort Sill was malaria and chronic diarrhea. Bode immediately got both. He was hospitalized for several months, first for dysentery, treated with opium pills, and then for malaria, treated with quinine. Opium pills were the military's cure-all for wounds and sickness, and, not surprisingly, addiction to opium was known as "the army disease." To his credit Bode soon realized the danger of opium and stopped taking the pills. He also put himself on a light diet that brought back his health and returned him to duty.[11]

Bode recognized pretty quickly that at a cavalry-heavy post like Fort Sill the infantry were often second-class citizens. "We were stationed in very neglected infantry quarters. . . . The only barracks there built of wood." In the army in general, the infantrymen were considered the laboring class, the jacks-of-all-trades, compared to the more glamorous cavalry or the technical-minded artillery. Water detail, weed cutting, trash hauling, fence building, and every other odd job fell to the infantry. "Take an [infantry] company of thirty-seven men," Bode wrote,

> and see how many really did garrison duty—that is guard duty and general fatigue. Subtract from these thirty-seven men: five sergeants, four corporals, two cooks, one or two servants (dog-robbers), two gardeners, one tailor and shoemaker, one clerk, about eight on extra duty detailed in the quartermaster department . . . add four or eight for daily duty in the fort and we have two to six men left to do military work for the company and fort. . . . In the cavalry companies, besides being stronger at seventy to eighty men per company, there are very few on extra or daily duty in the forts.[12]

Still, extra duty was in fact a bonus that Bode often sought to increase his income. In addition to their regular pay of thirteen dollars per month, soldiers detailed to extra duty longer than ten days as laborers, teamsters, assistant cooks, and clerks, among other positions, received twenty cents per day. For higher-skilled labor—orderlies, schoolteachers, mechanics, and carpenters—it was thirty-five cents per day.[13]

COMANCHES AND OFFICERS

In fact it was on extra duty as an assistant cook for the soldiers on guard at the Kiowa-Comanche Indian Agency that Bode soon encountered and became very familiar with the world of the reservation Comanches and Kiowas. He noted, "Many a battle had been fought by them for their liberty, but they had to gradually submit to their incarceration in the gilded cage of civilization." That a soldier such as Bode should express sympathy for the plight of Native Americans was not uncommon in the army. In fact, sympathy reached the highest echelons of the military, even those who often advocated violent measures to control independent Indians. Commanding the vast Division of the Missouri at the time, Gen. Philip H. Sheridan observed, "We took away their country and their means of support, broke up their mode of living, their habits of life, introduced disease and decay among them, and it was for this and against this they made war. Could anyone expect less?" Although known as an aggressive officer, Lt. Colonel George Armstrong Custer wrote, "If I were an Indian, I often think I would greatly prefer to cast my lot among those of my people adhered to the free open plains rather than submit to the confined limits of a reservation, there to be the recipient of the blessed benefits of civilization."[14]

In spite of this expression of sympathy, Bode must have been very aware that Indian wars were current events, not ancient history. Custer's fate at the Little Bighorn and in the hands of the Sioux had happened only the summer before, in June 1876. The fiercest warriors of Kiowas and Comanches, such as those belonging to the formidable Quahada band, had only been on the reservation a few years, since their defeat in September 1874 at Palo Duro Canyon by Colonel Mackenzie and his Fourth Cavalry. However, a Quahada group broke from the reservation in 1876 and, finally, corralled by the Tenth Cavalry, was returned to the reservation and imprisoned until August 1877. It was among this group Bode lived when detailed to the agency.[15]

Bode recounted that he was the sole soldier in this camp of Indians. "There were from twenty to twenty-five tepees in my section [which] stood in the shade of high trees on the banks of a clear cool stream, Cache Creek. . . . My abode was a picket house on the lower corner of the camp." Close by lived a young Indian by the name of Tasstaouy, whom Bode described as "the most good-hearted fellow I ever met out West." An impoverished refugee, he lived with his mother, two wives, brother, and sister, in a tepee "next to my picket house." The oldest wife "was about eighteen years of age and an exceptional beauty with very pretty eyes, but the youngest squaw the reverse of the first, in fact a mere child of eleven or twelve." Bode made a point of the fact that "we were naturally on good terms and mutual exchanges were frequent. I could enter their tepee at any time in the day or evening without running the risk of my modesty being shocked by the display of nude squaws lounging about. . . . They took their baths every day, dressed neat, and kept themselves very clean and tidy. They also used paint, like their civilized sisters, only they used red instead of black paint for the lids of their eyes."[16]

These remarks from his memoirs show how Bode had an insatiable curiosity and a keen eye for detail. He describes nearly every aspect of

Comanche life from tepees to food, to sport and hunting. Typical in its attention to detail is his image of the male fighters: "The men were well proportioned, with an awkward walk, being Plains Indians and always on horseback. They had projecting cheekbones and rather flat noses." Their dress, as may be expected, looked very curious and original to Bode. It consisted, for the men, of a breechcloth kept in place by a string or leather strap, held around the waist, while the ends fell below the knees. A pair of painted tight leggings with fringe on the seam were supported like the breechcloth and elegantly ornamented with beads. Then there was a buckskin or calico shirt and a red blanket that went around the warrior's waist when on horseback but covered the upper body and head when on foot. Their feet, Bode also noted, were covered "with a pair of beaded moccasins the style of which differed with the tribes."[17]

It seems that the appearance of Comanche warriors absolutely mesmerized Bode. Perhaps he thought he was making notes of a culture that was soon to disappear. He seemed to behave like the most astute of ethnologists when describing his new acquaintances. His narrative is extremely detailed and precise, and his attention is at times on things very intimate and personal. This was something one surely would not expect from an enlisted soldier. Bode penned, for instance, how the hair of Comanches fighters "parted in the middle and braided with cloth and scalps, ornamented with bear claws, eagle feathers, and panther teeth, was kept hanging over the left shoulder." He also noted, "Their cheeks, noses, eyelids, and tops of heads were painted with red, yellow, blue, and black circles and lines. As ornaments they wore five or six large earrings. An ornament made of bones or bear claws was frequently seen on the chest, running in four rows, each two inches wide, from throat to waist."[18]

Bode's experience was eye-opening for him in many ways. He fell for the beauty of Comanche women, thus showing his age and virility. And he portrayed the Native men as fine warriors, thus perhaps venting his frustrations and disappointments with his own military life, an experience that had proved a far cry from the kind of fighter's existence he may have dreamed of before enlisting. He also made friends among the Comanches and discovered a common humanity. If Bode had come to Fort Sill with preconceived notions of finding wild men of lower intelligence in this country, he instead found equally intelligent, generous people who welcomed him as a friend.

Although he enjoyed his time, mostly unsupervised, at the Comanche camp, Bode was eventually ordered back to duty at the fort and life in an infantry company with its routine and discipline enforced by sergeants and officers. He was not shy in opinions of officers, observing, "Lieutenants were generally good, even second lieutenants, after they lost their West Point ways." Rather curiously, he regarded the cavalry officers, as a rule, "more cordial and intelligent" than infantry officers. The former, he assured, "did not consider their West Point teachings supreme in a frontier campaign. They would listen to the suggestions of experienced enlisted men." On company commanders he had little good to say: "Among the captains were some great fellows who deserved to be put on ice instead of being in command of troops. . . . Most of the company commanders were of a kicking disposition . . . and my captain, H. A. Theaker, was one of the principal." On senior officers, Bode remarked how one of them was "a good and daring leader" but "without morals or character," while another proved "an opium and morphine eater under the strict leadership of his wife." His remarks seemed endless. He described Col. Ranald Mackenzie, "the three-fingered jack, one of the ablest fighters in the West, in my estimation the only man fit for command of troops amongst Indians. He was strict, but well liked by all his subordinates." Col. Edward Hatch of the Ninth Cavalry, he said, was a "perfect gentleman, probably a very clever general in civilized war, but against hostile Indians . . . was staying at headquarters." He noted that Col. Benjamin Grierson of the Tenth Cavalry "preferred the safe side" and that Maj. George W. Schofield of the Tenth "was a perfect gentleman, but the penny was his god."[19]

Lt. Henry O. Flipper, the first black graduate of the U.S. Academy at West Point, was stationed at Fort Sill with the Tenth Cavalry, one of two cavalry regiments with all African American enlisted men and white officers. Bode served with Flipper at Fort Sill in 1878, and again at Fort Davis, Texas, in 1881, so Bode had direct observation of and was present during the controversy involving Flipper at Fort Davis. Of the lieutenant, Bode wrote how he was met initially with contempt by his fellow officers and how "his tact kept him away from places where he was not wanted, that is, the officers' homes." Flipper's "superior knowledge and good tact soon brought him in close commune with his captain [Nicholas Nolan] who made him his confidential friend and advisor, and entertained him in his private home," Bode continued. Whenever the captain got into a scrape, his lieutenant was sure to get him out. Flipper "also proved his courage in a couple of engagements with horse thieves. While he was apparently enjoying the love of this officer and the respect of the men, his enemies were quietly at work laying snares and traps wherever he went. At last they succeeded."[20]

Bode's observation and sympathetic opinion, while admirable, does not alter the facts of the Flipper case. Like many other young and inexperienced officers, Flipper was the acting assistant quartermaster and the acting assistant commissary of subsistence at Fort Davis. Flipper discovered that he was short $1,440 in post commissary funds, possibly stolen by a servant. He covered the deficit with a personal check, but during weekly inspections led the post commander, Col. William Shafter, to believe that his status of accounts was in proper order. During an audit, the senior commissary of subsistence in Texas discovered the deficit and also the fact that Flipper lacked sufficient bank funds to cover the check. In the ensuing court-martial, Flipper was acquitted of embezzlement but was convicted and dismissed from the service for conduct unbecoming an officer and gentleman by lying to his post commander.[21]

Bode spent nearly three years at Fort Sill, a good part of it marching across the entire Indian Territory and parts of Texas. He was frequently on detached service, escorting quartermaster trains and hunting parties. During this time, he apparently neither partook nor saw many violent encounters. He became something of specialist at installing telegraph lines, however, building the line from Fort Sill to Fort Reno, and replacing with iron poles the wooden poles destroyed by prairie fire on the line from Fort Sill to Fort Richardson, Texas. The constant exposure to the risks of thunderstorms, lightning, tornadoes, bitter cold, poisonous snakes, accidental discharge of rifles, and high river crossings transformed and forged him into a seasoned and dependable veteran, evidenced by his promotion to corporal in November 1879.[22]

VICTORIO WARS

In February 1880, Company D was transferred to Fort Gibson, Indian Territory, arriving March 6, 1880, by overland march and then rail. Fort Gibson was established in 1824 near the convergence of the Grand, Verdigris, and Arkansas Rivers and served as a gateway to the Indian Territory and the frontier. The men of the company had barely unpacked and settled into barracks and quarters when they had to hastily repack their field gear and weapons in response to sudden telegraphic orders to join the Victorio campaign. On May 28th, 1880, Company D departed Fort Gibson, Bode marking his third anniversary in the service by going on an actual campaign.[23]

In 1877, Victorio, a man from the Chihenne band of the Chiricahua Apaches, with a group of three hundred, escaped the San Carlos reservation in Arizona and attempted to return to their homeland in the Mogollon Mountains and Black Range in New Mexico. Rounded up and held at Ojo Caliente, New Mexico, the group was being returned to Arizona in 1879 when Victorio made a second break and eventually established a base of operations in the mountains of northern Mexico. Leading a group of 150 in the winter and spring of 1880, Victorio raided mines, roads, and ranches in Arizona and New Mexico. Wounded by Indian scouts, Victorio returned to the mountains in Mexico in late May 1880, about the time Bode's infantry company was deployed to New Mexico. Then Victorio turned his attention to the West Texas border but was forced back to the mountains in Mexico after two bruising fights with Col. Benjamin Grierson's Tenth Cavalry.[24]

"Twenty-four hours after the notice was received we were speeding again over the country on the iron horse," Bode recorded. The train carried them due north to Emporia, Kansas, then west to Pueblo, Colorado, and south through Raton Pass, a roundabout journey of eleven hundred miles that ended on June 1, 1880, in Belin, New Mexico, just south of Albuquerque. From there it would be hard foot slogging, Bode remembered, "to do active duty against a hostile tribe of Indians who terrorized the southern section of the territory and committed depredations."[25]

Bode had no illusions about the skill of the foe. He recognized that the Chiricahua Apaches were mountain Indians and "could, when necessary, travel on foot faster than any body of whites in the country." As for their tactics, Bode did not find much to like, although he recognized the practical utility. "When on the warpath," the Chiricahua "either laid in ambush or sneaked up on his victim. . . . The Apache preferred to take their enemy unawares."[26]

Following the Rio Grande, Company D marched sixty miles south to Fort Craig, New Mexico, where the men camped, awaiting orders. At the end of June, Bode's company resumed the march, due west into the San Mateo Mountains to scout for Indians. Remote, rocky, and rugged, the San

Mateos brought tough hiking and isolation. "We experienced a feeling of separation from the rest of the world," Bode remarked. Establishing a base camp at Nogal Spring and now deep in Chiricahua country, Bode's company commander took proper protection measures for the bivouac, constructing rock breastworks, placing guards on high ground, and pushing pickets well out for early warning at night. Guarding the waterhole to prevent Victorio from using it, from this camp scouting parties scoured the mountains.[27]

After a few weeks of "running after shadows," as Bode put it, all the soldiers had to show for their efforts were half a dozen captured Apache ponies and a stray mule. Clearly, the everyday experience of borderlands soldiering had disappointed Bode once more. There were few prospects of battles, or even smaller fights, and glory seemed destined to evade Bode and his comrades indefinitely. Ordered to Knight's Ranch in the Burro Mountains of southwestern New Mexico, Bode's company was on the march once again, stopping at the first village it encountered to sell the captured Indian ponies for "ten dollars and a sack full of onions." A hundred-mile march, complete with thunderstorms and 100 degree heat, took the men through Fort Bayard, followed by the mining district centered around Santa Rita, Pinos Altos, and Silver City, where a number of soldiers got drunk as well as locked up in jail. Finally, during the second week in August, they arrived at Knight's Ranch.[28]

Knight's Ranch was a staging area for a three-hundred-man task force assembling to go into Mexico after Victorio. Commanded by Col. George P. Buell, Fifteenth Infantry, the expedition consisted of the Fourth and Ninth Cavalry companies, several companies of the Fifteenth and Sixteenth Infantries, and two Apache scout companies. Bode came to greatly admire the Apache enlisted scouts. He not only noted how "the constitution of these people and the amount of hardship they were capable of enduring was extraordinary" but also recognized that "this made them, as soldiers, superior to the white." Buell's expedition departed the last week in September and spent most of the month looking for Victorio before returning north of the international line. Meanwhile, Bode remained behind.[29]

"I was left . . . in charge of ten men to guard the ranch. Our position was not a very secure one. If the troops failed to capture the Indians they would [have] surely passed and probably given us a call," he noted. However, "being relieved of all restrictions from the presence of officers and superiors . . . we lived like lilies of the valley, nothing else to do but cook and eat." In spite of one scare when a scout found fresh signs of Indians nearby, Bode spent most of his time exploring and hunting bear and mountain lion, one of the latter of which he managed to kill.[30]

Although the Buell expedition had ended, Bode and his company spent most of October at Knight's Ranch before being ordered to return to Fort Gibson to pack for a transfer to Fort Davis, Texas. Also, in October 1880, the Victorio campaign finally concluded when a column of Mexican soldiers attacked and killed Victorio at Tres Castillos, Chihuahua. For Bode, the six-month campaign was over. Bode was somewhat cynical about the operation and the "useless occupation of chasing Indians from one section of the country to another." He had not seen any action himself and never fired his weapon against Victorio's Chihennes. Still, in the end, and in retrospect, he was also proud of what he had achieved, noting, "We started with the firm belief that some of our comrades would never return, paying the earth with their blood for the benefit of the country and its citizens. But we were safe and hearty without having received a wound from the enemy. . . . Although we were in the heart of dangerous country we had the satisfaction to know that our presence was sufficient guarantee for the safety of the inhabitants and sojourners."[31]

GARRISON LIFE AGAIN

Returning by rail to Fort Gibson in late November in a snowstorm, Bode and his company had but a few days to pack, departing for Fort Davis the first week of December 1880. With three other companies of the Sixteenth, D Company rode the rails 375 miles south through Dallas and Fort Worth, the rail ending at Eastland, Texas. From Eastland, the companies marched 250 miles on a route through Fort Concho, spending Christmas Day on the march at Grierson Springs near the Pecos River. The column traveled on to Fort Stockton, and then west on New Year's Day in the snow, arriving at Fort Davis the first week in January 1881. Established on Limpia Creek in 1854 by the Eighth Infantry, Fort Davis was one of the most important posts in the Trans-Pecos.[32]

Shortly after arriving at Fort Davis, Corporal Bode faced the most serious trial of his days on the frontier, literally a trial—by general court-martial. On the trip from Fort Gibson to Fort Davis, Bode had charge of some drunken soldier prisoners. He recounted, "During one of our rests one of the prisoners sufficiently sobered up to know what he was about, taking French leave. . . . I, as corporal of the guard, was held responsible by the officer of the day for the man's action and was subsequently tried but acquitted by a general court-martial." Bode was quite worried about the outcome, "which might have meant in this case reduced to the ranks and confined in the guardhouse for six months. I found there were some men in my company already aspiring for my [corporal's] place. . . . But they were to be disappointed in this respect." Bode was tried in February 1881 in a court-martial presided over by Capt. Nicholas Nolan of the Tenth Cavalry.[33]

This experience of court-martial was fairly common to the soldier and did not seem to affect his reputation or blemish his record. Bode's was one of nineteen general courts-martial in the Sixteenth Infantry in 1881, and one of 1,693 in the army, in addition to the 8,500 lesser regimental and garrison courts-martial for a total of 10,193 courts. On a per capita basis, this represents about 43 percent of the army's enlisted strength of 23,596 in 1881.[34]

The drain on army manpower to pursue the military judicial process is astonishing. The 8,500 garrison or regimental courts required three officers, a clerk, a defendant, probably a witness, and at least one guard for a minimum of seven personnel and at least one hour, more likely two or three. Not counting travel time, 8,500 courts, times seven personnel, times one hour equates to 59,500 man-hours or 7,437 modern man-days using the eight-hour day, of which the army worked more. The 1,693 general courts-martial required nine officers, although there were usually five to seven due to the difficulty of travel and shortage of available officers. They also required a clerk, an acting judge advocate, a defendant, several witnesses, and several guards—conservatively, fifteen personnel. These formal courts could drag on for weeks, but at a minimum took three hours to get through the legalities. Without travel time, 1,693 general courts-martial times fifteen personnel, times three hours equals 76,185 man-hours or 9,523 modern man-days. The 1881 garrison, regimental, and general courts-martial together equates to, conservatively, 135,685 man-hours or 16,960 modern man-days.[35]

Bode was at Fort Davis a few months, actually spending little time in the comfort of the fort and most of his time on detail in the field. First, he had escort duty to Fort Bliss at El Paso. Passing through a village near El Paso, he spied a bevy of Mexican beauties entering a Catholic church and he suddenly "experienced a strong longing for salvation." Entering the church,

Bode immediately drew the ire of the protective older matrons and found "the heavy cross-fire of black eyes was getting too hot for us and we beat a hasty retreat."[36]

Soon he was back to his old specialty of installing and repairing telegraph lines. Once in the West Texas mountains, he camped at a spring with a group of Texas Rangers. Bode recounted,

> They were all fantastically dressed. . . . As frontier soldiers they were far superior to [army] regulars, in fact twenty-five were . . . more efficient in and Indian outbreak than one hundred U.S. troops. . . . But this superiority was gained through their uncivilized treatment of the unfortunate beings of the Plains. Their orders were to kill every Indian on sight without pardon . . . while the U.S. troops endeavored to kill as few as possible and to capture alive if possible.[37]

While Bode was on telegraph detail in March 1881, his D Company was ordered to change station to Fort McKavett, Texas, the regimental headquarters for the Sixteenth Infantry, about three hundred miles east of Fort Davis. Fort McKavett, founded in 1852 in what was then the heart of Comancheria, was a large, comfortable post. It was also Bode's final duty station.[38]

A DOSE OF SOLDIERING

Bode was a philosophical and thoughtful individual, and once while on guard duty he reflected on what it meant to be a soldier. It was the existence of living

> far from any home, thrown in company with all classes of mankind, exposed to all kinds of weather, not knowing at what instance a bullet or arrow may pierce his heart. . . . If he has hard times for a while there are surely ninety percent sunny days coming. He is permitted to hunt and follow any pleasure he is inclined to. He can read books and papers, study all branches of science, and cultivate himself when in [the] fort. He has concerts, dances, and theaters, and selects his own companions. He does not need to worry his brains about the next meal, and if sick there is somebody to nurse him. There is no smiling

> and deceiving society to contend. . . . If he should die, no matter what place or time, he is buried with full military honors. . . . I was perfectly satisfied where I was.[39]

Corporal Bode was briefly promoted to sergeant before his discharge at Fort McKavett on February 28, 1882. On his discharge papers, the company commander noted that Sergeant Bode was "intelligent, temperate, trustworthy" and described his character as "excellent." In an era and army when one-third of the soldiers deserted and many were in the guardhouse, Emil A. Bode proved a loyal, stalwart soldier who saw his duty and did it well. Thus his five years on the borderlands came to close, five years of hard duty mixed with the occasional adventure and where, as he put it, Emil Georg Adolph Bode, "got a dose of frontier soldiering."[40]

After his discharge, Bode kept a notebook with undated draft letters to old army friends, detailed notations of very specific latitude and longitude of roads, mountain ranges, and rivers of the Southwest, as well as a hand-drawn topographic map of El Paso and part of New Mexico, as if they were the notes of a surveyor. It is apparent from the letters that he traveled by railroad, spending a lot of time in Dayton, Ohio, and Chicago. He wrote his memoir of frontier service sometime between 1884 and 1889 as he mentions that Col. Ranald Mackenzie was confined to an asylum. Mackenzie was committed in 1884 and died in 1889.[41]

Bode lived in San Antonio in 1891, working as a warehouseman for an oil company, and by 1894 was living in Philadelphia, where he remained for the next decade and a half until his death. He never married, living in boardinghouses as a lodger, listing his occupation variously as carver, sculptor, and woodcarver, the latter of which was recorded on his death certificate when he died on December 22, 1909, at age fifty-three in Philadelphia. He was buried in Baltimore, Maryland.[42]

NOTES

1. On Bode's birth and parents, see letter to author from Rolf Nowak, Archivpfleger des Kirchenkreises Uslar, Uslar, Germany, January 15, 1992.

2. *Leipzig* (ship) Passenger List, November 1869, and November 1871, Baltimore Passenger Lists, 1820–1948, M255, National Archives and Records Administration, Washington D.C. (NARA); Passenger Lists of Vessels Arriving at Baltimore, 1820–1891,

www.Ancestry.com (accessed November 11, 2011); Ninth Census of the United States (1870), Baltimore, Md., Ward 9, Household 214, M593, roll 575, NARA, at www.Ancestry.com (accessed September 26, 2012). All three documents provided by Mrs. Kathryn M. Newton, Buena Vista, New Mexico, September 26, 2012.

3. U.S. City Directories, 1821–1989, Cincinnati, Ohio, 1877, www.Ancestry.com (accessed March 14, 2014); Thomas T. Smith, ed., *A Dose of Frontier Soldiering: The Memoirs of Corporal E. A. Bode, Frontier Regular Infantry, 1877–1882* (Lincoln: University of Nebraska Press, 1994), 14 [quotation].

4. Register of Enlistments, vol. 72, 1871–1977, p. 198, Entry 118, Record Group (RG) 94, NARA; Muster Rolls, 28 February to 30 April 1882, Company D, Sixteenth Infantry, Regular Army Muster Rolls, RG 94, NARA; Smith, *Dose of Frontier Soldiering*, 4.

5. "Report of the Secretary of War, November 20, 1876," in U.S. War Department, *Annual Report of the Secretary of War* (*ARSW*), House Ex. Doc., No. 1, 44th Cong. 2d Sess., Serial 1742, 6 [first quotation], 12–13, 24, 40; "Report of the General of the Army, November 20, 1876," in *ARSW*, House Ex. Doc., No. 1, 44th Cong. 2d Sess., Serial 1742, 25; Smith, *Dose of Frontier Soldiering*, 7 [second quotation], 65 [third quotation].

6. Smith, *Dose of Frontier Soldiering*, 17–18 [first quotation], 123 [second quotation], 18–19 [third quotation], 19 [fourth and fifth quotations], 17 [sixth quotation], 19 [seventh quotation].

7. Regimental Returns (RR), Sixteenth Infantry, August 1877, Returns from Regular Army Infantry Regiments, M665, roll 175, NARA; Smith, *Dose of Frontier Soldiering*, 23, 25–26 [quotation].

8. Ibid., 29.

9. Sherry L. Smith, *The View from Officers' Row: Army Perceptions of Western Indians* (Tucson: University of Arizona Press, 1990), 55–91. See also Patricia Albers and Beatrice Medicine, *The Hidden Half: Studies of Plains Indian Women* (Washington D.C.: University Press of America, 1983). Smith, *Dose of Frontier Soldiering*, 79 [quotation].

10. Fort Sill, June 1877, Returns from U.S Military Posts 1800–1916, M617, roll 1174, NARA; RR, Sixteenth Infantry, June 1877, Returns from Regular Army Infantry Regiments, M665, roll 175, NARA; Smith, *Dose of Frontier Soldiering*, 33; Wilber S. Nye, *Carbine and Lance: The Story of Old Fort Sill* (Norman: University of Oklahoma Press, 1937), 59–123.

11. "Record of Medical History of Fort Sill, February 1873–May 1880," No. D62.137.140, Fort Sill Archives, Fort Sill, Okla.; Bernice Norman Crockett, "Health Conditions in the Indian Territory, from the Civil War to 1890," *Chronicles of Oklahoma* 36 (Spring 1958): 21–59; David T. Courtwright, "Opiate Addiction as a Consequence of the Civil War," *Civil War History* 24 (June 1978): 101–11; Smith, *Dose of Frontier Soldiering*, 42–45.

12. Smith, *Dose of Frontier Soldiering*, 32 [first quotation], 65 [second quotation].

13. Ibid., 20, 41, 43. On extra duty pay, see Edward M. Coffman, *The Old Army: A Portrait of the American Army in Peacetime, 1784–1898* (New York: Oxford University Press, 1986), 347; and Robert M. Utley, *Frontier Regulars: The United States Army and the Indian, 1866–1891* (New York: Macmillan, 1973), 88.

14. Smith, *Dose of Frontier Soldiering*, 31 [first quotation]; "Report of Lieutenant General Sheridan, October 25, 1878," in *ARSW*, House Ex. Doc., No. 1, pt. 2, 45th Cong., 3d Sess., Serial 1843, 36 [second quotation]; George Armstrong Custer, *My Life on the Plains; or, Personal Experiences with Indians* (Norman: University of Oklahoma Press, 1976), 22 [third quotation].

15. "Report of the Commissioner of Indian Affairs, November 1, 1877," in U.S. Office of Indian Affairs, *Annual Report Commissioner of Indian Affairs* (*ARCIA*), House Ex. Doc., No. 1, pt. 5, 45th Cong., 2d Sess., Serial 1800, 485; "Report of the Commissioner of Indian Affairs, November 1, 1878," in *ARCIA*, House Ex. Doc., No. 1, pt. 5, 45th Cong., 3d Sess., Serial 1850, 555.

16. Smith, *Dose of Frontier Soldiering*, 52–53.

17. Ibid., 54–55.

18. Ibid.

19. Ibid., 39–41, 165. Hugh Albert Theaker, from Ohio, was commissioned as a first lieutenant in the Sixteenth Infantry at the start of the Civil War and received a brevet promotion at the battle of Missionary Ridge. He spent his career in the regiment, rising to colonel and regimental commander in 1896. Francis B. Heitman, *Historical Register and Dictionary of the United States Army*, 2 vols. (Washington, D.C.: Government Printing Office, 1903), 1:952.

20. Smith, *Dose of Frontier Soldiering*, 39.

21. Theodore D. Harris, ed., *Negro Frontiersman: The Western Memoirs of Henry O. Flipper, First Negro Graduate of West Point* (El Paso: Texas Western College Press, 1963), vii, 18–20; Paul H. Carlson, *"Pecos Bill": A Military Biography of William R. Shafter* (College Station: Texas A&M University Press, 1989), 122–26; Bruce J. Dinges, "The Court-Martial of Lieutenant Henry O. Flipper: An Example of Black-White Relationships in the Army, 1881," *American West* 9 (January 1972): 12–17, 19, 21; Donald R. McClung, "Second Lieutenant Henry O. Flipper: A Negro Officer on the West Texas Frontier," *West Texas Historical Association Year Book* 48 (1971): 20–31.

22. Smith, *Dose of Frontier Soldiering*, 59–127.

23. Fort Gibson, March and May 1880, Returns from U.S Military Posts, M617, roll 406, NARA; Smith, *Dose of Frontier Soldiering*, 127–38; Brad Agnew, *Fort Gibson: Terminal on the Trail of Tears* (Norman: University of Oklahoma Press, 1980), 25–62.

24. Utley, *Frontier Regulars*, 369–74; Dan L. Thrapp, *Victorio and the Mimbres Apaches* (Norman: University of Oklahoma Press, 1974); Joseph A. Stout, Jr., *Apache Lightning: The Last Great Battles of the Ojo Calientes* (New York: Oxford University Press, 1974); Martin L. Crimmins, "Colonel Buell's Expedition into Mexico in 1880," *New Mexico Historical Review* 10 (April 1935): 133–42.

25. Smith, *Dose of Frontier Soldiering*, 139 [first quotation], 140–42, 143 [second quotation]; RR, Sixteenth Infantry, June 1880, Returns from Regular Army Infantry Regiments, M665, roll 175, NARA.

26. Smith, *Dose of Frontier Soldiering*, 144.

27. Ibid., 147, 148 [quotation]; National Park Service, *Soldier and Brave: Historical Places Associated with Indian Affairs and the Indian Wars in the Trans-Mississippi West.*

The National Survey of Historic Sites and Buildings, vol. 12, ed. Robert G. Ferris (Washington D.C.: U.S. Department of the Interior, National Park Service, 1971), 224–25; Robert W. Frazer, *Forts of the West: Military Forts and Presidios and Posts Commonly Called Forts West of the Mississippi River to 1898* (Norman: University of Oklahoma Press, 1965), 98.

28. Smith, *Dose of Frontier Soldiering*, 153 [first and second quotations], 154–57.

29. Ibid., 157–58 [quotation]; Crimmins, "Colonel Buell's Expedition into Mexico," 133–42; Thrapp, *Victorio and the Mimbres Apaches*, 208–209; Stout, *Apache Lightning*, 153–59.

30. Smith, *Dose of Frontier Soldiering*, 158 [first quotation], 159 [second quotation].

31. Ibid., 175 [first quotation], 162–63 [second quotation]; Utley, *Frontier Regulars*, 373; Thrapp, *Victorio and the Mimbres Apaches*, 208–209.

32. Smith, *Dose of Frontier Soldiering*, 168–75; Fort Gibson, December 1880, Returns from U.S Military Posts, M617, roll 406, NARA; RR, Sixteenth Infantry, December 1880 and January 1881, Returns from Regular Army Infantry Regiments, M665, roll 175, NARA; Fort Davis, January 1881, Returns from U.S Military Posts, M617, roll 298, NARA; Robert Wooster, *Frontier Crossroads: Fort Davis and the West* (College Station: Texas A&M University Press, 2006), 31–42.

33. Smith, *Dose of Frontier Soldiering*, 169 [first quotation], 182, [second quotation]; Register of the Records of the Proceedings of the United States Army General Courts-Martial, M1105, roll 7, vols. 15–16, PP–QQ, 1869–1883, Index No. 2285, RG 153, NARA.

34. "Report of the General of the Army, November 3, 1881," in *ARSW*, House Ex. Doc., No. 1, pt. 2, 47th Cong., 1st Sess., Serial 2010, 34, 73; "Report of the Judge-Advocate-General, October 1, 1881," *ARSW*, House Ex. Doc., No. 1, pt. 2, 47th Cong., 1st Sess., Serial 2010, 207–11; Coffman, *Old Army*, 378–79.

35. William Winthrop, *Military Law and Precedents*, 2nd ed. 2 vols. (Boston: Little, Brown, 1896), 2:1509–37; William B. Skelton, *An American Profession of Arms: The Army Officer Corps, 1784–1861* (Lawrence: University Press of Kansas, 1992), 57–58, 265–81; Coffman, *Old Army*, 197, 377–78; Robert Wooster, *Soldiers, Sutlers, and Settlers: Garrison Life on the Texas Frontier* (College Station: Texas A&M University Press, 1987), 94–97. For an excellent discussion of the practice and practicalities of these courts-martial, see Marcos Kinevan's notes and text in his treatment of the journals of Lt. John Bigelow. Kinevan, a retired brigadier, was a professor emeritus of law at the U.S. Air Force Academy. Marcos Kinevan, *Frontier Cavalryman: Lieutenant John Bigelow with the Buffalo Soldiers in Texas* (El Paso: Texas Western Press, 1998), 73–75, 79, 276n11, 277n27.

36. Smith, *Dose of Frontier Soldiering*, 180.

37. Ibid., 178–79.

38. RR, Sixteenth Infantry, March 1881, Returns from Regular Army Infantry Regiments, M665, roll 175, NARA; Fort McKavett, March 1881, Returns from U.S Military Posts, M617, roll 688, NARA; Smith, *Dose of Frontier Soldiering*, 186–87.

39. Smith, *Dose of Frontier Soldiering*, 105–106.

40. Register of Enlistments, vol. 72, p. 198, Entry 118, RG 94, NARA; Muster Rolls, 28 February to 30 April 1882, Company D, Sixteenth Infantry, Regular Army Muster Rolls,

RG 94, NARA [first and second quotations]; Smith, *Dose of Frontier Soldiering*, 5, 32 [third quotation].

41. Bode's original manuscript and typescript is at Texas A&M University, College Station, Texas, Sterling C. Evans Library, Special Collections, Western Box 2 W2. It was originally cataloged under the name Emil A. Baue. Special Collections purchased the material in 1986 from John H. Jenkins, The Jenkins Company Rare Books and Manuscripts, Austin, Texas; Smith, *Dose of Frontier Soldiering*, 5–6, 12.

42. U.S. City Directories, 1821–1989, San Antonio, Tex., 1891; Philadelphia, Pa., 1894–1899, 1901, 1904, both at www.Ancestry.com (accessed March 14, 2014); Twelfth Census of the United States (1900), Philadelphia, Pa., Ward 5, Enumeration District 102, Household 514, T623, roll 1454, NARA, at www.Ancestry.com (accessed August 14, 2014); Philadelphia, Pa., Death Certificates Index, 1803–1915, Philadelphia City Archives, at www.Ancestry.com (accessed June 3, 2014).

9
Mickey Free

Victoria Smith

In a territory renowned for memorable characters, few individuals proved to be as germane to Arizona history as the Apache captive, army scout, and government interpreter Mickey Free. While the struggle for control of the borderlands defined the fundamental relationship between Apaches and Americans from 1861 to 1886, Mickey Free played a singular and pivotal role in both the inception and the outcome of the historic contest. It was not a role he deliberately sought, nor was it one that rewarded him with fame or wealth. The illiterate Free left neither a written account of his life nor a recorded oral history. His story must be pieced together from the documents and personal memoirs that chanced to record him in his time and place.

As to his centrality to the era, there is no question, yet his remarkable life leaves one wondering how he did it. How could one boy find himself in the middle of three warring peoples—Apaches, Americans, and Mexicans—and remain the last man standing? In retrospect, resiliency of character and a measure of courage were keys to surviving a lifetime of violence and shifting identities in the borderlands. So was an uncanny ability to capitalize on the advantages at hand.

Mickey Free was born, probably around 1853, as Feliz Tellez Martinez. His home was just south of the new international boundary in the small community of Santa Cruz, Mexico, established in 1691 to convert the Sobaipuris—the easternmost and most militant of the O'odham people of southern Arizona, then a part of New Spain—to Catholicism. The village was located at the turbulent intersection of the O'odham and Hispanic domains around Tucson and San Xavier del Bac mission; the Western Apaches, who took up residence in mountainous central and eastern Arizona; the Chihenne band of the Chiricahua Apaches, who occupied western New

Mickey Free, 1885. Photo 1153. Courtesy Arizona Historical Society, Tucson.

Mexico; and the Chokonen band of the Chiricahuas, who had settled in today's southeastern Arizona and northern Mexico.[1]

Feliz was the son of Santiago Tellez and Jesusa Martinez. But to say he was born a Mexican would be too simplistic, for northern Mexico was an ethnically and racially complex borderlands. For example, 1831 Mexican census records show that Free's paternal grandfather was Juan Abad Tellez. His paternal grandmother bore the name Siriaca German.[2] In fact, the northern Mexican borderlands was awash with persons of various European descents. No matter what his racial origins, Feliz Martinez was born with comparatively pale skin, light eyes, and a reported red cast to his dark hair, facts that would play a defining role throughout his lifetime.[3]

Feliz's father, Santiago, was dead by 1858, possibly killed by Apaches.[4] In need of an income to support her children, Jesusa Martinez moved the household north across the American line to Tubac. Long a place of refuge from Apaches, by 1859 Tubac was home to Charles Poston, who would one day be known as "the Father of Arizona." In 1859, he was the deputy clerk of Doña Ana County, and Jesusa may have found employment with him.[5] Within a short time, she met Irish rancher John Ward and joined him at his ranch on the Sonoita Creek, near Fort Buchanan. The move signaled a turning point in the evolution of Mickey Free. Born a Mexican citizen on Mexican soil, red-headed Feliz Martinez made the transition to Felix Ward on the 1860 U.S. federal census.[6]

RED HEART

On January 31, 1861, Apaches raided the ranch. They took Ward's livestock and his stepson. The melee that followed Martinez's captivity became known to Arizonans as the Bascom Affair. Young Lt. George Bascom took command of the detachment sent to locate the boy. Convinced that Cochise, the most powerful Chokonen headman, was behind the raid, Bascom confronted him in Apache Pass.[7]

Cochise claimed to have no knowledge of the raid. He promised Bascom that he could locate the offending party. Skeptical, Bascom insisted on holding Cochise's family members as guarantee, but Cochise cut through the officer's tent and escaped. Bascom then hung Cochise's family in retaliation. Cochise responded by capturing and mutilating four American freighters.

The furious chief decried the notion that his word had been doubted for the sake of a Mexican boy.[8] There can be no doubt that Felix Ward had unwittingly become the boy who started a war. Among the Chiricahua, he would be called "the coyote whose kidnapping had brought war to the Chiricahua."[9] As Charles Poston aptly summed it, "The men, women and children killed; the property destroyed, and the detriment to the settlement of Arizona, cannot be computed. The cost of the war against Cochise would have purchased John Ward a string of oxen reaching from the Atlantic to the Pacific."[10]

In actuality, it was a band of Western Apaches who had raided the Ward ranch. Seventy years later, in the 1930s, the White Mountain Apache John Rope claimed that the boy had been given to his father Nayundiie, a headman among the Western Apache, as a gift. Rope considered the former captive to be his brother. In less than a decade, young Feliz Martinez had transited from the son of Mexican settlers into Felix Ward, the stepson of an American rancher; now, he was a *yodascin*, a Western Apache captive.[11] It was another step in the social construction of Mickey Free.

As a yodascin, Feliz Martinez would have adopted the clan of his captor/owner—the *ti-sie-dnt-i-dn*. Over time, the Spanish-speaking Martinez would have learned to speak Apache. As a member of Nayundiie's family, he would have heard the elder leader narrate stories of his own youth and of many raids into Mexico. At other times, Martinez would have led the daily existence of an Apache youth, training in military skills, herding livestock, and hunting rabbits and small game. And he would have depended on Nayundiie's two wives, cousins from the *biszahe* clan, to feed him.[12]

However, by 1861, powerful forces had begun to undermine Western Apache autonomy. Americans had disbursed trade goods to Apaches on the western slopes of the Santa Catalina Mountains north of Tucson in 1857, and again at Apache Pass, Chiricahua territory, in 1858. Soon thereafter, small bands had begun to collect rations intermittently at Fort Breckinridge, north of Tucson. Among the Western Apaches, hunger crept in as the newcomers stressed the Apaches' traditional hunting grounds. Hacke-ida-silah, one of the most powerful leaders of the White Mountain bands of Western Apaches, called a *nant-a-ya-ti*, a chief's talk, among the headmen, to discuss the threats to their game and water.[13]

The summer of 1864 brought drought and white prospectors seeking Apache annihilation to the region.[14] Weakened by hunger, the Apaches were unprepared for the brutal winter that followed, and, in March, 1865, Hacke-ida-silah took four hundred followers to Camp Goodwin. Among them were Nayundiie and his family, including John Rope and presumably Feliz Martinez, now about thirteen years old. Nayundiie's people had never seen white people before.[15]

At Camp Goodwin, soldiers had pity on the Apaches and fed them. According to Rope's memoir, the encounter marked the beginning of a series of changes to Western Apache political economy. He noted, for instance, how "somebody found some little sticks with red points on their ends. . . . Someone struck one against a basket. It caught fire and that was when we first knew matches." One of Rope's aunts acquired some flour from the soldiers but did not know what to do with it. Another aunt transformed it into bread in the fireplace ashes. Further, the Apache women gathered hay and kindling for the white men, and traded it for "this new food. . . . We didn't know what money was in those days."[16] After the women had traded for a substantial amount of beans and flour, Nayundiie's family returned north.[17] Later, ominously, Hacke-ida-silah surrendered land on the White River for the new Fort Apache. Significantly, the following year the chiefs promised to surrender the captives living among them.[18]

Now about to reach manhood, Feliz Martinez had watched the Apaches learn to eat white man's food and barter in an American economy that seemed to value women's labor as much or more than warrior's skills. He had learned the Apache language and had found a place in Nayundiie's family. He enlisted in the U.S. Army as an Indian scout.

BLUE COAT

The reorganization of the army following the Civil War provided for the enlistment of Indian scouts. Even prior to the reorganization, Brig. Gen. John Mason, commanding Arizona, had begged the quartermaster's department to allow him to hire Indian recruits. He claimed that he desperately needed the services of the Mexican guides, "who, having been prisoners of the Apaches, know their language and their haunts," conflating Indianized captives with Natives themselves.[19] In July 1866, the army appropriated funds for the enlistment of one thousand scouts. At the time, Arizona was allotted ninety scouts, most of them sedentary O'odhams and Maricopas, enemies of Western Apaches. A few Apache *mansos*, "tame" Apaches who had integrated into Hispanic society over the years, were also hired. This move formed part of a graduated plan to bring Indians under the regulation and control of the United States.[20] To Native men, scouting provided an income, a chance to earn warrior status, a relief from boredom in the absence of traditional venues for war, and the chance to take an active role in the protection of their families and communities. For former Mexican captives, the work capitalized on their bicultural skills. Additionally, many had married and created families among the Western Apaches, which they were reluctant to abandon.

On October 7, 1868, Gen. Thomas Devin set up headquarters at Tucson. His first order called for the mustering of a company of Indian scouts to patrol the mail route between Tucson and Mesilla, New Mexico.[21] On the same day, a manso Apache scout calling himself simply Feliz enlisted at the Tucson depot. A notation in the muster rolls indicates that this was Feliz's third three-month enlistment, implying that he had been enlisting since January 1868.[22] Though Feliz did not seem to arouse the attention of the enlisting adjutant, his reappearance in white society did not go unnoticed.

When Feliz returned to the Tucson depot to reenlist in January 1869, Capt. Reuben Bernard, who had been an enlisted man when Bascom had tried to seize Cochise as a ransom for the captured Feliz Martinez but had since been commissioned, had just arrived to take command of Fort Lowell at Tucson.[23] He alone, of all men posted in southern Arizona, would have been able to recollect the red-headed, blue-eyed, Apache-speaking scout labeled now as manso, for Bernard had been at Fort Buchanan on the Sonoita Creek at the time of Martinez's captivity in 1861. Within days, murmurs circulated about the notorious incident. On January 25, Colonel Devin recounted what he knew of the events of 1861 in a letter to a fellow officer.[24] In March, Bernard, in turn, sent a letter to Lt. William Winters, First Cavalry, the adjutant at the Tucson depot, sharing his version of the Bascom Affair.[25]

It seems likely that Feliz Martinez served in Bernard's Company G of the First Cavalry. If so, he would have been under the scout command of Manuel Duran, a manso who had been captured from Tubac about a decade before Martinez. Duran, who was older than Martinez and had a reputation for cruel violence, would initiate him into the life of Indian scouting.[26] The mansos would lay to rest some whites' fears that Indian scouts were bound to be cowardly, unreliable, undisciplined, and impulsive.[27]

In January 1870, smallpox broke out in southern Arizona. Maj. David Clendenin, commanding Camp Goodwin, sent all but a few scouts whom he had vaccinated to various posts to isolate them from the disease. Feliz Martinez was sent to Fort Whipple, near Prescott, for he next appears as enlisted scout with the Third Cavalry at that post on February 24, 1870, under the name Mickey Free. On March 1870, Free's company would transfer to Fort Grant.[28]

Irish novelist Charles Lever had published his best-selling second novel, *Charles O'Malley, the Irish Dragoon*, in the 1830s. In this work, a "loveable rogue of a man-servant" called Mickey Free played the foil to the "dashing young soldier" Charles O'Malley.[29] The character was a favorite with Irish readers, and the Arizona frontier was no stranger to Irishmen. With his red hair and light eyes, Feliz Martinez was a natural for the role, and the soldiers could not resist saddling the young captive-turned-scout with the nickname. Furthermore, at some point in his life, Martinez had lost the use of his left eye, adding to his roguish appearance.[30] The Mexican boy who became the stepson of an Irish-American rancher and the adopted yodascin of the Western Apaches, had now been reinvented as Mickey Free, an Irish Indian scout.

For the next fourteen months, Mickey Free served under Lt. Howard Bass Cushing while patrolling southern Arizona. As a very young scout, he could not have been in more enthusiastic, if pitiless, company. The indefatigable Cushing and his men reportedly killed thirty Chiricahuas who had attacked a wagon train in May 1870. The Apaches, Lt. John G. Bourke reported, were surprised by the presence of the manso scouts, unaware that they had resumed operations since the smallpox scare. Another attack on wagons in July spawned a reprisal by Cushing and his troops, although the reckless lieutenant almost drowned in the process. Two days after arriving in Tucson, they accompanied Governor Anson P. K. Safford on a scout in the San Pedro River valley, and in December they attacked Apaches at Mount Turnbull, where Bourke admired the way that Duran killed a warrior "the moment he exposed himself to his aim."[31]

Free was probably in the field when the rash Cushing—Arizona's iteration of George Custer—lost his life to an attack by the Chiricahua Apache leaders Juh and Geronimo in May 1871.[32] Free had also been in the field when the infamous Camp Grant massacre occurred in late April. The public outcry engendered when a party of civilians from Tucson butchered a sleeping camp of Aravaipa Apache women and children resulted in the assignment of Lt. Col. George Crook to the territory in June 1871.[33]

The presence of the U.S. Army, and Crook's aggressive enlistment of Indians, began to corrode the traditional balance of power among the White Mountain bands. The opportunity to attack traditional rivals under the aegis of the army or to intervene on behalf of family members, the entitlement to extra rations and a salary of thirteen dollars a month, and the ability to camp close to Fort Apache, as well as the opportunities for trade and socializing it entailed, lured Apache warriors out of their traditional power matrix. To Crook, however, such considerations were tactical: each enlistment represented one more Apache under military control, as well as one less Apache under civilian control, a serious consideration in the struggle for management of Indians between the War Department and the Indian Office. It also guaranteed the good behavior of the recruits' families on the reservation.[34]

In the fall of 1871, peace emissary Vincent Colyer derailed Crook's agenda. Colyer succeeded in establishing a reservation at Camp Verde for the Tontos and Yavapais, but after Tontos attacked a stage, Crook resumed scout enlistments in the area in November 1871. Washington responded by sending Gen. O. O. Howard, who mollified the Western Apache chiefs with promises of better management and rewarded the cooperative chiefs with a trip to Washington, D.C. In May 1872, Howard held a conference with the Aravaipa Apaches in an attempt to redeem the numerous children captured during the Camp Grant massacre the year before. Finally, in October 1872 he negotiated a reservation with Cochise, much to Crook's disgust.[35] When violence continued despite the new reservations, Crook proceeded with his long-delayed campaign. His efforts, which relied heavily on the ruthless efficiency of Indian scouts—including Mickey Free—in tracking and engaging the enemy, nearly annihilated the Tonto Apache and Yavapai resistance by April 1873.[36] Many white soldiers found themselves astounded at the proficiency and physicality of the Western Apache recruits.[37]

Posted at Camp Verde, Mickey Free, now in his early twenties, had served in the field under various commanders since his first enlistment in 1868. He had apprenticed under Manual Duran, had ridden with Cushing, and had served under Crook. He was now positioned to expand his role in the war for Arizona. On July 23, 1873, Free was promoted to sergeant of the scouts.[38] But it was at Camp Verde in 1875 that Free had the opportunity to demonstrate his exceptional value. In July of that year, the federal government ordered the Natives at Camp Verde to relocate to San Carlos. On the march, tensions erupted among the mixed company of Tonto Apaches, Yavapais, and Mojaves. The commanding officer later reported that through Mickey Free, who was fluent in both Apache and Spanish (his proficiency in English was debatable), he was able to address the leading men and diffuse the volatile situation. Not simply a scout and guide, Free could now claim the pivotal role of interpreter, a position that required that one understand what people believed and how they behaved.[39]

Free returned to Camp Verde, as testified by the quartermaster's records. There, he negotiated the cash-and-credit culture at the sutler's store for Natives still present at the fort. Between June and October 1875, Free visited the store no less than ten times, purchasing such items as buttons, hats, crackers, candles, hair oil, shirts, wallets, spurs, boots, pants, underwear, and tobacco. Clearly, his agency went beyond the bounds of army scouting.[40]

In September 1877, several Chiricahua chiefs who had been forcibly relocated from the Chiricahua (Chihenne) Reservation at Ojo Caliente in New Mexico fled San Carlos, led by Victorio.[41] The following year, in 1878, many of the Chokonens also left San Carlos, while other Apaches lined up to enlist for the campaign that was surely coming. This time, Free reenlisted with his adopted Apache brother John Rope. They reenlisted again in the fall of 1879, and for the first time, Chiricahua Apaches who had not left San Carlos enlisted with them. Now, the Chihennes and Chokonens would have to contend with Chiricahua scouts, their kin.[42]

As expected, Victorio was furious to learn that the Apache recruits were among the troops chasing and fighting him in New Mexico. He sent warriors to counterattack. At Ash Creek, east of Fort Apache, they butchered "Richard Bylas' uncle," a leading White Mountain man and his family, and continued on to San Carlos, but were unable to assault the scouts' families there. In May 1880, Gen. Edward Hatch mustered in one hundred scouts, among them Rope and Mickey Free.[43] They helped in pushing Victorio's outfit into Mexico, where Mexican troops eventually massacred the chief and his people at Tres Castillos.[44]

Following the Victorio campaign, Crook retained the best of his Apache force to function as Indian police on the newly reorganized reservations. Free enlisted with the San Carlos Indian Police in the spring of 1880. There, he found a corrupt system of trafficking in government rations with the nearby community of Globe. When he tried to intervene, Free was arrested by civilian Indian agent J. C. Tiffany in April 1881. Tiffany, however, soon found himself under federal investigation for fraud and corruption, on the spurious charge of "trafficking in agency stores."[45]

Mickey Free was not present at Cibecue in August 1881—probably because he was under arrest—when Western Apache scouts attempting to arrest a popular medicine man had to choose between loyalty to their military enlistment or loyalty to their culture and kinship relations. In the battle that followed, both Apaches and soldiers lay dead, and formerly loyal scouts found themselves outlaws on their own reservation. Americans were shocked to learn that the previously faithful White Mountain Apaches had seemingly betrayed the implicit pact with the military.[46]

Free next reenlisted on April 1, 1882, at Camp Verde, where records show that he lived with Tag Band E of the Eastern White Mountain Apaches under Chief Biulka, a successor of the aged Hacke-ida-silah. Free was listed as being of "mixed descent" and had a wife and six-year-old son.[47] He was among several companies assigned to track down the Cibecue mutineers who had escaped the melee, along with Tom Horn, a young protégé of Al Sieber, the chief of scouts at Fort Apache. The combined forces tracked the Cibecue scouts to Chevelon's Fork on July 6, 1882, where the troops dealt them a harsh blow, one that would prove to be the final battle between Apaches and the army on Arizona soil. Horn remembered, "Some of the soldiers afterwards said that there were a couple of wounded bucks, but that Mickey had stuck his knife into them. . . . I don't know if Mickey Free did this deed or not[,] but I am afraid that he did."[48]

Free, almost thirty years old, had learned to protect himself in a violent world through violence and cultivating a violent reputation. Furthermore, like the Western Apaches and the Apache scouts, Free's livelihood, identity, and future were vested in assisting the U.S. Army against those Apaches who resisted reservation realities. He could not allow room for his loyalties to be misunderstood.

CHASING CHIRICAHUAS

In March 1882, Geronimo and Chatto, two aspiring Chiricahua leaders, stopped at Ash Flat, east of Fort Apache, and brutally murdered Mexican sheepherders and their families working for White Mountain headman Dja-la-ta-ha, Ear Tips. They next made their way to San Carlos, where they compelled the Chihenne leader Loco, a strong peace advocate, and his people to flee the reservation.[49] After cutting the telegraph wires and beheading the chief of police Albert Sterling, they fled the reservation with a herd of White Mountain Apache horses, among which were the horses of Nayundiie. Nayundiie and his men pursued the raiders to the Gila River, where they found that the Chircahuas had attacked a freight train, leaving a barrel of whiskey at the scene. Nayundiie and his warriors trailed Geronimo's men until they lost the trail and then returned to the Gila and helped themselves to the whiskey. That night, Nayundiie and another of Rope and Free's relatives died in their sleep from unknown causes, presumed at the time to be related to drinking alcohol. Immediately, Apache companies were mustered in.[50] Free was already enlisted.

By the next night, scout companies and troops led by Al Sieber, Tom Horn, and Mickey Free were on the Chiricahuas' trail. By now, Free's reputation for ruthlessness was legendary. Horn observed that Free "was so reckless and loved to fight so well that he would have led those two troops right into any kind of trap and come out alright himself, for the fellow seemed to bear a charmed life." Free and the soldiers trailed the raiders across the line into Mexico, a technically illegal maneuver, but Maj. Tullius Tupper was, according to Horn, "spoiling for a fight." They engaged the Chiricahuas below the international line, and drove them into the hands of a large Mexican contingent that virtually annihilated them. The Chiricahuas had not only suffered serious defeats, but their Mexican territory, their final stronghold, had been invaded by the American enemy.[51]

In September 1882, General Crook returned to Arizona. He would place the San Carlos reservation under military control. Free would serve as first sergeant of scouts and interpreter under one of Crook's trusted men, Lt. Britton Davis. Crook also reissued General Order No. 13 of April 1873, which declared all Apaches off the reservation liable to be shot on sight.[52] The Apache enlistees, for their part, had not forgotten that the Chircahuas had murdered their kin. As clan members, they were obligated to avenge anyone murdered by outsiders.[53] At their forefront was Mickey Free, the coyote who had started the war.

However, Free's racial identity remained at issue. Prior to Crook's return, Free had enlisted in the San Carlos police again, and was listed as a half-blood. Less than six weeks later, he was discharged for "disrespectful language to the chief [of police]." The following day, Free reenlisted in the police, this time as Irish-American. Eventually the matter demanded the attention of Lt. Col. William Price, who sent a query to agent P. P. Wilcox: "Heretofor Mickey Free has been reported simply as a half-breed[;] in the descriptive list he is listed as 'Irish and Mexican.' Is he an Indian and a member of the tribe, as required by the rules governing the U.S. Indian Police Service?" Agent Wilcox replied, "He is of Irish and Mexican parentage, was born in Mexico, stolen by Indians when a child, adopted as a member of the tribe, a position he now holds in full fellowship."[54]

The boy who had been born to Mexican parents, raised by an American stepfather, adopted by an Apache father, and renamed as an Irish literary figure was now a full-fledged Irish-Mexican member of the White Mountain Apache tribe, as far as the army and Indian Office were concerned. The social construction of Mickey Free was complete.

The men he worked with admired him. Sgt. Fred Platten who was posted with Mickey Free at Camp Verde prior to his transfer to San Carlos, wrote that the "H Troop had an Indian company of thirty scouts under Mickey Free . . . [who] was said to be the indirect cause of Cochise going on the warpath years before. . . . [He] was kidnapped by a band of White Mountain Apaches who raised him. . . . Cochise tried to reason with the soldiers and explain that it was not his tribe but another that kidnapped the boy. But . . . his protestations availed him nothing." If Free's history had become the subject of common speculation, his character was also under constant scrutiny. According to Platten, "Mickey Free was a valuable ally. When it came to tracking, or other scouting duties, he had no peer. To the government, he was First Sergeant Free, scout attached to H Troop, Sixth U.S. Cavalry." It is worth noting that Platten's observations coincide with another return of Capt. Reuben Bernard, who had spent recent years fighting Natives in Oregon and Idaho, to Arizona.[55]

In March 1883, Chiricahua raiders led by Chatto captured six-year-old Charlie McComas, son of an Irish father and a Mexican mother. General Crook now had the compelling reason he needed to wrestle permission from Mexican authorities to enter Mexico in pursuit of the Chiricahuas. He recruited a record quota of Apaches, foremost among them Mickey Free, John Rope, and Nayundiie's kinsmen, and staged the campaign from the far southeast Arizona border on May 1, 1883. Free was under special orders to learn of Charlie McComas's whereabouts. Ironically, the so-called Irish-Mexican scout who had inadvertently started a war was now searching for an Irish-Mexican captive boy on a campaign that marked the final stages of Chiricahua resistance.[56]

Crook's forces followed the Chiricahuas deep into the Sierra Madre. In late May, with Mickey Free serving as interpreter, Geronimo surrendered and promised to return to San Carlos, although there was no word of Charlie McComas.[57]

Free returned with Crook to San Carlos in June 1883. There, he was surprised by a visit from his biological half-brother, Santiago Ward, a mere baby when his brother had been "stolen," as he later termed it, by Apaches. Ward left a brief recollection of what must have been a poignant reunion. "I did not know him at first but he looked very much like his sister, fair with grayish eyes. They called him Mickey Free. I do not know why." The pair spent the following year escorting the straggling bands of surrendered Chiricahuas from the border to San Carlos. At the end of what must have been an extraordinary year for both men, Santiago asked his brother to return with him to Tucson. "I tried to get him to come home and see the family but he never would do it, always made some excuse. He wanted me to stay with him."[58] Santiago did not understand what his brother knew all too well—there would be no demand in Tucson for a former-captive-turned-Indian scout and interpreter with a reputation for violence and an Apache family.

Geronimo kept his word and surrendered at the international line in March 1884. It was only fitting that Mickey Free was among those troops who escorted the Chiricahuas back to San Carlos. Rumors about Charlie McComas's presence in the crowd proved untrue, and the boy was never heard from again. But the truce with the Chiricahuas was short-lived.[59]

Tensions between military and civilian administrators of the Apaches were soon at an all-time high. On May 14, 1885, Free found himself interpreting at a dispute between a military officer and Apache chiefs over the production of the alcoholic beverage tiswin, and the concomitant violence that accompanied drinking, on the reservation. "Tell Fat Boy that he can't advise me how to treat my women. He is only a boy. I killed *men* before he was born. . . . We drank tiswin all last night. . . . What are you going to do about it?" a surly Chihuahua challenged the officer. The unpleasant exchange, mediated by Free, led to an exodus of a sizable portion of the

Chiricahuas on May 17. Once again, the Chiricahuas were hunted by the army and Free.[60]

By December, Free was serving as interpreter attached to Capt. Emmett Crawford's mobile offensive command, which consisted mainly of Apache enlistees in Mexico. When the column fell upon an Apache camp, Tom Horn testified to the commitment of Apache recruits: "One thing that worked against me was the eagerness of my scouts. I talked to them and warned them to try to keep from starting the fight as long as possible to give us better light, but they were all mad because of the raid that the renegades had made on the reservation and the killing of women and children."[61]

Geronimo surrendered once again, and in March the parties sat down to negotiate. Geronimo insisted that Free was contributing to the Chiricahuas' troubles at San Carlos, though he did not level specific charges. At day's end, some Chihuahuas returned, but Geronimo and his small following slipped back across the border. When Crook reached Fort Bowie, he resigned, deeply frustrated with the Apache situation. He was replaced by Gen. Nelson Miles, who immediately dismissed most of the Apache scouts but retained Free.[62]

With a scant thirty scouts to accompany the troops, Miles sent white cavalry into Mexico. After trailing the Chiricahuas a thousand miles south, the column lead by Capt. Henry W. Lawton was augmented by a peace envoy consisting of two reservation Chiricahuas and Lt. Charles Gatewood, who finally extracted promises from Geronimo to return by telling the chief his women and children had already been shipped by train to the East. Again, Geronimo protested that Mickey Free was responsible for his troubles at San Carlos, but to no avail. But Miles must have had his doubts. He declined to use Free as the interpreter at the proceedings. The defeated chief surrendered for the last time on September 4, 1886.[63]

Miles ensured that Free would not interfere with the negotiations by sending him with a delegation of Chiricahuas to Washington, D.C. There, Free pleaded passionately with Secretary of War William Endicott on behalf of the San Carlos Chiricahuas not to send them to the East.[64] Leaving the capital, the train headed west. At Fort Leavenworth, Kansas, it was rerouted, transporting the Chiricahua delegation to Fort Marion, Florida, where they—former scouts included—were imprisoned at Castillo San Marcos. They were soon joined by Geronimo's people and former Chiricahua scouts and their families from San Carlos. On October 15, 1886, on his return trip from Florida, Mickey Free requested and received a discharge from the army at Fort Wingate in New Mexico, and returned to his home at Fort Apache.[65]

Now about thirty-six years old, Free was not yet ready to settle into retired life. He reenlisted in May 1887, mostly policing the reservation.[66] He also assisted in the hunt for Massai, a Chiricahua warrior who had jumped the eastbound train in Missouri, and for the Apache Kid, a former scout who had shot aging Al Sieber in the leg and spent the rest of his life running from the law.[67] With age, Free lost the last of his sight, and death followed, most likely in 1915. He was interred at the cemetery at Fort Apache and later removed to an undisclosed site by his family.[68]

Mickey Free's extraordinary life was defined by a violent battle for control of transnational boundaries—Mexican, Apache, American—and by shifting personal identities born of three nations wrestling for control of the territory once known as Apacheria. Captured as a child, labeled as the cause of war by warring societies, forced to rely on violence and on arbitrarily assigned identities for survival, and all the while trapped in an apparently white man's body while identifying as a Native American, the one-eyed Mexican boy Feliz Martinez triumphed over adversity by exercising resiliency in the face of challenging circumstances and by maximizing his unique tricultural skills to their fullest advantage.

NOTES

1. Kieran McCarty, comp., *Desert Documentary: The Spanish Years, 1767–1821* (Tucson: Arizona Historical Society, 1976), 92n2; Juan Nentvig, *Rudo Ensayo: A Description of Sonora and Arizona in 1764* (Tucson: University of Arizona Press, 1980), 24–25, 79, 108–10, 139–41; Herbert Eugene Bolton, *The Rim of Christendom: A Biography of Eusebio Francisco Kino, Pacific Coast Pioneer* (Tucson: University of Arizona Press, 1984), 136, 182.

2. Eugene L. Sierras and Kieran McCarty, *Mexican Census: Pre-Territorial [Arizona]*, vol. 1, *Pre-territorial Tucson, Tubac and Santa Cruz*, and vol. 2, *Pimeria Alta* (Tucson: Arizona State Genealogical Society, 1986); Edwin R. Sweeney, *Cochise: Chiricahua Apache Chief* (Norman: University of Oklahoma Press, 1991) 71, 415n39. See Cynthia Radding, *Wandering Peoples: Colonialism, Ethnic Spaces, and Ecological Frontiers in Northwestern Mexico, 1700–1850* (Durham: Duke University Press, 1997).

3. Santiago Ward Manuscript (SWM), Arizona Historical Society, Tucson, Arizona, 2. Santiago Ward was Free's younger half-brother, and claimed that both Free and one of their sisters had red hair and gray eyes.

4. See Sweeney, *Cochise*, 71, 415.

5. A. Kinney Griffith, *Mickey Free, Manhunter* (Caldwell, Idaho: Caxton Printers, 1969) 24; Allan Radbourne, "Salvador or Martinez? The Parentage and Origins of Mickey Free," *English Westerners Brand Book* 14 (January 1972): 6.

6. U.S. Bureau of the Census, *Federal Census: Territory of New Mexico and Arizona, 1860, 1864, 1870* (Washington, D.C.: Government Printing Office, 1965); SWM, 1. Free's siblings on the 1860 census included a ten-year-old sister, Teodora, and a baby, Mary Ward. Although Free is listed as twelve years old, it is unlikely, since his mother was listed on the 1852 Sonoran census as the single head of household of her siblings, with no mention of a son. It is more likely that Free was about seven or eight at the time of his abduction. *Saint Louis Missouri Republican*, February 28, 1861.

7. Sweeney, *Cochise*, contains the most cogent evaluation of the Bascom Affair.

8. Sweeney, *Cochise*, 144–67, cites at least five instances of Cochise angrily recalling the incident between 1861 and his death in 1874.

9. Eve Ball, *In the Days of Victorio: Recollections of a Warm Springs Apache* (Tucson: University of Arizona Press, 1970), 155.

10. Charles Poston, "Building a State in Apache Land: The Story of Arizona's Founding Told By Arizona's Founder," *Overland Monthly* (July–October 1894): 293–94.

11. White Mountain, Cibecue, San Carlos, and Tonto Apaches represent the main groups of Western Apaches. Grenville Goodwin, *The Social Organization of the Western Apache* (Tucson: University of Arizona Press, 1969) 95–96, 106, 600–601, 613, 666–67; Grenville Goodwin, *Western Apache Raiding and Warfare*, ed. Keith H. Basso (Tucson: University of Arizona Press, 1971), 93, 135, 284–87.

12. Goodwin, *Social Organization*, 106, 600–601, 610, 613, 651, 654, 666–68.

13. Ibid. 5, 13–14, 22–23, 617–18; Lori Davisson, "New Light on the Cibecue Fight: Untangling Apache Identities," *Journal of Arizona History* 20 (Winter 1978): 423–44; Edwin R. Sweeney, *Merejildo Grijalva: Apache Captive, Army Scout* (El Paso: University of Texas Press, 1992), 10–11.

14. Goodwin, *Social Organization*, 14, 600, 658, 672–73, 675–76, 685; Charles Meketa and Jacqueline Meketa, *One Blanket and Ten Days Rations: 1st Infantry New Mexico Volunteers in Arizona, 1864–1866* (Globe, Ariz.: Southwest Parks and Monuments Association, 1980), 62–63; Constance Wynn Altshuler, *Chains of Command: Arizona and the Army, 1856–1875* (Tucson: Arizona Pioneers Historical Society, 1969), 37.

15. Meketa and Meketa, *One Blanket*, 64–65; Altshuler, *Chains of Command*, 44–51; James Gorman to R. C. Drum, April 5, 1865, *The War of the Rebellion: A Compilation of the Official Records of the Union and Confederate Armies* (*OR*) (Washington, D.C.: Government Printing Office, 1880–1901), series 1, vol. 50, pt. 2, 1180; Fort Goodwin, March 1865, Returns from U.S. Military Posts, 1800–1916, M617, roll 410, National Archives and Records Administration, Washington D.C. (NARA); *Santa Fe Gazette*, April 22, 1865.

16. Goodwin, *Western Apache Raiding*, 98–100.

17. Goodwin, *Social Organization*, 10, 95; Goodwin, *Western Apache Raiding*, 100.

18. Davisson, "New Light," 428; Constance Wynn Altshuler, *Cavalry Yellow and Infantry Blue: Army Officers in Arizona Between 1851 and 1886* (Tucson: Arizona Historical

Society, 1991), 144; Charles Collins, *Apache Nightmare: The Battle at Cibecue Creek* (Norman: University of Oklahoma Press, 1999), 7.

19. John Mason to Drum, June 18, 1865, *OR*, series 1, vol. 50, 1261–63.

20. A. M. Gustafson, ed., *John Spring's Arizona* (Tucson: University of Arizona Press, 1966), 99; General Orders (GO) No. 56, August 1, 1866, Adjutant General's Office (AGO), Record Group (RG) 94, NARA; Thomas L. Dunlay, *Wolves for the Blue Soldiers: Indian Scouts and Auxiliaries with the United States Army, 1860–1890* (Lincoln: University of Nebraska Press, 1982) 224–25.

21. Fort Lowell, October, November 1868, Returns from U.S. Military Posts, M617, roll 653, NARA.

22. *Registers of Enlistments of Indian Scouts*, M233, roll 70, vol. 150, RG 94, NARA.

23. Altshuler, *Cavalry Yellow*, 31–32, 375.

24. Thomas Devin to Sherbourne, January 25, 1869, Letters Sent, Department of Arizona (DA), RG 94, NARA. Sherbourne is not listed in Altshuler's *Cavalry Yellow*; consequently, Sherbourne's first name is unknown. There is some possibility that he is actually William L. Sherwood, a lieutenant who served at Camp Goodwin and Camp Lowell from 1869 to 1870. See Altshuler, *Cavalry Yellow*, 301.

25. Reuben Bernard to William Winters, March 23, 1869, Letters Received (LR), AGO, RG 94, NARA.

26. Mentions of Duran can be found at (first name unknown) McCormick to Devin, September 30, 1869, Medical Director's Office, Headquarters, Department of California, Misc. Microfilm 0214, Arizona Historical Society, Tucson (AHS); John Green to Assistant Adjutant General (AAG), Department of California, August 20, 1869, LR, AGO, RG 94, M619, roll 737, NARA, copy in University of Arizona Special Collections, testifies to his violence. These sources document him on detachment duty from Fort Grant in April 1869. Duran also appears on the Tucson census of 1870.

27. David D. Smits, "Fighting Fire with Fire: The Frontier Army's Use of Indian Scouts and Allies in the Trans-Mississippi Campaigns, 1860–1890," *American Indian Culture and Research Journal* 22 (Spring 1998): 73–116.

28. David Clendenin to Devin, March 18, 1870, Misc. Microfilm 0214, AHS. Record of Martinez's (Mickey Free's) presence at Fort Whipple is found in an original page from a Quartermaster's Account Book, in Mickey Free, the Hayden Arizona Pioneer Biography Files, Arizona State University, Tempe. The ledger page is signed by Lt. Howard Bass Cushing and dated February 24, 1870; a copy is in the author's files. Regimental Returns, Third Cavalry, March 1870, Returns from Regular Army Cavalry Regiments, M744, roll 30, NARA, reports that the company arrived at Grant on March 18, 1870. Altshuler, *Cavalry Yellow*, 91, states that Cushing and his troops arrived at Grant on March 19, 1870.

29. *Diary of John G. Bourke*, Microfilm vol. 46, prior to August 29, 1881, entry, Arizona Historical Society, Tucson; Allen Radbourne, "The Naming of Mickey Free," *Journal of Arizona History* 17 (Autumn 1976): 341–46 [quotation on 343]; Charles Lever, *Charles O'Malley, The Irish Dragoon* (London: Chapman and Hall, 1857); Lionel Stevenson, *Dr. Quicksilver: The Life of Charles Lever* (London: Chapman and Hall, 1939).

30. Packer and scout Tom Horn described Free as having "long, fiery red hair" and "one good eye," the other having been hooked by a deer. Tom Horn, *Life of Tom Horn, Government Scout and Interpreter, Written by Himself, Together with His Letters and Statements by His Friends: A Vindication* (Norman: University of Oklahoma Press, 1964), 17. One of the 1880 census enumerators, Charles Connell, said that Free had "long, tawny hair." He believed that a bear was responsible for Free's eye injury. Charles T. Connell, "The Apache, Past and Present," *Tucson Citizen*, February–July 1921 (esp. April 10, 1921). Connell did more than any one man to cast Mickey Free as an untrustworthy mixed-blood. Free's Apache brother John Rope described him as having long, red hair. Goodwin, *Western Apache Raiding*, 135. His half-brother Santiago Ward said that he had brown hair, a family trait. SWM, 1.

31. Kenneth A. Randall, *Only the Echoes: The Life of Howard Bass Cushing* (Las Cruces, N.Mex.: Yucca Tree Press 1995), 50–51, 55–59, 62–64; John G. Bourke, *On the Border with Crook* (Lincoln: University of Nebraska Press, 1971), 21–22, 33, 35, 52–65, 97, 100–103.

32. *Prescott Arizona Miner*, February 5 and February 19, 1870; Fort Whipple, January 1870, and Camp Lowell, February 1870, Returns from U.S. Military Posts, M617, rolls 1425, 653, NARA; Letter to Devin (author not clear), March 3, 1870, Misc. Microfilm, 0214, AHS; Randall, *Only the Echoes*, 50–51, 62–64; Dan L. Thrapp, *Juh: An Incredible Indian* (El Paso: University of Texas, 1973), 10–11.

33. *Fort Lowell, Arizona Territory, Letters and Telegrams Sent, 1868–1891*, RG 98, rolls 1–2, vols. 12–21, 23, NARA, in Microfilm 3748, Arizona Historical Foundation, Tempe. See Woodworth Clum, *Apache Agent: The Story of John P. Clum* (Lincoln: University of Nebraska Press, 1978), 60–61, for the Aravaipas' side of the story.

34. Smits, "Fighting Fire with Fire," 73–109.

35. George Crook, *General George Crook: His Autobiography*, ed. Martin F. Schmitt (Norman: University of Oklahoma Press, 1960), 168; Dan L. Thrapp, *The Conquest of Apacheria* (Norman: University of Oklahoma Press, 1967), 102–107; Bourke, *On the Border*, 166–67; Angie Debo, *Geronimo: The Man, His Time, His Place* (Norman: University of Oklahoma Press, 1976), 84.

36. Bourke, *On the Border*, 176–82; Thrapp, *Conquest*, 133–40, *Registers of Enlistments of Indian Scouts*, M233, roll 70, vol. 151, RG 94, NARA; Free enlisted in December 1872.

37. Bourke, *On the Border*, 183, 187, 188–201, 203, 210; H. B. Wharfield, *Apache Scouts* (n.p., 1964), 5.

38. *Registers of Enlistments of Indian Scouts*, M233, roll 70, vol. 150, RG 94, NARA.

39. Regimental Returns, Third Cavalry, March 1875, Returns from Regular Army Cavalry Regiments, M744, roll 30, NARA; Mason to AAG, March 1, 1875, Letters Sent, DA, RG 94, NARA, copy in the Mickey Free file, Fort Verde Museum; Dan L. Thrapp, *Al Sieber, Chief of Scouts* (Norman: University of Oklahoma Press, 1964), 162–69; Frances Karttunen, *Between Worlds: Interpreters, Guides, and Survivors* (New Brunswick: Rutgers University Press, 1994), xi, xii, 76, 79, 241. Free's use of English was said to be limited, for official purposes, although it is reasonable to presume that he acquired at least some use of the language.

40. Transcripts of entries on Mickey Free in the 1874–75 Ledger of the Camp Verde Sutler's Store, Verde File, Fort Verde Museum.

41. Debo, *Geronimo*, 115–17; Thrapp, *Conquest*, 177–79.

42. Debo, *Geronimo*, 117–18; Clum, *Apache Agent*, 263; John Rope, as told to Grenville Goodwin, "Experiences of an Indian Scout From the Life of John Rope, An 'Old-Timer' of the White Mountain Apaches," pt. 1, *Arizona Historical Review* 7 (January 1936): 42–50. *Registers of Enlistments of Indian Scouts*, M233, roll 70, vol. 151, RG 94, NARA.

43. Thomas Cruse, *Apache Days and After* (1941; repr., Lincoln: University of Nebraska Press, 1987), 80–81, 83–84; Rope, "Experiences," pt. 1, 58; Rope, "Experiences," pt. 2, *Arizona Historical Review* 7 (April 1936): 42, 58; Goodwin, *Western Apache Raiding*, 31n63, 103.

44. Ball, *In the Days of Victorio*, 8–60, 113; Debo, *Geronimo*, 123–25; Thrapp, *Al Sieber*, 217; Thrapp, *Conquest*, 202–203, 208–209; Shelly Bowen Hatfield, *Chasing Shadows: Apaches and Yaquis along the United States–Mexican Border, 1876–1911* (Albuquerque: University of New Mexico Press, 1998), 39.

45. Radbourne, "Salvadore or Martinez?," 20; Records of the San Carlos Indian Police, June–October 1881, vol. 153, RG 75, NARA. These records indicate that Free was abruptly discharged after a two-and-a-half-month enlistment on June 30, 1881. He did not reenlist again until October 1, 1881; this irregularity probably reflects the dates of his incarceration. See also V. Keith Thorne, *White Eyes, Long Knives, and Renegade Indians* (Sedona, Ariz.: Thorne Enterprises, 1993), 30; Collins, *Apache Nightmare*, 222; Thrapp, *Conquest*, 257–59.

46. Horn, *Life of Tom Horn*, 78; Thrapp, *Conquest*, 21, 226, 232; Thrapp, *Al Sieber*, 220–21; William B. Kessell, "The Battle of Cibecue and its Aftermath: A White Mountain Apache's Account," *Ethnohistory* 21 (Spring 1974): 123–34; Cruse, *Apache Days*, 11, 53, 54, 118–19; Collins, *Apache Nightmare*, 67, 242n47, 249n23; Dan L. Thrapp, *The Encyclopedia of Frontier Biography*, 3 vols. (Lincoln: University of Nebraska Press, 1991), 3:1289; Will C. Barnes, *Apaches and Longhorns: The Reminiscences of Will C. Barnes* (Los Angeles: Ward Ritchie Press, 1941), 55–56; Bourke, *On the Border*, 178–79.

47. *Records of the San Carlos Indian Police*, vol. 153, RG 75, NARA. Both Free and Rope enlisted at San Carlos under Lt. Wallace Clark—Free as a sergeant on April 1, 1882; Horn, *Life of Tom Horn*, 80, 93; Goodwin, *Social Organization*, 577; *Tucson Arizona Daily Star*, October 24, 1882.

48. Horn, *Life of Tom Horn*, 87.

49. Thrapp, *Conquest*, 235–38; Thrapp, *Al Sieber*, 223–24; Rope, "Experiences," pt. 2, 44; Goodwin, *Social Organization*, 579, 658, 676.

50. Rope, "Experiences," pt. 2, 44–48.

51. Horn, *Life of Tom Horn*, 48, 63; Horn confused the Tupper Battle with the Battle of Chevelon's Fork.

52. Thrapp, *Conquest*, 259–61, 263–64; Thrapp, *Al Sieber*, 259, 264; Bourke, *On the Border*, 435.

53. Goodwin, *Social Organization*, 97, 179, 673.

54. Photocopies of this exchange, taken from *Records of the San Carlos Indian Police*, RG 75, NARA, form the core of the Mickey Free manuscript collection at Arizona Historical Society, Tucson.

55. Fred Platten, *Ten Years on the Trail of the Redskins* (Williams, Ariz.: Williams New Press, 1959), 28. I have corrected his spelling. On Bernard, see Altshuler, *Cavalry Yellow*, 32.

56. Devine manuscript, first name unknown, origin unknown, most likely The Arizona Historical Foundation, file mark 11, ff4, D519, copy in author's possession; Thrapp, *Conquest*, 257, 270.

57. SWM, 2; Rope, "Experiences," pt. 2, 68–71; Thrapp, *Conquest*, 288–91; John G. Bourke, *An Apache Campaign in the Sierra Madre* (New York: Scribner's, 1958), 82–99; GO No. 10, DA, reprinted in *Arizona Daily Star*, June 20, 1883, states that Free was among several men commended by Crook for their roles in the campaign.

58. SWM, 3.

59. *Phoenix Arizona Gazette*, May 1, 1884. The unknown fate of Charley McComas led to years of speculation among Arizonans both Apache and white, and ranged from death at the hands of the Chiricahuas to his survival deep in the Sierra Madre. Subsequent decades spawned several attempts by private parties to locate his presumed descendants in Mexico. See, for example, Victoria Smith, *Captive Arizona, 1851–1900* (Lincoln: University of Nebraska Press, 2009), and Grenville Goodwin and Neil Goodwin, *The Apache Diaries: A Father-Son Journey* (Lincoln: University of Nebraska Press, 2000), for details.

60. Britton Davis, *The Truth about Geronimo* (New Haven: Yale University Press, 1929), 138–46 [quotation on 138]; Ralph. H. Ogle, *Federal Control of the Western Apache, 1848–1886* (Albuquerque: University of New Mexico Press, 1940), 227–28.

61. Davis, *Truth about Geronimo*, 197; Horn, *Life of Tom Horn*, 175–76, 184–96.

62. Bourke, *On the Border*, 476; Davis, *Truth about Geronimo*, 200–18; Horn, *Life of Tom Horn*, 201; John Bigelow, Jr., *On the Bloody Trail of Geronimo* (Los Angeles: Westernlore Press, 1998), 182–83.

63. Davis, *Truth about Geronimo*, 220–24; Anton Mazzanovich, *Trailing Geronimo* (Los Angeles: Gem Publications, 1926), 51–56; Debo, *Geronimo*, 291–98.

64. "Apache Indians," Senate Ex. Doc. No. 35, 51st Congress, 1st Sess., Serial 2682, 35–36, 41, 44, 48; "Report of the Secretary of War, November 30, 1886," in U.S. War Department, *Annual Report of the Secretary of War*, House Ex. Doc. No. 1, 49th Cong., 2d Sess., Serial 2461, 14.

65. Debo, *Geronimo*, 276–78, 316; *Registers of Enlistments of Indian Scouts*, M233, roll 70, vol. 153, RG 94, NARA.

66. *Registers of Enlistments of Indian Scouts*, M233, roll 70, Vol. 154, RG 94, NARA; Rope, "Experiences," pt. 2, 73.

67. Thrapp, *Al Sieber*, 320–41; Jason Betzinez, with Wilbur Sturtevant Nye, *I Fought with Geronimo* (1959; repr., Lincoln: University of Nebraska Press, 1987), 144–45; Frederick Remington, *Crooked Trails* (New York: Harper, 1923).

68. Radbourne, "Salvadore or Martinez?," 24n62; Griffith, *Mickey Free*, 217.

10
John Rope

Janne Lahti

In April 1883, hundreds of U.S. Army troops flocked to the San Bernardino Ranch in southeastern Arizona near the Mexican border. Set to embark on a potentially perilous campaign, their destination was the lofty Sierra Madre of northern Mexico. Their target: the Chiricahua Apaches, who, after rejecting reservation life in the United States, had executed such effective raids across the borderlands that the federal authorities regarded them a serious danger to the development of white settlement and industries in the region. One of the men at San Bernardino was John Rope, a White Mountain Apache and already an experienced enlistee. In fact, the majority of U.S. troops who left San Bernardino for Mexico were Apaches. Rope later told the ethnologist Grenville Goodwin, who interviewed Rope and many of his contemporaries in Arizona in the 1930s, that he was at the ranch "in order to help the Whites against the Chiricahuas because they had killed a lot of people."[1]

WHITE MOUNTAIN APACHE WORLD IN TRANSITION

Tlodilhil ("black rope") or John Rope was born around 1855 (and possibly as late as 1863) somewhere between the Black River and Old Summit in what is today central Arizona south of the Mogollon Rim. Although he lost his mother while still young, Rope grew up with many siblings, one of whom was the adopted captive Mickey Free. His father, Nayundiie, was a leader in the *ti-sie-dnt-i-dn* clan. For the most part, Rope's White Mountain Apache local group lived at Cedar Creek, west of what would become Fort Apache and east and north of many other Western Apache communities.[2] While the land Rope and his community occupied was broken into deep valleys and high timbered ranges with relatively limited rainfall, it was still rich in diversity. Streams allowed an opening for farming corn, pumpkins, squash, and other crops, and as a young man Rope grew to comprehend the importance of spring planting, digging of ditches, and building of dams, communal affairs in which both the women and the men took part. When corn formed ears, Rope and his people usually traversed south of the Black River to gather acorns, from where they returned for the corn harvest. Later in the fall they organized outings to pick juniper berries, while the gathering of mescal at its most optimal locations peaked at springtime.[3]

It was usually easier for Rope and his community to obtain a livelihood near home by planting, gathering, and hunting than by raiding distant peoples. Still, raiding and military skills mattered a great deal even though Rope's homelands were somewhat removed from the Spanish communities and the hotbeds of borderlands violence at Santa Rita, along the Rio Grande, and in northern Sonora and Chihuahua. Rope learned early in life that each Apache community inhabited its own territory and made its own choices when it came to war and peace. He also saw how the interaction between different Apache peoples and between the Apaches and their indigenous and Hispanic neighbors constantly evolved between avoidance, cooperation, and antagonism. While clan relations mattered and clan members from different Western Apache communities could be close, Rope remembered that in his childhood only important men, such as his father, were allowed to visit "with outside people" like the San Carlos Apaches or the Zuni Pueblos. It is more than likely that, before his enlistment, Rope had little if any personal relationships with the Chiricahua Apaches—who did not have clans—he would later fight against.[4]

Learning his kin and communal obligations, Rope, like most Apache boys, was expected to master rigorous fighter training. The Apache regimen was more than a fitness program for personal health; it was a community-driven, well-ordered, and methodically planned and executed maintenance for struggle and conflict today and tomorrow. From an early age, Rope went through a preparation that involved lots of running and climbing designed to advance endurance, as well as wrestling and practice fights to improve muscle strength and coordination. Riding, weapons crafting and use, and lessons on natural bounty and terrain were also part of the repertoire performed under the supervision of veteran trainers. So was mental coaching and tactical instruction on different combat scenarios. Rope must have realized that to be a respectable adult in his community he needed to learn warrior skills. He also needed to comprehend that, while a man should only trust himself in a world filled with enemies, he was still to behave in a manner that would contribute to the material welfare and reputation of his family and community. Training also grew steadily more challenging until it climaxed with the *dikohe* trials during which a youngster, by excelling in four raids, proved he had what it took to become a man.[5]

When interviewed by Goodwin, Rope and his fellow Western Apaches spoke plenty of daring raids into Mexico. While only a few of them had any personal experience, Goodwin's informants showed how stories of Apache exploits in Mexico circulated and how these accounts were passed from one generation to the next. Rope described how, as a young man, his father had wanted to prove his worth and had first "tried himself out," testing his strength and endurance on his own at home to see if he was ready for Mexico. "I was tough enough for it, and I showed them," Rope remembered his father saying. Ignoring the objections others raised of his young age and lack of experience, Rope's father not only went to Mexico but raided successfully. As a consequence, he, in Rope's words, gained respect and a good reputation, proving that he was a man to be taken seriously and someone who could be considered a leader. The implications in Rope's narration are apparent: for a White Mountain Apache man, raiding in Mexico was not merely a bold and thrilling endeavor but something of a requisite element of his manhood.[6]

By the time Rope was old enough to raid in the mid-1870s, the traditional avenues had all been blocked by the Americans and their reservation system. In fact, Rope identified the last time his people raided in Mexico as sometime in the mid-1860s. It had been a miserable failure with several Apaches killed, thus serving as a warning of the risks involved.[7] Whether his timing is accurate or not, it is obvious that Rope had missed out. In addition, Rope could not claim his manhood by raiding the O'odhams, Navajos, or Yavapais, who were all subject to American control by the 1870s. The Hispanic and Anglo communities were also off limits, at least for an Apache who did not want to fight the U.S. Army troops occupying the territories. Rope had to seek alternate paths to manhood than the traditional ones sought by the previous generation.

Rope was yet a boy when he noticed the white newcomers as they established Camp Goodwin in 1864 on the Gila River between the Gila Mountains and the Santa Teresa Mountains. It was not military pressure or violence but curiosity that, according to Rope, drove his people to the scene. "We had never seen any White people before. We went up on the side of the bank and watched them," he said. While he acknowledges that "long ago" some whites used to come to trade his people for the contraband the Apaches had taken from Mexico, Rope's account to Goodwin indicates that his community had lived relatively free from interactions with white hunters, traders, explorers, and soldiers, whose incursions into the Western Apache domain had been tentative until the mid-1860s. Moreover, while many Western Apaches who Goodwin interviewed connected the arrival of whites with violence, treachery, and hatred, and as a consequence told him how they dreaded entering Camp Goodwin, in Rope's account whites are represented as amicable and generous. He remembered how Apache women traded hay to the white soldiers for food, while he and other young boys received gifts of clothing, bread, beans, and meat at the post.[8]

Rope declined to associate the arrival of white soldiers with devastation and displacement or to underscore hunger and diplomatic needs as factors driving his people to Camp Goodwin. Whether he actually realized it or not as a boy, the world around the White Mountain Apaches was ablaze in the mid-1860s. In the late 1850s, normal Western Apache life had been such that families could usually build their camps where they wished, sleep peacefully, plan and organize ceremonies ahead, plant and harvest on schedule, gather wild plants in season, and find game to hunt in their mountain ranges. Inside a few years, that would all change. After refuting the Confederate invasion, the U.S. government expanded from its previous concentration on the Rio Grande toward Pinos Altos and Western Apache lands. In April 1863, the word of the mineral discoveries made by Joseph R. Walker's party in the San Francisco Mountains of central Arizona, a Yavapai-Tonto Apache territory previously free of Anglo residents, spread the latest version of the familiar western gospel of incredible treasures awaiting takers in remote (to whites) places. The news led to a burgeoning mining concentration around Prescott, which was made the capital of the newly created Arizona Territory in 1864. It also unleashed a wave of terror into Western Apache and Yavapai communities as they found themselves pitted against ruthless outfits composed of local Hispanics, O'odhams, and

Anglo civilians operating by themselves or side by side with the California Volunteers or regular army troops. Sometimes the outfits—the most notorious led by King Woolsey—did not shy away from acknowledging that they worked on the "broad platform of extermination," slaughtering Apache men, women, and children or using perfidy and poisoned food as their weapons.[9]

For his part, Gen. James Carleton, commanding the California Volunteers, had overpowered the Mescalero Apaches in 1862–63 and the Navajos the next winter. In 1864, Carleton made plans for the forced removal (to Bosque Redondo) or extermination of Chiricahua and Western Apaches in an all-out war. His design called for thousands of American civilians and soldiers, Mexican troops, and the O'odhams and other indigenous allies to work in concert against the Apaches. Luckily for Rope, Carleton's ideas never fully materialized. But his men did set up Camp Goodwin before being replaced by the regular troops.[10]

Encircled by swelling waves of violence, Rope's people were saved from the worst. But they heard and witnessed enough to be deeply alarmed. Rather than wait for a disaster, some White Mountain and Cibecue Apaches turned Camp Goodwin into an opening for diplomacy. After initial nurturing of contacts, they welcomed the soldiers to build a new fort on their lands. In the vicinity of the new post, named Camp (later Fort) Apache in 1871, Rope's people received rations and lived independently but relatively close to the army. It was not unheard of for officers and their wives from the post to visit nearby Apache camps for hunting, dancing, and feasting, and vice versa. The daughters of important Apache leaders Hashkee-yànilti-dn (Pedro) and Hacke-ida-silah also married white interpreters/traders aligned with the military. Furthermore, these Apaches contributed a steady supply of men who helped the army in 1872–74 to defeat the other Western Apaches as well as Yavapais and to force the survivors to reservations.[11]

JOINING THE ARMY

"We lined up to be chosen," Rope said as he remembered the scene at San Carlos where many Yavapais, Tonto Apaches, San Carlos Apaches, and White Mountain Apaches had gathered in 1878. By then the federal government had concentrated most of the Apaches and Yavapais to San Carlos, an unhappy move done for the sake of administrative efficiency and monetary savings. The civilian agent John Clum had even forced the majority of White Mountain and Cibecue Apaches to vacate Fort Apache for the more barren Gila River location. The move unsettled the cycle of farming, gathering, and hunting that Rope's people practiced, and although many of his people soon returned to the vicinity of Fort Apache, their worsening situation did not go unnoticed for Rope. There were many quarrels between Apaches who had been traumatized by war and by the loss of their homes and loved ones, and who detested their new living place and the proximity of so many people. Drunkenness, hunger, diseases, and general hopelessness became very much chronic problems. The corruption of reservation agents or the government attack on Apache culture—the government tried to make the Apaches into Christian farmers and alter their familiar gender roles—did not make things any easier.[12]

Linking one's fate with the army increased the likelihood of retaliation from those Chiricahuas who continued to uphold their independence. It also generated discord and factions among the reservation residents, some of whom resented fighting for the whites and others who, when struggling to provide for their families, were jealous of those chosen for the army. Enlistment nevertheless had many factors in its favor. Only superficially interested in integrating its indigenous workforce, the army wanted to use the military skills of the Apaches to its advantage and thus allowed Apache recruits great latitude. Although labeled "scouts," Apaches like Rope functioned primarily in similar combat roles as their white or black peers. But they were not drilled, dressed, or made to do manual labor in the manner that white and black soldiers were. As for military training, there was a chronic shortage of it in the army in general, and training for the Apache recruits proved no exception. On the other hand, they hardly needed any more training, being primed for combat since childhood. The Apache recruits received equal wages with white and black troopers, but their periods of recruitment were more flexible and shorter.[13]

Importantly, the freedom of Apache recruits in the field was extensive. White junior officers who led the Apaches in person were told by their superiors—most significantly by Gen. George Crook, who commanded the Department of Arizona from 1871 to 1875 and again from 1882 to 1886—that under no circumstances were they to suppress the Apaches' sense of independence but instead were to give them general directions and let the

Apaches do their work in their own way. As a result, the Apache recruits often operated much like a raiding party would. They walked, ran, or rode horses as it fitted them, advancing at their own pace and using their own formations. They moved "with no semblance of regularity," one officer observed during the 1883 Sierra Madre campaign.[14] Dreading any surprises, the Apache soldiers could also take the routes that suited them, conceal their tracks, and post rear, front, and flank guards in their own fashion if it seemed right to them. They could also usually pause, rest, and eat when they deemed it proper and determine a rendezvous point for the day's end if necessary.

Apaches also had the liberty to organize different dances when in service, a practice of theirs done for social reasons and in preparation for war and following a military triumph. Thus on several occasions, for example at the San Bernardino Ranch prior to leaving to the Sierra Madre, the nightly silence and order of U.S. Army encampments was disrupted as the places came alive and moved to the rhythm of Apache drumming and singing. Furthermore, regardless of the army's official goals for the campaigns, the Apaches enlistees could set their own agendas, which usually revolved around acquiring material property and exacting revenge.[15] It was hardly unexpected that all this made military service appealing to Apaches trapped in the reservations and thirsting for opportunities to showcase their skills and bravery.

When his opportunity came, Rope was eager to get chosen and was more than ready to serve. "My brother was the first one picked," he recalled of the tense selection process. It was his brother—perhaps Free, who had enlisted before—who advised the white officers doing the recruiting to more closely examine Rope. They "looked me over to see if I was all right. They felt my arms and legs and pounded my chest to see if I would cough," Rope recalled. Happily, "I was all right, so they took me." Hiring forty men that day, the officers had to leave out many hopefuls to wait for the next time. As others lamented the missed opportunity, Rope prepared to leave the reservation the next day. His first patrol would take Rope toward the Chiricahua lands in southeastern Arizona.[16]

Advancing via Forts Thomas, Grant, and Bowie to the Chiricahua Mountains and the Guadalupe Canyon, it did not take long for Rope, an inexperienced fighter, to feel somewhat sore and stiff. Soon, his training started to show, however. Not only did he feel lighter but the whole ordeal seemed much easier. Overall, the first impressions of life on a patrol were positive. Eating twice a day, in the morning and evening, traveling all day over desert terrain and skirting or climbing mountains, or, if stationary, scouting the vicinity of the camp, being alert all the time, and learning to cope with the officers, no matter how little one thought of them, was Rope's new routine. Hunting deer and other game was his passion, and this he pursued whenever possible. Except for the officers' presence, Rope could imagine he was on a raid with his fellow Apaches in search of Chiricahua prey. Despite all his hard marching and energetic efforts, Rope did not make contact with the Chiricahuas during his first tour. Still, not all raids were successful either. The most dramatic event, which made Rope sick inside, saw the accidental drowning of two officers, Lt. Austin Henely and Lt. John Rucker, in a flash flood in the southern section of the Chiricahua Mountains on July 1878.[17]

Despite this tragic accident, Rope's first experiences as a soldier had proven very valuable. He had found an outlet for hunting game, a skill held in high esteem in the Apache community yet curbed by the barrenness of San Carlos and the rules of reservation life. It is probable that Rope was in better shape after than before his first enlistment. Spending the bulk of his time in the field, he had plenty of exercise. In the army he also had better nutrition and more to eat than in the shortage-stricken San Carlos. Rope in fact emphasized this side of military life to Goodwin. For example, he noted that he killed "lots of deer" as a soldier and that in service there was "lots of food with us." By enlisting, he had also made life a little easier for his family and relatives. Rope divided much of his pay among his kin and used some of the money he earned to buy horses or supplies that would benefit not only himself but those close to him. He also put much emphasis and effort in bringing back captured booty. Furthermore, the military allowed the families of its Apache soldiers to draw extra supplies from the commissary.[18]

In the army, Rope had also garnered the respect of other Apache men. Rope was proud how his relatives admired his performance and work effort. Among the youngest in the company, Rope was commended by the kinsmen of his unit for his individual initiative, for his diligent action within the group, and for doing much camp work—getting food and water, building fires, and cooking. He had behaved in a manner similar to that expected not so much from white or black recruits—who were required to show little initiative but instead to follow orders emotionlessly and machine-like—but from an Apache youngster during his very first raids. Before he enlisted, Rope's older male relatives had even reminded him that he must work hard while a soldier, or otherwise it "would be no good." Rope had also found camaraderie among a group of men. As the enlistment was about to expire, the Apaches had held a big dance, being merry, doing some drinking, and bonding in the process.[19]

In sum, Rope had made military service suit his needs. He had escaped outsider control on the reservation, gained a source of income in times of dreadful poverty, and used what the service offered to suit his own ideas of manliness. Furthermore, he had gained valuable knowledge of the Chiricahua territory, where he would soon return.

FROM ONE VIOLENT CRISIS TO THE NEXT

Based on his own testimony, Rope stayed home for a year before reenlisting. Then he again took to investigating the area between Fort Bowie and Guadalupe Canyon. Once more, he did not get to fight any Chiricahuas. But now he at least met some of them, including Geronimo, as they arrived to Fort Bowie to discuss coming to San Carlos in the closing weeks of 1879. Rope's encounter with the Chiricahuas was far from a tense one. In fact, it was very jovial and enjoyable. There was plenty of talking, eating, playing games, and dancing. In the process, Rope gained much information on Chiricahua thinking, leaders, and even their dances, which, he said, "We [White Mountain Apaches] didn't know how to do." A few years later Rope served for a spell with some Chiricahuas and seemed to enjoy their company as his narrative is, again, filled with references to hunting, games, and socializing. One of the Chiricahua leaders, a man known as Chihuahua, Rope even came to regard as a close friend.[20]

This kind of joviality was far from Rope's mind when Victorio's Apache group invaded the reservation and violently slayed one White Mountain Apache leader and his family on May 1880. For Victorio and his men, this act represented revenge against the Western Apaches who had recently served against him in the army, stealing Chiricahua horses and killing some of their people. For White Mountain Apaches, the incident embodied a brutal and unjust butchering.[21]

Rope and his fellow Apaches craved payback, but their effort proved one of taxing disappointments. On the trail of Victorio's men, the mixed command of white and Apache troops encountered many recently vacated ranches and slayed inhabitants. They also nearly ran out of water, and Rope had to rescue some of his relatives who could not keep up on their own. Much to Rope's disappointment, a few of the younger Apache recruits found military service too hard for them. Some apparently even collapsed along the route and had to be aided by the others. Souring the mood further, there were all sorts of clashes with the officers. The most heated question seemed to be when it was acceptable to hunt deer and how would the meat the Apaches killed be shared between the officers, white soldiers, and Apaches. This kind of quarreling and small-mindedness disgusted Rope. But worse times were yet to come. Not finding their targets, the exhausted men engaged in drunken brawls and witnessed a fistfight between an officer and a trooper. Morale hit a new low when the Apaches, feeling unjustly treated, threatened to quit if two of them were to be discharged for shooting a burro without authorization. While the officers changed their minds on that occasion and the two Apache recruits were spared for the moment, soon many Apaches were in fact discharged from service. Others simply quit in protest, having had enough of the ill-fated campaign. Disappointed and angry, Rope went home to recuperate. Army service had just shown its uglier side to him.[22]

Worse times would follow after the Cibecue crisis in Autumn 1881. The reservation Apaches at Cibecue, near Fort Apache, like so many peoples throughout world history, had sought solace in religion from their everyday misery and emotional confusion resulting from the sweeping changes forced upon them by colonial policies. They turned to religious revivalism in search of hope of a better tomorrow, but found violence. After troops from Fort Apache arrested the Apache preacher Noch-ay-del-klinne in his village on Cibecue Creek, violence erupted between his followers and the troops en route back to the fort. Apparently some Western Apache enlistees had switched sides and betrayed the army during the violent clash. Soon unfounded news of a general uprising spread like wildfire across the United States, and the government responded by hurrying reinforcements to Arizona to hunt the Western Apaches. The military buildup made things chaotic and confusing at San Carlos, to say the least.[23]

Rope also had his hands full with ugly duty. Back on the government payroll, he was sorting out killings and chasing and catching renegades

John Rope, ca. 1930s. Photo 18527. Courtesy Arizona State Museum, University of Arizona.

for several months following the Cibecue fight. Rounding up suspects and guarding them—some of whom he knew and some to whom he was related—made this a very stressful period for Rope. Going against those close to him was not what he had signed up for, but as long as he remained in the army Rope knew he had little choice on the matter. He knew that his work now brought him enemies too close to home. He slowly began to question military service in general and to absolutely loathe the duty inside the reservation boundaries.[24]

Then in April 1882 came the independent Chiricahuas from the Sierra Madre led by Geronimo and Chihuahua, men familiar to Rope. Entering San Carlos to take their relatives to Mexico, the Chiricahuas created plenty of confusion, panic, and anxiety among the Western Apache residents. They placed some Western Apaches under guard, taunted others, and took their horses. They also killed the head of police at San Carlos and scared off some freighters on their way. To their misfortune, Rope's father and another relative found the barrels of whiskey the freighters had abandoned. They started drinking heavily. And they apparently did not stop until they passed out dead. The brave raider and respected leader Nayundiie had met a most inglorious end. If Rope contemplated quitting the military after this, he did not share his thoughts with Goodwin. But he was only too glad to get away from San Carlos when he reenlisted in 1883.[25]

TO THE SIERRA MADRE

Rope's military career culminated with the U.S. Army's campaign to the Sierra Madre of northern Mexico in May and June of 1883. Previously home to one of the four Chiricahua bands, the Nednhi, the Sierra Madre turned into the focal point of the borderlands wars during the 1880s. The mountain hideouts of the remaining independent Chiricahuas promised rough campaigning with their plunging, steep-sided canyons, oak and pine forests above five thousand feet, humid and thickly vegetated outer slopes, and nearly barren inner slopes. While winters were mild, the summers could be very rainy and hot. Using the U.S.-Mexico borderline and its rugged topography to their advantage, the Chiricahuas had made the Sierra Madre a launching pad for their raids to geographically scattered targets in Sonora and Chihuahua as well as Arizona and New Mexico. In American and Mexican military minds, the Sierra Madre came to equal a formidable barrier they needed to wrestle from Apache control.

Gen. George Crook believed that any free Chiricahua hiding in northern Mexico constituted a risk to American security. He felt that the Apaches could lay low and strike at unexpected times and places for years to come, while the U.S. Army would face an impossible task of defending the vast desert border region and its growing settlements. Already by 1883, the Tombstone mining boom and the transcontinental railroads had brought thousands of whites to the Chiricahua lands in southeastern Arizona in a short time. The vulnerability of American interests had become evident in March 1883 when a small Chiricahua party crossed the border to Arizona to acquire weapons and ammunition for their American-made guns. For the first days, the soldiers remained confused and passive while the Chiricahuas hit miners, prospectors, ranchers, merchants, and civilian packtrains—out-of-the-way targets that usually carried tempting quantities of goods. On their way, the Chiricahuas cut the telegraph wire; split, united, and split again; took cover in the mountain ranges; and kept up a breakneck speed. On March 28, the raiders spotted easy victims, the traveling party of Judge H. C. McComas, his wife, Juanita, and son Charlie riding a buckboard on their way to Lordsburg, New Mexico, from Silver City. Ambushing and slaying both parents, Apaches took the six-year-old Charlie captive and stole everything, from the driving whip to raincoats, they could transport. Regardless of an extensive and much-publicized search that lasted for years, Charlie was never seen again. By now aware that the troops had become active, the Chiricahuas, split into several parties and transporting a supply of ammunition, guns, and other provisions, headed south of the border. During the nine-day-long raid, the Apaches, writes historian Marc Simmons, covered, in their zigzag advance, somewhere between two hundred to four hundred miles. They suffered just one casualty, shot by a miner.[26]

The March 1883 raid left the soldiers humiliated. Meanwhile, Crook had already dispatched emissaries across the border to gather intelligence and open communications with the Chiricahuas concerning surrender. Having recovered from his earlier disappointments, Rope, whose options were limited, still saw military service as his best choice in securing a better life for himself and his kin. Possessing a good service record, he was chosen to be among Crook's messengers. Together with five other Apache recruits, Rope escorted two Chiricahua women who had recently returned to San Carlos from the Sierra Madre. In northern Mexico, this small party canvassed terrain that proved unfamiliar to Rope, who, while relieved for being out in the field again, felt somewhat uneasy and edgy. After all, he was deep in Mexico, where most of the locals tended to fear and hate the Apaches regardless of whether they were Chiricahuas or not. He was also uncertain what would be the Chiricahua reaction to their mission. However, he never found that out, as the efforts to open contacts with the independent Apaches proved futile. Rope and his colleagues could not find any of them.[27]

While still in the field, new orders reached Rope that he was to report at San Bernardino Ranch and there to join the command that consisted of 42 white cavalrymen and 193 Apache soldiers supplied by a massive packtrain. After the necessary preparations, which included a big dance, this force crossed the international line on May 1, 1883.

While American troops prepared the take the field, the Chiricahuas had dispersed after successfully holding off a Mexican force in late April. On May 15, 1883, the Apache recruits found and hit one of their camps, belonging to Chihuahua and his followers, in the Sierra Madre. The troops took possession of the village, killing an estimated nine people and seizing most of its materials. Other residents took flight to the surrounding mountains. This time Rope also saw action. During the fight, his detachment of Apache soldiers had spotted a few Chiricahuas herding horses and approached them. Hiding in the bush, Rope and the other Apache soldiers waited until the targets "were right opposite us." Then they jumped the Chiricahuas, capturing two children and shooting at three Chiricahua men, who now bolted off in the direction of pine woods. "I was wearing two belts of fifty cartridges each, but I did not shoot more than three times because I was satisfied with having helped to catch these two Chiricahuas [children]," Rope later revealed.[28]

Going over the skirmish site, Rope soon found yet another Chiricahua boy hiding in the bushes as well as a little girl behind a tree. While the other Apache soldiers wanted the boy, Rope was determined to keep his new male captive. The girl he gave to another Apache recruit. Feeling triumphant, as did most of his peers, Rope also collected for himself a thick cowhide, some dry meat, grease, and mescal, as well as a rope, a silver cross, and an old Mexican saddle and a bridle from the battle site.[29]

During and after the fight, Rope's focus had been on captured items, not on killing or destroying the enemy. He coveted for material articles and captives as proof that he was a brave fighter. He took care to place all he had taken neatly together at the side of the camp. In this way, he wanted to make sure that others knew that these things were his and his alone. The items would serve as symbols for the occasion when the courageous Rope and his peers had engaged and triumphed on Chiricahuas' home ground. What made it all the more significant was that this had been Rope's first true fight; it would also be his last. Excelling on such an occasion, Rope tried to make certain that everybody would know he had done well and had fought in the front. Importantly, he wanted it known that he was not one of those Apache recruits, who, Rope later noted, had "started to say their knees hurt" before the fight so they could keep to the rear because they "were afraid."[30] That he killed no one scarcely mattered, as Rope and his fellow Apaches, except when seeking revenge, did not place so much value on killing the enemy than they did on capturing material wealth and the prestige that went with it. As Rope saw it, they were in the Sierra Madre to catch the Chiricahuas, impress and fight them if need be, and then make them come back to San Carlos.

At the time of the attack, the majority of the Chiricahua combatants were actually raiding in Chihuahua, hoping to find captives to exchange for those Apaches the Mexicans had taken the preceding year. Still, both the Mexican and American attacks had turned San Carlos into an attractive choice. Tired of the fighting, more and more Chiricahua women started to approach the military camp in the Sierra Madre after they realized it was a safe thing to do. By May 19, one hundred Chiricahuas already camped with Rope and his fellow enlistees, and more followed in the days to come. The camp was fast turning into a refugee center. Rope remembers how they gave lots of rations to the Chiricahua women to make them feel more at ease and receptive to peace offers. Soon these women approached the Western Apaches more freely as well, wanting to be on friendly terms.[31]

Still, the tensions ran high as the stalemate in the Sierra Madre remained potentially explosive. As the Chiricahua fighters gradually returned, soldiers not only switched campsites repeatedly for the sake of forage and to avoid possible Apache assault, but remained uncertain of what to do next. On May 20, a peculiar incident occurred. While Crook failed to mention it, Rope noted how the general went hunting that day and was evidently caught by the Chiricahuas. Obsessed with hunting, Crook made himself an easy target, perhaps intentionally to open talks with the Apaches. Geronimo and Crook apparently talked for a few hours and then came to camp to continue discussions.[32] Rather than demand an unconditional surrender, Crook offered amnesty for past crimes and return to the reservation. Furthermore, being in a hurry to depart before some unfortunate clash of violence might undo everything, Crook indicated that his troops were running short on rations and could not wait for the Chiricahuas to gather all their people, who the Chiricahuas claimed had dispersed after the fight. In reality, historian Dan Thrapp observes, Crook had no means, except psychological pressure, to make the Apaches to return to the United States. He had to take with him those who were already there and be willing to leave and accept the Chiricahua headmen's word that the rest would return to Arizona at their own pace. This proved acceptable for the Chiricahuas.[33]

After the talks ended, the camp assumed a surprisingly jovial atmosphere. According to Rope, "Now we all mixed with the Chiricahuas like friends." Curiously, the Chiricahuas even held a victory dance. Rope added that, as the party started back to San Carlos, the Western Apaches arranged a social dance with the Chiricahuas every night and "had lots of good times." The Apaches also played the Apache game hoop and poles together and seemed to get along very well. Still, the danger was not over. One night, Rope claims, the Chiricahuas suggested that their women could dance freely with the Western Apache soldiers. Rope felt that this was a plot to ambush and kill the unsuspecting Western Apache men while they danced. While the dance got started, the white chief of scouts, Al Sieber, who was most likely oblivious to the plot, refused permission for the Apache recruits to participate as one of them had died that day. The dance was stopped and, according to Rope, a potential massacre avoided.[34]

TOWARD RETIREMENT

As the outfit reached San Carlos, the place was buzzing with anticipation. Crowds watched as the caravan of several hundred Chiricahuas and Apache and white soldiers reached the Gila River and made camp. The rest of the Chiricahuas would arrive in the following spring. While most would adjust to reservation life near Fort Apache, a vocal and militarily powerful minority would not tolerate white control over their lives. On May 1885, they would leave the reservation, head for the Sierra Madre, and start raiding again. This would mark the start of the much-publicized Geronimo campaign.[35]

Upon returning from the Sierra Madre, Rope went home. He was probably pleased with what he had accomplished. Some two months later he again enlisted, but this time he spent much of his time on the reservation.

Although Rope enjoyed seeing more of his relatives, including Mickey Free, his enlistment turned sour quickly. If anything, it was worse than before the Sierra Madre campaign. Arresting and jailing Apaches the whites saw as potential troublemakers, and seeing them being sent off to distant lands (to Alcatraz Island, for instance) for imprisonment, was not to Rope's liking. Neither was working with Apache spies who operated undercover in the reservation informing on other Apaches. But perhaps the worst kind of duty was chasing after renegades and murderers. "This being stationed at San Carlos all the time was no good, as there was always somebody killing someone else, and we were having to go out after them," Rope told Goodwin.[36]

In all, the chaos of the reservation made Apache futures in Rope's eyes seem perhaps more uncertain and more vulnerable than ever before. When one of Rope's peers was murdered by a reservation Apache, it made him question his choices seriously. Rope served until his discharge, but then no more. Asked at least three times to reenlist, he remained firm. He simply told Goodwin, "I would not do it." There was nothing that would get him back to the army. The job had become too stressful, too ugly, and too risky. Creating enemies inside the reservation was not what Rope wanted. He would not risk having someone take revenge on him and his family on the account of what he had done as a borderlands soldier.[37]

Rope lived at the small community of Bylas on the White Mountain Apache reservation to be an old man, probably dying from pneumonia in 1944. His military experiences had apparently made him into a man who wanted to mind his own business while protecting those dear to him. As with the other men in this study, Rope's life as a soldier attests to the complexities of borderlands violence and U.S. settler colonialism. Raised to become a warrior in a violent time and region, Rope never fought against the whites, the Mexicans, or the O'odhams. He had only clashed with other Apaches, although some of them were his friends and his kin. Additionally, Rope patrolled, campaigned, and policed extensively during several years of military service. He heard stories of vicious deeds, witnessed desperate incidents, and tried to make sense of brutal violence. He never shut his eyes from the violent reality around him, but he did not do any killing himself. Neither did he participate in numerous battles and skirmishes. Furthermore, when on the payroll of the U.S. government, Rope behaved much like he would on a raiding party. He displayed little intent or desire to kill the enemy and had other concerns. Rope wanted honor and personal reputation the way Apache raiders preferred to have it: by outwitting and outperforming the enemy and pilfering his material supply. Balancing personal ambition with communal needs, he sought to secure the survival of his family and kin as they negotiated the impacts the U.S. settler invasion had on their lives. What mattered for Rope was securing a livelihood, respecting Apache conducts of manliness, and carving such relations with the whites that would enable his people to persist and prosper in the future.

Rope's exploits allows us a particular perspective to the complex shapes of borderlands manliness and violence. It is noteworthy that Rope's narratives to Goodwin emphasize things like hunting, socializing, and adventure instead of murder and mayhem. It seems that, while Rope was far from naïve, he wanted to see the positive side of things and emphasize the good in the everyday. He certainly could have narrated a much grimmer story to Goodwin. He had the materials for it, the killings, misery, destitution, and desperation. On another level, Rope's story offers a window into a world where the lines between "us" and "them" were seldom self-evident. Rope did not see the world foremost in terms of a racial dichotomy. For him, humanity and human interactions did not follow a simple white-nonwhite, Anglo-Apache, division. Life on the borderlands was much too complicated for that. It had always been so.

NOTES

1. Grenville Goodwin, *Western Apache Raiding and Warfare*, ed. Keith H. Basso (Tucson: University of Arizona Press, 1971), 154. Much of my analysis of Rope's life relies on transcripts of Goodwin's interviews housed at the Arizona State Museum in Tucson and published in part in Goodwin, *Western Apache Raiding*, 93–186. Grenville Goodwin was born on Long Island, New York, in 1907, and his interest in the Southwest led him to study anthropology at the University of Arizona. Not coveting academic degrees, Goodwin devoted his whole attention on the Apaches and went to live for better part of the year at the White Mountain Reservation. There he extended his acquaintance with the Apaches for a decade, studying various communities, including Bylas, Arizona, where John Rope lived. Goodwin died suddenly in June 1940, his work left badly unfinished. On Goodwin, see Morris E. Opler, ed., *Grenville Goodwin among the Western Apache: Letters from the Field* (Tucson: University of Arizona Press, 1973); and Grenville Goodwin and Neil Goodwin, *The Apache Diaries: A Father-Son Journey* (Lincoln: University of Nebraska Press, 2000).

2. Rope's mother came from the *biszahe* clan. According to Goodwin, she and her sister, who was also married to Rope's father, died on subsequent days. On Rope's childhood and his family, see Grenville Goodwin, *The Social Organization of the Western Apache* (Chicago: University of Chicago Press, 1942), 588–89, 600, 610, 613, 664–65, 668–69; John Rope interview, Folder 33, Box 3, Grenville Goodwin Papers (GP), Arizona State Museum, Tucson. Probably the largest Apache major group with four thousand to eight thousand people, the Western Apaches were divided into White Mountain, Cibecue, San Carlos, and Tonto Apaches. Goodwin, *Social Organization*; Opler, *Grenville Goodwin*, 53.

3. Ian W. Record, *Big Sycamore Stands Alone: The Western Apaches, Aravaipa, and the Struggle for Place* (Norman: University of Oklahoma Press, 2008), 38–43, 69; Goodwin, *Western Apache Raiding*, 93–98; Opler, *Grenville Goodwin*, 44–45, 52, 55. On Western Apache subsistence, see also Sherman Curley interview, Anna Price interview, both in Folder 33, Box 3, GP; Walter Hooke interview, Folder 34, Box 3, GP.

4. Goodwin, *Social Organization*, 669 [quotation]. Clan affiliation held an important role as Western Apaches engaged those around them. Layered across the basic territorial units, the clans formed a cross strata of relationships, a far-flung web that ran through the several local groups, bands, and groups. While there existed no clan government, all members of the same clan were regarded as relatives, and clan members were expected to help each other by military and other means in time of crisis. Grenville Goodwin, "The Social Divisions and Economic Life of the Western Apache," *American Anthropologist* 37 (January–March 1935): 55–60; Grenville Goodwin, "The Characteristics and Function of Clan in a Southern Athapascan Culture," *American Anthropologist* 39 (July–September 1937): 394–407; Harvey Nash-kin interview, Folder 32, Box 2, GP; Walter Hooke interview, James Nolan interview, both in Folder 34, Box 3, GP.

5. John Rope interview, Folder 33, Box 3; Harvey Nash-kin interview, Folder 32, Box 2 and Folder 33, Box 3, GP.

6. Goodwin, *Social Organization*, 664–66 [quotations on 664]. For personal accounts of Western Apache raiding in Mexico, see Barney Tisle interview, Palmer Valor interview, both in Folder 33, Box 3, GP.

7. Weapons, Raids, and Warfare, Folder 44, Box 4, GP.

8. Goodwin, *Western Apache Raiding*, 98–101 [quotation on 99]; John Rope interview, Barney Tisle interview, both in Folder 33, Box 3; Nancy Wright interview, Folder 34, Box 3, GP.

9. Karl Jacoby, "'The Broad Platform of Extermination': Nature and Violence in the Nineteenth Century North American Borderlands," *Journal of Genocide Research* 10 (June 2008): 249–67; William Four, "A Young Man's Life in the West," typescript, 150–94, 202–209, 226, Folder 5, Box 1, William Four Papers; Augustus Brichta, "Reminiscences of an Old Pioneer" typescript, 1–10, Folder 2, Box 1, Augustus C. Brichta Papers, both in Arizona Historical Society, Tucson; John Nicholson, ed., *The Arizona of Joseph Pratt Allyn, Letters from a Pioneer Judge: Observations and Travels, 1863–1866* (Tucson: University of Arizona Press, 1974); Daniel E. Conner, *Joseph Reddeford Walker and the Arizona Adventure* (Norman: University of Oklahoma Press, 1956); Timothy

Braatz, *Surviving Conquest: A History of the Yavapai Peoples* (Lincoln: University of Nebraska Press, 2003).

10. On Carleton's plan, see *The War of the Rebellion: A Compilation of the Official Records of the Union and Confederate Armies* (Washington, D.C.: Government Printing Office, 1880–1901), series 1, vol. 34, 387–89; and *Indian Tribes and Their Treatment*, S. Rep. No. 156, 39th Cong., 2d Sess., Serial 1279, 172–73, 176–81.

11. Goodwin, *Western Apache Raiding*, 100–102; Allan Radbourne, "Great Chief: Hashkeedasillaa of the White Mountain Apaches," *Journal of Arizona History* 50 (Spring 2009): 28, 30, 32–36, 44; Lori Davisson, "New Light on the Cibecue Fight: Untangling Apache Identities," *Journal of Arizona History* 20 (Winter 1979): 428–34; Samuel George interview, Folder 35, Box 4, GP. On Apache-army social interactions at or near Fort Apache, see, for example, William D. Fuller, "An Evening with the Apaches," in *Eyewitnesses to the Indian Wars, 1865–1890*, vol. 1, *The Struggle for Apacheria*, ed. Peter Cozzens (Mechanicsburg, Pa.: Stackpole Books, 2001), 94–95; Martha Summerhayes, *Vanished Arizona: Recollections of the Army Life of a New England Woman* (Lincoln: University of Nebraska Press, 1979), 90–96.

12. Goodwin, *Western Apache Raiding*, 101–103, 116 [quotation on 103]. On San Carlos, see, for example, Donald E. Worcester, *The Apaches: Eagles of the Southwest* (Norman: University of Oklahoma Press, 1979); Davisson, "New Light"; Thomas Cruse, *Apache Days and After* (1941; repr., Lincoln: University of Nebraska Press, 1987).

13. Janne Lahti, "Colonized Labor: Apaches and Pawnees as Army Workers," *Western Historical Quarterly* 39 (Autumn 2008): 283–302; Janne Lahti, *Cultural Construction of Empire: The U.S. Army in Arizona and New Mexico* (Lincoln: University of Nebraska Press, 2012): 224–31; Thomas W. Dunlay, *Wolves for the Blue Soldiers: Indian Scouts and Auxiliaries with the United States Army, 1860–90* (Lincoln: University of Nebraska Press, 1982).

14. John G. Bourke, *An Apache Campaign in the Sierra Madre* (1886; repr., Lincoln: University of Nebraska Press, 1987), 17–18, 21–37 [quotation on 22].

15. John G. Bigelow, Jr., *On the Bloody Trail of Geronimo* (Tucson: Westernlore Press, 1986), 43–44; Cruse, *Apache Days*, esp. 55–56; Harvey Nash-kin interview, Folder 32, Box 2; Walter Hooke interview, Folder 34, Box 3, GP.

16. Goodwin, *Western Apache Raiding*, 103–104.

17. For Rope's first campaign, see ibid., 104–108; and John Rope interview, Folder 32, Box 2, GP.

18. Goodwin, *Western Apache Raiding*, 104, 108. See also John Rope interview, Folder 32, Box 2, GP.

19. Goodwin, Western Apache Raiding, 108; John Rope interview, Folder 32, Box 2, GP.

20. Goodwin, *Western Apache Raiding*, 110–13, 115–16, 130–35 [quotation on 112]; Allan Radbourne, "The Juh-Geronimo Surrender of 1879," *English Westerners Brand Book* 21 (Summer 1983): 1–18; Edwin R. Sweeney, *From Cochise to Geronimo: The Chiricahua Apaches, 1874–1886* (Norman: University of Oklahoma Press, 2010), 138–45.

21. Sweeney, *From Cochise*, 152–55, 179; Goodwin, *Western Apache Raiding*, 116; Kathleen P. Chamberlain, *Victorio: Apache Warrior and Chief* (Norman: University of Oklahoma Press, 2007), 188–89.

22. Apparently white officers suspected that some Apache enlistees were helping the Chiricahua party that the troops were chasing. Goodwin, *Western Apache Raiding*, 116–26.

23. Davisson, "New Light," esp. 440–42; John R. Welch, Chip Colwell-Chanthaphonh, and Mark Altaha, "Retracing the Battle of Cibecue: Western Apache, Documentary, and Archaeological Interpretations," *Kiva* 71 (Winter 2005): 133–63; Alchisay et al., "The Apache Story of the Cibicue," in Cozzens, *Eyewitnesses*, 1:295–310; Cruse, *Apache Days*, 93–145. Charles Collins, *Apache Nightmare: The Battle at Cibecue Creek* (Norman: University of Oklahoma Press, 1999), is a thorough look on the military operations and thinking.

24. Goodwin, *Western Apache Raiding*, 135–40; John Rope interview, Folder 32, Box 2, GP.

25. Goodwin, *Western Apache Raiding*, 140–48; Jason Betzinez, with Wilbur Sturtevant Nye, *I Fought with Geronimo* (1959; repr., Lincoln: University of Nebraska Press, 1987), 56–64; Bud Shapard, *Chief Loco: Apache Peacemaker* (Norman: University of Oklahoma Press, 2010), 152–86.

26. Marc Simmons, *Massacre on the Lordsburg Road: A Tragedy of the Apache Wars* (College Station: Texas A&M University Press, 1997), 84–130; Sweeney, *From Cochise*, 290–97; "Report of Brigadier General George Crook, September 27, 1883," in U.S. War Department, *Annual Report of the Secretary of War* (*ARSW*), House Ex. Doc. No. 1, 48th Cong., 1st Sess., Serial 2182, 161–63, 173–74.

27. Goodwin, *Western Apache Raiding*, 148–53; John Rope interview, Folder 32, Box 2, GP.

28. Goodwin, *Western Apache Raiding*, 159–60.

29. Ibid., 158–61; John Rope interview, Folder 32, Box 2, GP. For the attack, see also Bourke, *Apache Campaign*, 68–78.

30. Goodwin, *Western Apache Raiding*, 159.

31. Ibid., 163–65; Bourke, *Apache Campaign*, 78–84.

32. Goodwin, *Western Apache Raiding*, 167–68; John Rope interview, Folder 32, Box 2, GP.

33. "Report of Brigadier General George Crook, September 27, 1883," in *ARSW*, 166, 176–78; Bourke, *Apache Campaign*; David Roberts, *Once They Moved Like the Wind: Cochise, Geronimo, and the Apache Wars* (New York: Simon and Schuster, 1993), 235–38; John Rope interview, Folder 32, Box 2, GP; Dan L. Thrapp, *General Crook and the Sierra Madre Adventure* (Norman: University of Oklahoma Press, 1971), 148–67.

34. Goodwin, *Western Apache Raiding*, 168–69 [quotations on 168].

35. See, for instance, Odie B. Faulk, *The Geronimo Campaign* (New York: Oxford University Press, 1969); Sweeney, *From Cochise*; and Roberts, *Once They Moved*.

36. Goodwin, *Western Apache Raiding*, 184.

37. Ibid., 173–85 [quotation on 185]; John Rope interview, Folder 32, Box 2, GP.

Contributors

Lance R. Blyth is the command historian of the North American Aerospace Defense Command and U.S. Northern Command and a research associate in the Latin American and Iberian Institute at the University of New Mexico. He is the author of *Chiricahua and Janos: Communities of Violence in the Southwestern Borderlands, 1680–1880* (2012).

William S. Kiser is an assistant professor of history at Texas A&M University, San Antonio. He is author of two books on the nineteenth-century Southwest. His most recent work is the award-winning *Dragoons in Apacheland: Conquest and Resistance in Southern New Mexico, 1846–1861* (2013).

Janne Lahti is an adjunct professor of general history and a Finnish Cultural Foundation Fellow at the University of Helsinki. His research interests cover the histories of colonialism, borderlands, the American West, indigenous peoples, transnationalism, the German empire, and Western movies. His publications include *Cultural Construction of Empire: The U.S. Army in Arizona and New Mexico* (2012).

James N. Leiker is a professor of history and chair of the History and Political Science Department at Johnson County Community College in Kansas. He has written, among other titles, *Racial Borders: Black Soldiers along the Rio Grande* (2002) and, with Ramon Powers, *The Northern Cheyenne Exodus in History and Memory* (2011).

Andrew E. Masich is president and chief executive officer of the Senator John Heinz History Center and chairman of the Pennsylvania Historical and Museum Commission. He is also an adjunct professor of history at Carnegie Mellon University. His publications include *The Civil War in Arizona: The Story of the California Volunteers, 1861–1865* (2006) and, with David F. Halaas, *Halfbreed: The Remarkable True Story of George Bent* (2004).

Megan Kate Nelson is a writer, historian, and cultural critic based in Lincoln, Massachusetts. She is the author of two books, *Ruin Nation: Destruction and the American Civil War* (2012) and *Trembling Earth: A Cultural History of the Okefenokee Swamp* (2005). Her blog, Historista (www.historista.com), examines the surprising, cool, and weird ways that people engage with history in everyday life.

Thomas T. Smith is a retired U.S. Army colonel and an executive officer of the Central Region Installation Management Command at Fort Sam Houston in Texas. He has written extensively on western military history. One of his books is *The U.S. Army and the Texas Frontier Economy, 1845–1900* (1999).

Victoria Smith is an associate professor of history and ethnic studies and the coordinator of Native American Studies in the Institute for Ethnic Studies at the University of Nebraska–Lincoln. A merited teacher and scholar of indigenous history, her publications include *Captive Arizona, 1851–1900* (2009).

Jerry D. Thompson is Regents Professor of History at Texas A&M International University. He has written or edited over twenty-five books on the Southwest borderlands. His most recent publications include the award-winning *Cortina: Defending the Mexican Name in Texas* (2013) and *A Civil War History of the New Mexico Volunteers and Militia* (2015).

Robert Wooster is a Regents Professor of History at Texas A&M University, Corpus Christi. He has published extensively on western and military history. His books include *The Military and United States Indian Policy, 1865–1903* (1988) and *The American Military Frontiers: The United States Army in the West, 1783–1900* (2009).

Index

References to illustrations appear in italic type.